BASIL RATHBONE

Also by Michael B. Druxman:

Paul Muni: His Life and His Films
Make It Again, Sam

Basil Rathbone
HIS LIFE AND HIS FILMS

Michael B. Druxman

South Brunswick and New York: A. S. Barnes and Company
London: Thomas Yoseloff Ltd

© 1975 by Michael B. Druxman

A. S. Barnes and Co., Inc.
Cranbury, New Jersey 08512

Thomas Yoseloff Ltd
108 New Bond Street
London W1Y OQX, England

Library of Congress Cataloging in Publication Data

Druxman, Michael B.   1941–
   Basil Rathbone.

   1.   Rathbone, Basil, 1892–1967.
PN2598.R35D7   791.43′028′0924 [B]   74-3611
ISBN 0-498-01471-1

First printing March, 1975
Second printing February, 1976

Printed in the United States of America

For my son,
David
—who likes to "sword fight"

CONTENTS

ACKNOWLEDGMENTS

Grateful acknowledgment is made to the many individuals and organizations who gave of their time, their knowledge, loaned films for viewing purposes, and/or helped gather stills in the preparation of this book:

Academy of Motion Picture Arts and Sciences, Brian Aherne, American Broadcasting Company, American Film Institute, American-International Pictures, Bill Atoris, Audio/Brandon Films, Lew Ayres, Azteca Films, James Bacon, Howard S. Benedict, Henry Blanke, Eddie Brandt, George Brent, British Film Institute, Hillary Brooke, Budget Films, Red Buttons, Robert J. Callen, John Carradine, Jack Carter, Cherokee Book Shop, Booth Colman, Columbia Broadcasting System, Columbia Pictures, Brian Conigliaro, Roger Corman, Peter Cowie, Jeanne Crain, Bing Crosby, George Cukor, Robert Cummings, Jane Bryan Dart, Laraine Day, Olivia deHavilland, Andy Devine, Walt Disney Productions, Faith Domergue, Billie Dove, Terry Druxman, Paul Ecenia, George Edwards, Douglas Fairbanks, Jr., Films, Inc., Sylvia Fine, Milton Goldman, Diane Goodrich, Gale Gordon, Huntz Hall, Bridget Hanley, Curtis Harrington, Louis Hayward, Bob Hope, Vickie Horne, John Howard, Walter E. Hurst, Ronnie James, Danny Kaye, Al Keller, KHJ-TV, Jonathan Kidd, Patric Knowles, Martin Kosleck, KTTV, Fernando Lamas, Paul Landres, Larry Edmunds Bookshop, Kenneth G. Lawrence, Reginald LeBorg, Rowland V. Lee, Frank Lieberman, Gary Lockwood, Los Angeles Public Library, *Los Angeles Times*, Ida Lupino, Fred MacMurray, Fredric March, Memory Shop, Metro-Goldwyn-Mayer, Robert Middleton, Cameron Mitchell, Movie Star News, Museum of Modern Art, Alan Napier, National Broadcasting Company, National Telefilm Associates, Richard Newton, Paul Myers of the New York Public Library, *New York Times*, Pat O'Brien, Barbara O'Neill, Paramount Pictures, James Robert Parish, Jean Porter, Vincent Price, Aldo Ray, Bob Red, Allen Reisner, RKO Radio Pictures, Ginger Rogers, Cesar Romero, George Schaefer, Randolph Scott, *Seattle Times*, Ray Smith, Gale Sondergaard, Sandra Steele, Milburn Stone, Glenhall Taylor, Teleworld, Inc., Wayne Thomas, Richard Thorpe, Claire Trevor, Twentieth Century-Fox, United Artists, Universal Pictures, Charles Van Enger, Joe Van Winkle, *Variety,* Hal Wallis, Wayne Warga, Warner Brothers, Paul Francis Webster, Arthur Whitelaw, Esther Williams, and Bernard Woolner.

Also, a very special thanks to Mrs. Ouida Bergere Rathbone, a very gracious lady, who was kind enough to share with us some personal memories of her late husband.

BASIL RATHBONE

I
Profile of a Nice Guy

He was the screen's supreme villain and his "rogue's gallery" of sophisticated scoundrels includes some of the most despicable characters ever recorded on film. Mr. Murdstone of *David Copperfield;* the Marquis St. Evremonde from *A Tale of Two Cities;* Sir Guy of Gisbourne in *The Adventures of Robin Hood;* Richard III from *Tower of London;* and Captain Esteban Pasquale in *The Mark of Zorro*—all were vivid portraits of evil incarnate.

He was also highly regarded as an all-round character actor, turning in such brilliant performances as Pontius Pilate in *The Last Days of Pompeii;* Major Brand of *The Dawn Patrol;* and Louis XI from *If I Were King.*

Fernando Lamas recalls him as: "a powerful personality. It was impossible to look at anybody else when he was on the screen."

Allen Reisner directed the performer in a 1954 teleplay for "Studio One Summer Theatre," *The House of Gair:* "He spoke to you with a wisdom that you don't hear from people anymore."

The comments are typical of the admiration that the motion picture industry as a whole felt for this distinguished actor.

Throughout a good portion of his film career, Basil Rathbone was the victim of "type-casting." The problem first manifested itself as a result of his realistic interpretation of the sadistic stepfather in *David Copperfield.* Producers were so impressed with the portrayal that, for the next few years, he was seldom cast as anything but a "heavy."

In a 1936 interview with the *Los Angeles Times,* the actor expressed his discontent: "Murdstone has haunted me ever since I played him. I am one of the best equipped actors today, because of my experience. Comedy, romance, tragedy, farce, burlesque . . . I can portray them all. But it's closed instead of opening doors to me. Producers forget so quickly or remember so long."

As Louis XI in If I Were King.

Even more damaging was his definitive portrayal of fiction's greatest detective—Sherlock Holmes. Rathbone essayed the role in fourteen films, a long-running radio series, a stage production, and on television. It was a characterization that satisfied audiences, but frustrated the artist, as it ultimately overshadowed the more impressive accomplishments of his career.

Rathbone had occasionally been able to garner a *good* sympathetic character role, prior to his taking up residency at 221-B Baker Street. But, after playing the sleuth for eight years, he became so identified with *that* part that producers refused to consider him for anything else. They'd lost sight of the fact that the performer had a very impressive stage and motion-picture background and was also the recipient of two Academy Award nominations.

What disturbed Rathbone most was that, even off screen, he began to lose his own identity. Instead of people addressing him as "Mr. Rathbone," fans would say, "Hello, Sherlock" or "May I have your autograph, Mr. Holmes."

Although he was eventually able to overcome this "jinx," and begin working once more, the actor's "star" never rose again to the heights it had achieved during the late 1930s and mid-40s. True, he managed to keep busy for the last twenty years of his life, doing New York plays, summer stock, one-man dramatic readings, television, and an occasional film, yet, with the exception of his success in the

The definitive **Sherlock Holmes.**

1947 stage production of *The Heiress,* he was never offered another opportunity to play an *important* role in a *major* project.

Basil Rathbone may not have been a *great* actor, but he was a *very good* one. It is unfortunate that the general public is seldom reminded of his more important contributions to the dramatic art and, instead, remembers him only as Sherlock Holmes. The man had so much more to offer than a single characterization.

* * * * * * * * * * *

Rathbone was a British subject. He was educated at Repton School, served during World War I with the Liverpool Scottish Regiment, and resided for more than thirty years in the United Kingdom. His manner was that of a gentleman and he spoke with an accent, which betrayed his origins. However, he was not the typical Englishman.

According to George Cukor, who directed him in both *David Copperfield* and *Romeo and Juliet*: "Basil was an *uniquely* nice man —not bland or boring—just nice. His nature was simple and he had a joy of life."

In a 1936 interview with *Motion Picture* magazine, the actor explained why he felt "confined and defeated" living in his homeland: "I am a born enthusiast, but I found that enthusiasm, generally speaking, is bad manners in England. I couldn't stand the conventional British chill."

Rathbone decided to live his life in the United States, though he chose not to become a citizen of his adopted country, explaining: "I work here . . . I pay my taxes here . . . I invest my money here. But, I fought for England and my brother died for it. I can't abandon those roots that easily."

The Hollywood community respected Rathbone's point of view. They knew him as a man of integrity, who also felt an allegiance to the United States and its people.

Gale Gordon, one of the several actors to play Inspector Lestrade on the "Sherlock Holmes" radio program, remembers an incident: "Basil got angry at an announcer who'd made a nasty remark about the United States and, in front of the entire cast, he went into one of the most beautiful dissertations on Americanism I've ever heard. It was very moving."

Actor Jonathan Kidd (*aka* Kurt Richards) had worked with Rathbone in the 1950 New York production of *Julius Caesar*. On a winter morning in 1955, Kidd was between trains in Washington, D.C. It was just before dawn and he decided to visit the Lincoln Memorial. At the base of the monument, he ran into the British performer, staring at the shrine—with tears in his eyes. Rathbone, in town for a day to do a reading with Helen Gahagan Douglas, accounted for his presence at such an early hour: "I cannot come to Washington without seeing this man."

He was a sensitive individual—not afraid to bare his emotions. When, in 1942, the S.S. *Normandie* burned in New York Harbor, witnesses reported they observed Basil weeping as he viewed the sight.

Rathbone liked people and, according to his widow, "didn't have an enemy in the world."

He always seemed to be going out of his way to help somebody. For the above-mentioned production of *Julius Caesar,* Jonathan Kidd was given a costume that he felt was inconsistent with his character. Pleas to the producers seemed to fall on deaf ears, so Kidd resigned himself to wearing the "rag"—until Rathbone became aware of the problem.

Reporting for rehearsal one day, Kidd found a very expensive costume hanging in his dressing room. He realized that the garment must have been rented by Rathbone—and paid for out of the star's own pocket. When he thanked Basil, the actor replied, "Well, the play's the thing, isn't it?"

Vincent Price was always grateful to his friend, Rathbone, for a kindness the Britisher had shown his son during the early 1960s. Basil was then doing a regular spot on the NBC radio series "Monitor," reading poetry—both classical and contemporary.

Barrett Price, a poet and resident of New Mexico, was contacted by Rathbone, who requested that he send him some of his work. Price complied and the poems were, subsequently, read by the actor on his program. Rathbone had sought out the young man on his own volition—*not* as a favor to his father.

In his autobiography, *In and Out of Character,* Basil described himself as a frustrated writer/poet. "Monitor," on which he would often read the poetry of young people, helped him to cope with that discontentment.

Rathbone's fascination with the young might best be illustrated with a passage from a letter he wrote in 1945 to Glenhall Taylor, a director for the "Sherlock Holmes" radio show. The occasion was Taylor's marriage: ". . . I do hope you will decide to have a child. Personally, I don't think any place can be called home for long that lacks a child's voice about it. And of all mystery stories, nothing is comparable to trying to figure out what one's child really thinks . . ."

He was, himself, a devoted father, constantly taking his adopted daughter, Cynthia, on outings, such as to the beach or the zoo. When the girl grew older, she accompanied him on his summer-stock tours.

Rodion, Basil's natural son from his first marriage, became a

With son, Rodion, and Ouida.

member of the Rathbone household during the late 1930s. Separated since 1919, the father and son were able to achieve a close relationship in the two years they lived together.

The actor's second wife, Ouida, was responsible for the reunion. Unknown to her husband, she had made friends with his former spouse, as well as Rodion. The boy, ultimately, moved from England to Hollywood, where his father got him a job at Warner Brothers in the editorial department. Rathbone commented in a 1938 *Photoplay* interview: "Ouida brought us together again. Now my happiness is complete. And I owe this, as I owe everything, to her."

Rodion stayed with Basil and Ouida until Britain became involved in World War II, at which time he returned to his country to serve in the military.

Before he'd met the former Ouida Bergere, Rathbone suffered from, as he put it, "the worst inferiority complex Dr. Freud ever imagined." Conversations with people terrified him. He was, in fact, afraid to express his own thoughts. Ultimately, this mental attitude hampered the actor's progress in his profession.

His problem became apparent after the end of World War 1.

Rathbone recalled: "I came out of the war comparatively untouched. That is, I wasn't shell-shocked or scarred up. But I had lost all sense of life's realities.

"Somehow I expected to be taken care of—as I had been in the army. I shrank from decisions. I never went after things I wanted. I hated any sort of battle or argument. I just wanted to be let alone— to vegetate. I was completely negative."

Miss Bergere's strong and definite personality was the complete antithesis of her husband's. According to Basil, she taught him some very important things: ". . . that you are as important as you make yourself; that you must have respect for yourself or no one will respect you; that an actor, particularly, must be aggressive; that it's all very well to expect and accept breaks and good fortune, but it's not enough. You must back yourself up."

Rathbone went along with Ouida's advice—and his career prospered. She also assisted him in conquering his social fears to the point

Rathbone in a Metro-Goldwyn-Mayer publicity shot.

where he garnered a reputation as a most charming conversationalist.

It was a great love affair between the two. Certainly, their marriage was one of the happiest in show business.

The Rathbones enjoyed throwing gala parties and, during the period from the late 1930s until the mid-1940s, they were known as the foremost host and hostess on the Hollywood social scene. The actor credited his wife for the success of these elegant functions: "I come to my own parties as a guest. Ouida does it all and, when Ouida does anything, she does it right."

Lew Ayres recalls attending one of these popular events: "I walked into the house and found myself among this great sea of personalities."

Guest lists for the parties were virtually a "Who's Who" of the entertainment industry and the arts. Regular callers were Ronald Colman, Max Reinhardt, Edward G. Robinson, Henry Blanke, Charles

Publicity shot: Basil and Ouida.

Boyer, Nigel Bruce, Boris Karloff, Norma Shearer, Douglas Fairbanks, Jr., Merle Oberon, Cesar Romero, Ida Lupino, Vincent Price, Mary Pickford, David Niven, Ralph Forbes, Laurence Olivier, Arthur Rubenstein, and Jascha Heifitz, as well as their respective spouses.

An orchestra was in attendance for the events and, if artists such as Rubenstein or Heifitz were present, they would, of course, play something.

Each gathering had its own theme. On one occasion, it was a costume ball. Another time, Ouida had a solid "blanket" of gardenias laid over the lawn. For Christmas, the house and grounds were covered with artificial snow to compensate for a lack of the real thing.

Needless to say, the parties were both lavish—and expensive. Indeed, friends of the Rathbones often expressed their concern that the couple might be living beyond their means by hosting such functions.

In a 1964 television interview, Basil described the affairs as ". . . not fantastic . . . but in very good taste."

Producer Henry Blanke remembers an incident that took place at one of the events: "Errol Flynn was there and, as might be expected, he was drunk. For some reason, he got the 'hots' for the homely daughter of another guest . . . an Italian banker. He followed her home and passed out on her living room couch. Late that night, the banker delivered Flynn back to Rathbone's house and left him unconscious on the lawn.

"The next morning, Basil and Ouida were having breakfast on the patio, when the gardener turned on the sprinklers. Who should spring up from the grass, but a hung-over Errol Flynn. The Rathbone's sat—mouths agape—as Errol bid them a cheery 'Good morning,' then departed for home."

Many people were surprised to learn that Basil Rathbone had a marvelous sense of humor. The cast and crew on his various films enjoyed listening to his funny anecdotes, which he told regularly.

He also had a reputation as a practical joker, finding his greatest enjoyment in playing gags on Nigel Bruce, his Dr. Watson from the "Sherlock Holmes" series and a very close friend. "Willy," in turn, would have a delightful time retaliating.

Bob Red, who for a period of time produced the "Holmes" radio show, reflects that "both Rathbone and Bruce had crazy senses of humor. While on the air, they would constantly be trying to break each other up. If one of them had a long speech to deliver, the other would lay his script down and make funny faces."

Glenhall Taylor considers the program one of the most enjoyable he ever directed: "Whenever Basil or Nigel disapproved of a direction I gave them, they would throw their doughnuts at me. By the time rehearsal was over with, the glass front of my control booth was filthy."

Gale Gordon: "Every time Nigel would go out of the rehearsal studio, Basil would either mess up the pages of his script or write nasty words in it. Willy would come back, start to read his lines, then become totally flustered when he discovered Basil's prank. It was always a very funny scene."

Bruce, not to be bested by Basil's antics, found ways to turn-the-tables on his friend. Gordon continues: "The three of us were having lunch together in a drugstore across the street from the radio studio. There was an open barrel of walnuts by the door and, as we walked out, Basil reached down and took a couple . . . stuffing them into his pocket. Bruce turned around, a twinkle in his eye, and called out to the proprietor, 'I say, my friend is pinching your nuts!'

"Rathbone ran like a scared rabbit."

Taylor relates another incident: "We'd done the show from San Francisco one week to promote the sale of War Bonds. The company took the night train back to Los Angeles and, the next morning, we were all having breakfast in the dining car.

"Rathbone's wife and little girl, Cynthia, were there and, after he'd finished eating, Basil picked up his newspaper and started to leave. Willy was sitting across the aisle and, with a knowing look, he asked the child, 'Cynthia, where's your daddy going?'

"The girl answered in her innocent, but loud voice, 'Daddy's going to make after-breakfast plop plops.' Basil made a quick exit."

Boris Karloff was another performer Rathbone enjoyed working with. George Schaefer remembers directing them both in the "Hallmark Hall of Fame" production of *The Lark*: "They were best of friends, but each of them had ideas on how the other should play his role. From time-to-time, either Boris or Basil would call me aside and make a suggestion . . . 'George, I think that Boris would be more effective if he. . . .' I didn't mind it a bit. In fact, it was all rather amusing."

Rathbone was an Episcopalian who worked at his religion. In a 1936 interview with the *Los Angeles Times,* he commented: "Any religion is marvelous. All people, and particularly artists, must have some faith to cling to."

He believed in ESP—and had good reason to, as his life had been affected more than once by unexplained events.

When the actor was almost four years old, his family booked passage on a ship sailing from South Africa to England. Prior to its departure, his mother, Barbara, had a dream that foretold of the vessel's sinking in the Bay of Biscay. Disturbed, she convinced her husband that they should take a later boat. It was the right decision. Their original ship did, in fact, go down with all hands—at the exact spot prophesied in the vision.

1930: Rathbone with his dog, Moritz.

Another incident occurred during the First World War. Basil experienced a nightmare in which his brother, John, was killed in battle. A few weeks later, the performer was in a dugout when he had a premonition that something was "not right" with John. He was unable to do anything about it at the time, but afterward, Basil learned that his brother had met his death—at the same moment he'd become conscious that there was something amiss.

Rathbone's interests were varied. He loved baseball, having become addicted to it shortly after moving to the United States. He also liked swimming, riding, football, tennis, golf, and cricket, and, from a more intellectual standpoint, was an avid reader and had a great love for music.

There was always a book of poetry with him on the set, which he would read when he wasn't otherwise occupied. Then, at mid-afternoon, filming would halt for a few minutes, while Rathbone and the cast enjoyed tea.

The actor was fond of good food. As he once told Robert Cummings, "I like to eat luxuriously."

Rehearsing the duel for the motion picture version of Romeo and Juliet.

Publicity shot.

He loved dogs, and at times there were several living in the Rath-bone household. His favorite was a black German Shepherd, Moritz, which he acquired during the mid-1920s. The animal was with Basil for eleven years. It was a source of constant pleasure and, occasionally —embarrassment.

One evening, Rathbone was walking with the dog along New York's 46th street, when Moritz, unable to find a lamp post, decided to relieve himself on the leg of a woman pedestrian. Basil, red-faced and at a loss for words, could barely sputter out an apology. Luckily, the woman was so impressed at meeting Basil Rathbone, that she told him to forget the whole matter and went on her way.

The actor was one of Hollywood's finest swordsmen, having studied with the best fencing instructors in the business. Although, on the screen, actors like Errol Flynn and Tyrone Power would, ultimately, run him through with their rapiers, Basil contented himself with the knowledge that he, in fact, could have killed any of his opponents with one thrust.

Rathbone was not afraid to make sport of himself. Actually, he rather enjoyed it. A regular guest on the various radio and television comedy programs, he acted as a foil for some of the top clowns in the entertainment industry.

Producer Arthur Whitelaw met Rathbone in 1955, when the actor was appearing at the Seacliffe Summer Theater on Long Island, New York. Whitelaw was serving as an apprentice with the group and, on this particular evening, was working the box office.

Rathbone arrived at the theater early. To pass the time, he joined Whitelaw in the box office, asking if he could help.

The phone rang. Basil answered it: "Hello. . . . Tonight, madame, we are presenting *The Winslow Boy* starring Razzle Bathbone. . . . that's right, *Razzle Bathbone!*" Whereupon he hung up the receiver.

Basil Rathbone may have frightened audiences in darkened movie houses, but, off the screen, he was completely unlike that villainous image. Douglas Fairbanks, Jr. sums up the performer quite succinctly when he describes him as "a charming, gentle, intelligent, and thoroughly 'nice guy.' "

II
Biography

Unlike many show business personalities of his era, Basil Rathbone was *not* "born in a trunk." Nor was he a child of poverty. The actor's family tree was, in fact, a distinguished one.

The paternal side boasted a cousin, Eleanor Rathbone, the first woman ever to be elected to British Parliament, and Uncle Herbert Rathbone, Lord Mayor of Liverpool. On the other hand, Mother was a descendant of King Henry IV. Relatives also included poets Stephen Phillips and Lawrence Binyon, as well as the noted actor/manager, Sir Frank Benson. Finally, the Rathbones were the shipping firm of Holt and Company and the Liverpool, London, and Globe Insurance Company.

In the wake of all this, Philip St. John Basil Rathbone was born in Johannesburg, South Africa, on June 13, 1892. His parents were Edgar Philip Rathbone, a mining engineer of English/Scotch ancestry, and Irish-born Anna Barbara (George) Rathbone, a talented violinist. A daughter, Beatrice, joined the family two years later.

It was early January of 1896 when the Rathbones departed Johannesburg for Durban—a three-hundred-mile journey by train. The Boer War was in progress and Edgar, who had been employed in the South African gold fields, was suspected of being a British spy. The trek to the coast through enemy territory was relatively uneventful, although, during several inspection stops, at which time Boer soldiers boarded the train, Father was forced to hide under a seat.

Upon their arrival in Durban, Mrs. Rathbone and the two children came down with typhoid fever. The trio spent several weeks in the hospital, but, eventually, the family sailed for England on the *Walmer Castle*, taking up residence in London. Sometime later, another son, John, was born.

The Rathbones were a close-knit family, in spite of the fact that Edgar, an adventure-loving man, would occasionally leave home to pursue his profession. In 1897, he traveled to Alaska, to become one

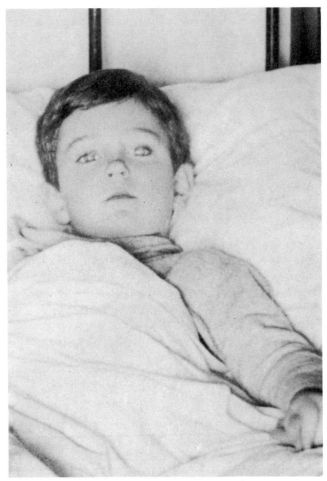

Rathbone at age three in a hospital in Durban, South Africa.

of the first men to reach the Klondike during the famous gold rush. Yet, he remained a devoted husband and father and Basil's memories of childhood were pleasant ones.

"Ratters," as young Basil was called by his classmates, received his education at the Repton School, where he was a member of both the debating and musical societies. It was at that institution that the lad wrote his first play, *King Arthur*. Nevertheless, he kept his interest in the theatre to himself, fearing that his teachers and classmates in such a sports-minded school might think him to be a "queer one."

Following his graduation in 1910, Basil announced to his parents that he intended to become an actor. Edgar, not enthusiastic over the choice, suggested that his son try the business world for a year to see how he liked it. The young Rathbone agreed to the compromise and, with the help of his father, obtained a position as junior clerk in the main office of the Liverpool, London, and Globe Insurance Company.

For a young man who'd aspired to become a part of the theatre since the age of seven, one year of dull office work was not enough to alter his ambition. Ergo, on the final day of his "servitude," Basil met with his cousin, actor/manager Frank Benson, founder of the annual Stratford-Upon-Avon Shakespeare Festival and "father" of British Actors' Equity.

His audition, a scene from *The Merchant of Venice*, left much to be desired, but Benson felt the youth had potential and assigned him

Rathbone at age four with his sister in London.

Rathbone at age five with sister, brother, and mother in Sussex.

With Brother John (center) and Sister Beatrice.

to tour England, Scotland, and Ireland for a year with his number-two Shakespearean company.

The repertory experience proved invaluable to Basil, as it afforded him the opportunity to play a variety of secondary roles, in addition to teaching him the fundamentals of diction, fencing, deportment, and makeup. His professional debut was as Hortensio in a production of *The Taming of the Shrew* at the Theatre Royal in Ipswich. The date was April 22, 1911.

Benson was impressed with his cousin's work, and the following year Basil was selected to play the important juvenile parts in the manager's own company at Stratford-Upon-Avon. He appeared in such

As Orsino in Twelfth Night **for Sir Frank Benson.**

As the Duke of Aumerle in Richard II for Sir Frank Benson.

As Laertes in Hamlet **for Sir Frank Benson.**

As the Dauphin in Henry V **at the Shaftesbury Theatre.**

varied roles as Orsino in *Twelfth Night,* the Duke of Aumerle from *Richard II,* and Laertes in *Hamlet.* When the company toured the United States in 1913, Rathbone went along, essaying Paris from *Romeo and Juliet,* Fenton in *The Merry Wives of Windsor,* Silvius in *As You Like It,* and Lorenzo from *The Merchant of Venice.* His salary was thirty shillings, the equivalent of $4.50 per week.

The actress playing opposite Rathbone in both *The Merchant of Venice* and *As You Like It* was Ethel Marion Foreman, who, in October of 1914, became his first wife.

That same year, Basil made his London stage debut as Finch in Stephen Phillips's *The Sin of David,* which played the Savoy Theatre for a brief run. The play, starring H. B. Irving and Miriam Lewes, was an updated adaptation of the David and Bathsheba biblical story, set in 1643.

Returning to Shakespeare, the actor did the role of the Dauphin in *Henry V,* presented at the Shaftsbury Theater, after which, in 1915, he played Lysander in a production of *A Midsummer Night's Dream* at the Royal Court Theater.

In July 1915, a son, Rodion, was born to the Rathbones. Soon thereafter, Basil decided to do his part in the war effort, enlisting in the British Army. He completed his basic training at a camp near London, then was sent to an officers' training school, located at Gailes in Scotland. Commissioned a second lieutenant, he was assigned, as per his request, to the Liverpool Scottish Regiment.

A distinguished service record in France resulted in Basil being awarded the Military Cross in September of 1918. Interviewed years later, he modestly dismissed his First World War actions, explaining: "All I did was to disguise myself as a tree and cross no man's land to gather a bit of information from the German lines. I have not since been called upon to play a tree."

Rathbone's return to civilian life was tinged with sadness. Not only had his brother, John, fallen in battle, but, while he was away, his mother had also passed on. The marriage to Marion Foreman was not going well either and, shortly after being mustered out of the service, he and his wife separated.

Lonely and broke, Basil borrowed some money from friends and moved into a one-room flat in Kensington. August of 1919 brought an offer from W. H. Savery, who had replaced Sir Frank Benson as manager of the New Shakespeare Company at Stratford-Upon-Avon. Rathbone was signed at five pounds per week to appear in four plays for the autumn season. The parts were good ones: Cassius in *Julius Caesar;* Ferdinand in *The Tempest;* Florizel from *The Winter's Tale;* and, most important, Romeo in *Romeo and Juliet*— his favorite Shakespearean role.

The performer's only other activity in 1919 was as the Aide-de-Camp in a short-lived production of Herbert Trench's *Napoleon*, which played the Queen's Theater in London. A. E. George starred in the title role.

1920 was a lucky year for the 6'11½" actor. Constance Collier, the well-known British star, had seen Basil play Romeo at Stratford and, when casting began for the London production of *Peter Ibbetson*, she sent for him. The interview with the actress was a good one and Rathbone departed—positive that he would be playing the title role.

The next day, he was having a drink in a London pub with fellow Thespians Henry Daniell and George Ralph. It didn't take long for the trio to discover that all of them were up for the same part and that each felt the role was his—until, of course, they started to compare the respective salaries they'd agreed to work for.

Ralph had quoted twenty-five pounds per week and Daniell's price was twenty. But, low man was Rathbone at ten pounds and *that* figure assured his being cast in the important project.

As Romeo in Romeo and Juliet **for the New Shakespeare Company.**

With Constance Collier in Peter Ibbetson.

John N. Raphael's dramatic adaptation of George DuMaurier's romantic novel opened at the Savoy Theater in February of 1920. Although the play was considered a failure by the British critics, performances were generally praised. Of the actor in the title role, the *Athenaeum* said: "Mr. Basil Rathbone is prettily sincere."

Peter Ibbetson was the break that Rathbone had been waiting for and, in June, he was chosen to appear opposite Mrs. Patrick Campbell in Philip Moeller's *Madame Sand* at the Duke of York's Theater. The plot dealt with the romance between French novelist George Sand and poet Alfred de Musset. Unfortunately, the material was poorly received. According to the *Athenaeum:* "The author is a trifle more successful with some of the minor characters. The Alfred de Musset, indeed, is poor, despite Mr. Basil Rathbone's fine performance. We get the absinthe and the nerves without the genius. . . ."

Legend has it that Mrs. Campbell was the party who christened Rathbone "the actor with a face like two profiles stuck together," then improved her description by calling him "a folded umbrella taking elocution lessons."

Certainly, the actress was not known for her tact. At the dress rehearsal for *Madame Sand,* she took one look at Rathbone's makeup and inquired, "What are you made up as . . . a rocking horse?"

Basil then *starred* as Major Wharton, a man who'd lost his faith in God. The play was *The Unknown* by W. Somerset Maugham, which opened in August of 1920 at the Aldwych Theater. The reviewer from the *London Morning Post* said: "Basil Rathbone as John, the unbeliever, did not impress. His bearing was no advocacy of his cause." The production's run was not a long one.

Next, the actor was cast as Harold Glaive in another poorly received drama, *Every Woman's Privilege* by J. Hastings Turner, which played the Globe Theater. The *London Observer* commented: "Mr. Basil Rathbone, as a middle-class Socialist of a type that never was on land or sea, displayed the shyness and indifference that the part required."

Rathbone's final assignment of 1920 was a revival of *Fedora,* Victorien Sardou's vehicle for Sarah Bernhardt. With Marie Lohr in the title role, the production opened to disastrous reviews at the Globe Theater in early November. Said the *Athenaeum:* "She [Miss Lohr] ought to borrow a leaf from Mr. Basil Rathbone's book and take her part with the easy contempt (and competence) with which he gets through the ·imbecile character of Louis Ipanoff."

Basil's stage work had attracted the attention of motion picture producer/director Maurice Elvey, who set the actor to star in two silent films for the Stoll Company. The first to go before cameras was *The Fruitful Vine,* a triangle love story, which co-starred Valya and Robert English. It was released in September of 1921.

Although shot after *The Fruitful Vine, Innocent* was the first of the two projects to go into theaters. Appearing with Madge Stuart, Rathbone played a painter who wins the heart of the film's heroine, then callously discards her. It was adapted by William J. Elliott from a story by Marie Corelli. The release date was March 1921.

Neither of the Elvey pictures helped to further Basil's career, so,

after he'd finished working on them, the performer signed with the
Royal Court Theater to star in two Shakespearean plays—*King Henry
IV, Part 2* as Prince Hal, and *Othello* as Iago. Of his performance in
the latter production, which had Godfrey Tearle essaying the title
role, the *Saturday Review* said: "Mr. Basil Rathbone's Iago was also
a notable performance. Here we had little or nothing of the grand
manner. Even the 'Divinity of hell!' verses were spoken almost con-
versationally, though their import was heightened by a sinister smile;
but the spite and devilish ingenuity of the character were clearly
brought out. Here too, as in the 'Othello,' the effect of the actor's
performance became more intense as it proceeded. It was never a
great Iago, but it was always vivid and convincing, with the subtle
Italianate touch."

On the opening night of *Othello*, Rathbone developed an un-
controllable case of the hiccups about halfway through the performance. But, instead of being laughed off the stage, as he'd feared, his
exit drew loud applause from the audience. In fact, a London reviewer commented that he thought Rathbone's interpretation of a
"drunk" Iago was "brilliant."

Early in August of 1921, the actor opened at The Garrick in a
production of *The Edge O' Beyond*, Roy Horniman and Ruby Miller's adaptation of Gertrude Page's romantic novel. E. Holman Clark
produced the well-received play. Of Rathbone, the *Stage* said: "The
strongest and most emotional work devolves upon Mr. Rathbone as
Lawson."

Producer Gilbert Miller then signed Rathbone to make his Broadway debut in a ten-year-old Hungarian comedy by Melchior Lengyel
and Lajos Biro, *The Czarina*, which dealt with Catherine the Great.
Basil and Miller sailed for the United States aboard the S. S. *Olympic*
on December 21, 1921.

Opening late in January at the Empire Theater, the production
received good notices from critics, but, unfortunately, was only a
modest success. Commenting on Rathbone, who played Count Alexei
Czerny to Doris Keane's Catherine, Alexander Woollcott said in the
New York Times: "And there is this young Basil Rathbone, who
emerged from the provinces two years ago to play *Peter Ibbetson* in
London. His is an excellent performance—as full of bounce as the
ballet in 'Prince Igor.'"

Following the close of *The Czarina*, the actor returned to London
to star as George Conway in Grossmith and Malone's production of
W. Somerset Maugham's *East of Suez* at His Majesty's Theater. Basil
Dean directed the script, which the *Saturday Review* described as "a
quite insincere play."

The Maugham drama ran for almost a year, after which Dean
convinced Rathbone to move over to St. Martin's Theater and play

Publicity shot from The Czarina.

Harry Domain in *R. U. R.*, Karel Capek's play about robots. Also
in the cast were Leslie Banks and Frances Carson. The *Saturday Review* said of the star: "Mr. Basil Rathbone did very pleasantly and
manfully."

Basil's third motion picture, an adaptation of Richard Brinsley
Sheridan's *The School for Scandal*, was released in August of 1923.
Bertram Phillips directed the costume comedy, in which Rathbone
portrayed Joseph Surface.

Gilbert Miller recalled the actor to America in the fall to co-star
with Eva Le Gallienne and Philip Merivale in Melville Baker's trans-
lation of Ferenc Molnar's comedy, *The Swan*. The production opened
on October 23, 1923 at the Cort Theater in New York. As Dr. Nicholas
Agi, the tutor in love with a princess, Rathbone garnered excellent
notices from reviewers. Said John Corbin in the *New York Times:*
"The tutor, a character that exalts the dignity and might of learning
and its mastery over all princes in the modern world, is as evenly and
vigorously sustained by Basil Rathbone."

The Swan was a tremendous success, playing a total of 255 performances. Most important, it made Rathbone a Broadway star.

About a month after the play opened, Basil was invited by actor Clifton Webb to attend a party being thrown by Ouida Bergere, a top Hollywood script writer and the former wife of director George Fitzmaurice. She, incidentally, had written *Forever*, the silent movie version of *Peter Ibbetson*.

With Eva Le Gallienne in The Swan.

Although she'd never met him, Miss Bergere was already an admirer of Rathbone. In fact, after seeing him in *The Czarina,* she informed her escort that it was her intention to marry the handsome dark-haired actor.

Basil and Ouida took to each other immediately and, following a weekend spent together with several other guests at her house in Great Neck, Long Island, the couple knew that they were in love.

However, before he could marry Miss Bergere, Basil had to obtain a divorce from Marion Foreman—a task that delayed the wedding for three years.

In the meantime, Rathbone's career was keeping him busy. *The Swan* was playing to full houses and, during the latter part of February 1924, he appeared with Eva Le Gallienne at the Cort in three special matinee performances of *The Assumption of Hannele* by Gerhart Hauptmann. The play, in which he portrayed Gottwald, received poor notices from the critics.

He also made his American film debut in 1924. *Trouping with Ellen,* an Eastern Production, starred Helene Chadwick and Gaston Glass. Rathbone's role in the insignificant photoplay was that of Tony Winterslip, scion of a rich family.

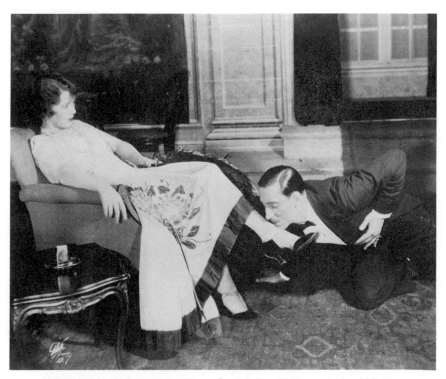

With Elsie Ferguson in The Grand Duchess and the Waiter.

From September of 1924 through Spring of the subsequent year, Rathbone made a successful tour of the major cities in the United States, repeating his Broadway role in *The Swan*. After this, Hollywood beckoned and Basil was signed by Metro-Goldwyn-Mayer to appear as a villainous apache dancer in *The Masked Bride*, starring Mae Murray and Francis X. Bushman. It was a pleasing melodrama, but, once again, it did nothing for his career.

He returned to New York in October as the co-star of *The Grand Duchess and the Waiter*, a comedy by Alfred Savoir, with staging by Frank Reicher. Other cast members included Elsie Ferguson, Alison Skipworth, and Frederic Worlock.

Rathbone's role was that of Albert, an aristocrat forced to assume the guise of a waiter in order to win the woman he loves. Said the *New York Times:* "In the part of the waiter, Mr. Rathbone enacts the stiff, bewildered, obedient suitor common to that type of entertainment, and with no little skill." The show closed after only thirty-one performances.

Port O' London, a melodrama by George W. Oliver, played a scant twenty-four performances at Daly's 63rd Street Theater during February, 1926. Thompson Buchanan staged the production, which starred Rathbone, Alison Skipworth, and Walter Kingsford. According to the *New York Times:* "Basil Rathbone as the sidewalk artist was an appealing and *almost* tragic figure. Not quite tragic, somehow."

Rathbone's divorce from Marion Foreman became final early in 1926, and on April 18th he wed Ouida Bergere at the home of a New York architect, Joseph Thomas. It was a good marriage, enduring until the actor's death forty-one years later.

The couple's interests and tastes were virtually identical. Both had a sentimental nature, and every year on their wedding anniversary, they would make it a point to repeat their marriage vows to each other.

Even before they were married, Ouida took a strong interest in Basil's career. He'd been paid only five hundred dollars per week for his role in *The Swan*, but after the attractive Miss Bergere began to advise him, his salaries increased steadily.

Believing that a *successful* marriage could have only one "breadwinner," the fifteen-hundred-dollar-per-week screenwriter had asked for a release from her pending contracts. Producer Samuel Goldwyn tried to talk Ouida out of her decision, arguing: "Why sacrifice your career to marry a 'ham' actor?"

To this, she replied: "Basil Rathbone is *not* a 'ham' actor, but a gentleman."

The performer's only picture in 1926 was released to theaters in August. *The Great Deception,* from a novel by George Gibbs, had Basil playing a German agent who menaces stars Ben Lyon and Aileen Pringle. The film was a moderate success.

Near the end of that year, Basil Rathbone was arrested—for offending public morals.

He'd been set by Gilbert Miller to star with Helen Menken and Arthur Wontner in *The Captive,* adapted by Arthur Hornblow, Jr.,

Mr. and Mrs. Basil Rathbone at their wedding.

from a French play, *La Prisonniere* by Edward Bourdet. Opening to excellent reviews at the Empire Theater in late September, the drama concerned a woman involved in a homosexual relationship. Needless to say, Lesbianism was a *very* controversial subject in 1926.

Of Rathbone's contribution to the play, which ran 160 performances, Brooks Atkinson of the *New York Times* said: "And Mr. Rathbone acts with rare dignity and understanding; without a single histrionic flourish, his Jacques Virieu indicates profound emotion and the torture of conflicting emotions."

The production had been playing to good houses for seventeen weeks when, after an evening's performance, the entire cast was arrested by the police, taken to night court, and booked on the aforementioned morals charge. Rathbone's bail, posted by the management of the theater, was set at one thousand dollars.

Eventually, all charges were dismissed, but the producers were forced to agree not to reopen the production, the play having been "dark" since the night of the arrest.

The closing of *The Captive* angered Rathbone. With a city election coming up in the near future, he felt the actions of the New York officials were politically motivated and that the censorship was a grave injustice to a fine play, which dealt with a serious social problem.

1927 started out with the actor refusing the male lead in a Gloria Swanson film, *The Love of Sunya*—the role eventually going to John Boles. Instead, he spent the year appearing in three plays on the New York stage.

Love Is Like That, a comedy by S. N. Behrman and Kenyon Nicholson, opened on April 18th at the Cort Theater and played a total of twenty-four performances. Atkinson of the *New York Times* commented: "Mr. Rathbone, who is always attractive and accomplished, gives the proper courteous distinction to the exiled prince." As for the play itself, the critic labeled it "dreary entertainment."

June found Basil moving over to the New Amsterdam Theater to play Cassius again in an eight-performance run of *Julius Caesar*. Described as "a curiously ill-assorted production" by the *New York Times,* the offering was directed by John Craig and had Tyrone Power, Sr., Frederic Worlock, and Harry Davenport in the cast.

On September 21st, he opened at the Longacre Theater—as Gaston, in *The Command To Love,* a bedroom comedy, adapted from the German of Rudolph Lothar and Fritz Gottwald by Herman Bernstein and Brian Marlow. Staging was by Lester Lonergan. Aside from Basil, the cast included Henry Stephenson, Violet Kemble Cooper, Mary Nash, and Ferdinand Gottschalk. In the *New York Times,* Brooks Atkinson said: "Mr. Stephenson, Mr. Rathbone, and Mr. Gotts-

With Mary Nash in The Command to Love.

chalk play with capital tact and relish—dry, sardonic, and worldly
wise."

A critical and financial success, *The Command To Love* played
247 performances on Broadway, then went on national tour for a
full year.

Rathbone had been intrigued with the character of Judas Iscariot
since his teens. It was during the New York run of *The Command
To Love* that he met Walter Ferris, a teacher who shared his interest
in the betrayer of Christ, and the two men decided to collaborate
on a play about the biblical figure.

They presented their central character as an intellectual reformer,
unable to grasp the meaning of Jesus' ultimate weapon—love. According to their play, which was written in one month, Judas betrayed Christ in order to force him into violent action against the
Romans. Believing that reform could only come through conquest by
the sword, the traitor had hoped to save Jesus from himself.

Judas, produced by William A. Brady, Jr. and Dwight Deero Winan, opened on January 23, 1929, at the Longacre Theater, under the direction of Richard Boleslawski. Of course, Rathbone played the title role.

The production was poorly received, playing only a dozen performances before closing. Said the *New York Times:* "Both the play *Judas* and Mr. Rathbone's acting of the part are, to this chronicler, presumptuous."

Publicity shot from the stage production of Judas.

1929: With Ouida at a costume ball at the Beverly Hills Hotel.

Following the demise of his play, Basil received two intriguing offers. The first was to star in the Broadway production of *Death Takes a Holiday*. However, more enticing was a bid from Metro-Goldwyn-Mayer to co-star with Norma Shearer in one of the studio's first talking pictures, an adaptation of Frederick Lonsdale's comedy about an adventuress in Monte Carlo—*The Last of Mrs. Cheyney*.

Ouida was instrumental in negotiating the Metro deal, which gained for her husband a salary twice the amount he had been paid on either of his previous Hollywood pictures. She advised him *not* to sign a long-term contract with the studio, feeling that he could do better as a free-lance performer. Their ultimate goal was to build his salary from five hundred to five thousand dollars per week. The "dream" became a reality in the latter part of the 1930s through the mid-1940s, when Basil was one of the most sought-after character actors in films.

The Last of Mrs. Cheyney, an August 1929 release, was directed by Sidney Franklin. It was one of the year's major successes and made Rathbone a "hot" actor in Hollywood.

Talkies were "the thing" and movie producers were seeking performers with trained voices. During 1930, the filmgoing public had the opportunity to view Rathbone doing leads in no less than seven features.

The Bishop Murder Case was released by Metro in February and had Basil playing S. S. Van Dine's suave detective, Philo Vance, a role previously essayed in a more relaxed manner by William Powell.

In April, he co-starred as the violinist husband of Billie Dove in *A Notorious Affair*, a triangle love story for First National. Lloyd Bacon directed. Miss Dove recalls that "working with Basil Rathbone was a sheer delight. He was a finished actor and always a perfect gentleman—one with charm, consideration, and an innate sense of humor."

Ruth Chatterton and Ralph Forbes appeared with the performer in his next picture, again a Metro project. *The Lady of Scandal* was based on another Frederick Lonsdale play, *The High Road,* and had Sidney Franklin for its director. The feature was a June release.

The following month, another M.G.M. film, *This Mad World,* appeared on the scene. This time, Rathbone was a French spy, romancing Kay Johnson, the wife of a German general. The director was William DeMille.

August ushered in a comedy from First National, *The Flirting Widow,* with Dorothy Mackaill. It was based on a play by A. E. W. Mason. Rathbone's amusing role was that of a British Army officer.

Universal's *A Lady Surrenders* was a September release. John Stahl directed the adaptation of John Erskine's novel, *Sincerity.* The stars were Genevieve Tobin, Conrad Nagel, Rathbone, and Rose Hobart.

His final movie of the year was *Sin Takes a Holiday,* a November release from Pathé. Rathbone, doing the role of a playboy, supported Constance Bennett and Kenneth MacKenna in this romantic comedy.

Unfortunately, none of these program pictures impressed either critics or audiences and, by the end of the year, Basil Rathbone was back in New York.

At the beginning of December, he opened at the Fulton Theater in *A Kiss of Importance,* a comedy adapted by Arthur Hornblow, Jr., from Andre Picard and H. H. Harwood's play, *Monsieur St. Obin.* Lionel Atwill directed. Of Basil's portrayal of Christian Saint Obin, a professional correspondent, the *New York Times* said: "Mr. Rathbone, fortunately, is a suave and knowing actor, and his performance, while suffering from overeagerness, could be worse." The production closed after twenty-four performances.

Art director Cedric Gibbons, Basil Rathbone, Kay Johnson, and director William DeMille on the set of This Mad World.

In February, the Britisher starred with Henry Daniell and Selena Royle in Roland Pertwee's *Heat Wave,* which played fifteen performances at the Fulton. Atkinson of the *New York Times* dismissed the project with: "Worse plays appear on Broadway from time to time, but seldom are they duller."

Two months later, Basil was starring at the Ethel Barrymore Theater with Edna Best in *Melo,* a play by Henri Bernstein, adapted from the French by Arthur Pollock. The plot had the actor portraying a violinist involved in an affair with the wife of an old friend. Atkinson commented: "Basil Rathbone plays with fervent clarity as Marcel." This show played sixty-seven performances.

Toward the end of 1931, he returned to Hollywood to replace an ailing Laurence Olivier as Pola Negri's dashing lover in the RKO picture *A Woman Commands.* Released in January of 1932, the production seemed to please the critics, although most felt that Rathbone was a bit too reserved as Captain Alex Pasitsch. The film served to confirm the suspicions of some "tinsel-town" producers that the actor was *not* the ideal choice to play a romantic lead on the screen.

Concurrent with the premiere of the Negri picture, he opened

With Edna Best in Melo.

on Broadway at the Selwyn Theater in Benn W. Levy's *The Devil
Passes,* co-starring Diana Wynyard. The premise of the religious
comedy was an interesting one, as it had Satan, in the guise of a
minister, visiting a group of civilized moderns, who are spending a
weekend at a country house. Brooks Atkinson of the *New York Times*
said: "Basil Rathbone is dapper and constricted as the evangelical
devil." *The Devil Passes* played a total of ninety-six performances.

The actor was set for Metro's *Reunion in Vienna* when he received a more lucrative offer to return to England for a series of stage
and screen projects.

Back in his homeland, he starred as the Unknown Gentleman in
Tonight or Never by Lili Hatvany, which played at the Duke of
York's Theater in London. Then, in the early part of 1933, he was
seen as Julian Beauclerc in a revival of Victorien Sardou's *Diplomacy*
at the Prince's Theater.

Filmmaking also kept him busy while he was in England. During the first half of 1933, he was seen in three British-made features:

Rathbone played a cad in *One Precious Year,* a slow-moving picture, starring Anne Grey and Flora Robson, with direction by Henry Edwards. It was never released in the United States.

He was next seen in another playboy role. The film was *After the Ball,* a Fox release, which teamed him with Esther Ralston. The project lacked most of the attributes of the original German film upon which it was based.

The third picture proved to be one of the best of Basil's career. *Loyalties,* John Galsworthy's play about anti-Semitism among London's upper social classes, was sensitively directed by Basil Dean. The first-rate cast, headed by Rathbone, who was magnificent as de Levis, the proud Jew, included Heather Thatcher, Miles Mander, and Alan Napier.

Fall 1932: Rathbone accepted an offer from Katharine Cornell to

A Woman Commands.

join her the following season for a seven-month tour of the United States in three repertory productions: *The Barretts of Wimpole Street* by Rudolf Besier, *Candida* by George Bernard Shaw, and *Romeo and Juliet* by William Shakespeare—the latter play to eventually open on Broadway. Basil was to portray Robert Browning, Morrell, and Romeo, respectively.

The eighty-six-city tour began in October of 1933 in Buffalo, New York, with a performance of *Romeo and Juliet,* followed the next night by *The Barretts of Wimpole Street.* Miss Cornell's husband, Guthrie McClintic, directed the three plays and the performing company included Orson Welles, Brenda Forbes, George Macready, and Helen Walpole.

Rathbone came down with a throat infection during dress rehearsals, which was to plague him for the entire tour. Yet, thanks to the nursing of his wife, the actor never missed a performance.

Basil received good notices while he was on the road. In reference to his portrayal of Morrell in *Candida,* the Columbus, Ohio, *Journal* said: "In the thankless role of the pastor husband, Basil Rathbone gave his usual finished performance, laboring with the long speeches that gave evidence of tedious and painstaking study."

Of his work in *The Barretts of Wimpole Street,* the same paper commented: "Basil Rathbone, always a reliable and skillful player on the stage and screen, gives a delightful performance of Robert Browning. The character is expertly conceived as a foil for Elizabeth, creating a fine light and shade, and Rathbone plays it with every regard for its nuances. His readings are those of an actor who knows his art well."

The tour concluded in May of 1934 with performances at the Brooklyn Academy of Music. The following month, Rathbone entered St. Luke's Hospital in New York to have his tonsils removed.

In July, he received an offer from producer David O. Selznick to come to Hollywood to play Mr. Murdstone in a screen version of Charles Dickens's *David Copperfield,* which was being filmed at Metro-Goldwyn-Mayer. The cast included W. C. Fields, Lionel Barrymore, Freddie Bartholomew, Maureen O'Sullivan, Roland Young, and Lewis Stone. George Cukor was the director.

Rathbone accepted the role of the tyrannical step-father and the move proved to be a smart one. After the picture was released in January of 1935, the actor once again found himself in demand by film producers. However, this time they wanted him for *important* projects.

In the meantime, Basil had rejoined Miss Cornell for the Broadway opening on December 20, 1934, of *Romeo and Juliet* at the Martin Beck Theater. Also with the company for the limited run was Brian Aherne as Mercutio and Edith Evans as Nurse. Orson

Publicity shot from The Barretts of Wimpole Street.

Welles, who'd essayed Mercutio on tour, took over the part of Tybalt.

The New York papers were not as kind to the British actor as the out-of-town sheets had been. Said the *New York Times:* "Mr. Rathbone is a neat and tidy actor with an immaculate exterior. Within those limitations, he plays a sufficient Romeo. The verse needs more virtuosity in speaking than he has at his command, for he is not always intelligible. When fortune goes against Romeo, Mr. Rathbone can raise his voice in vigorous lamentation, but he lacks the emotional range to play the part all the way through."

Brian Aherne, working with Basil for the first time, recalls him as "a fine actor . . . one of the best in the profession. He was also a fine man . . . good . . . kind . . . intelligent . . . humorous . . . and beloved by all who knew him."

David Copperfield opened around the country in January. Almost immediately thereafter, Rathbone was hired again by Selznick—this time to play Karenin, the insensitive husband, in *Anna Karenina,* being filmed at Metro with stars Greta Garbo and Fredric March. Clarence Brown directed the project, which gave Rathbone his best screen role to date.

In an interview with *Motion Picture* magazine, the actor said: "My

With Elizabeth Allan on the set of David Copperfield.

With Katharine Cornell in Romeo and Juliet.

own attitude toward Karenin is that he was a man who honored the institution of marriage, and there was no brutality about him. He was an upstanding citizen, married to a very physical wife, whose tragedy was nothing compared to his. He is, indeed, the central character of the story."

With numerous offers for film work pouring in, Basil and Ouida moved to Los Angeles and became a part of what was affectionately

Anna Karenina.

The Last Days of Pompeii: **As Pontius Pilate.**

known as Hollywood's British Film Colony. Members included such performers as Ronald Colman, Nigel Bruce, David Niven, Reginald Denny, C. Aubrey Smith, Brian Aherne, and Herbert Marshall. The Rathbones rented a house at 5254 Los Feliz Boulevard, in which they resided with their seven dogs for three years.

Merian C. Cooper next brought the actor over to RKO to play Pontius Pilate in his screen version of *The Last Days of Pompeii,*

With his dogs in front of the house on Los Feliz.

starring Preston Foster. With the exception of Rathbone's performance, the picture had little to recommend it.

Columbia Pictures hired him to co-star with Pauline Lord in *A Feather in Her Hat,* a minor little film, which was directed by Alfred Santell. After this, he returned to M.G.M. for the short, but impressive, role of the cruel Marquis St. Evremonde in the lavish *A Tale of Two Cities,* directed by Jack Conway, and starring Ronald Colman.

Moving over to Warner Brothers, he starred in his first swash-buckling film and his first of three pictures with Errol Flynn—*Captain Blood,* directed by Michael Curtiz. The actor was impressive in the relatively small part of Levasseur, the pirate, his duel on the beach with Flynn being the high point of the production.

Rathbone's seventh picture to be released in 1935 was a programmer. Based on Edward Chodorov's play, *Kind Lady,* the Metro thriller co-starred Aline MacMahon.

Publicity shot from A Tale of Two Cities.

Early the following year, Twentieth Century-Fox enlisted the actor's services for one of their insignificant features, *Private Number,* starring Robert Taylor and Loretta Young. Rathbone was cast as a sinister butler.

Frustrated that he'd been typed as a "heavy" ever since he'd played Murdstone, the actor lashed out at Hollywood casting methods in the aforementioned 1936 interview with *Motion Picture:* "The average producer hasn't freed himself yet from the mentality of the small town of twenty-five years ago. He still thinks the public likes a pretty boy hero, a pretty heroine, and a bad man. He gives the public a heavy, expecting the audience to react to him as such, but they don't. On the contrary, they *like* him. Why? Because usually the hero and heroine have no character, while the heavy is a real human being. And when, as it sometimes happens, he is led to death and prison, they don't hate him. He is a man who has failed, and most people have failed. There is a bond of understanding sympathy.

"We should, if possible, throw out all the 'heroes,' 'heroines,' and 'heavies,' and have nothing but characters. In other words, portray the mental instead of the physical. And all characters should be kaleidoscopic. After all, we are trying to work out the complete reproduction of life on the screen. We have the picture, the sound, and, before long, we might have the third dimension. It will be the task of the actor to reproduce with perfection the emotions of the character he is portraying. But as things are now, they buy personalities and not acting. This business is full of personalities. True, what gets you first is personality, but what lasts is acting. Personalities come and go; good actors remain. Chaplin, for instance, remains because he is not only a great personality, but also a great actor."

Rathbone's next picture, Metro-Goldwyn-Mayer's production of *Romeo and Juliet,* garnered him his first of two Academy Award nominations—in the category of Best Supporting Actor. His portrayal of Tybalt and Norma Shearer's Juliet were the most memorable performances in the uneven George Cukor-directed film. The Oscar that year, however, was won by Walter Brennan for *Come and Get It.*

Selznick signed the actor again, this time for his first Technicolor production, *The Garden of Allah,* starring Marlene Dietrich and Charles Boyer. Richard Boleslawski directed this, the third and best film version of Robert Hichens' tragic love story. Rathbone was competent in the rather bland role of Count Anteoni.

On January 15, 1937, Rathbone and actor John Miltern, a close family friend, were out walking Basil's seven dogs. Returning home, Miltern was struck by a hit-and-run driver, as he attempted to cross Los Feliz Boulevard. The badly injured actor died shortly after being brought to a hospital.

The Garden of Allah: **As Count Anteoni.**

Early in March, Basil and his secretary, Harry Dausman, were instrumental in capturing a former employee of the Rathbone household, who was suspected of stealing money and jewelry. The ex-butler had locked the actor in a room, then fled. Upon being released by Dausman, Rathbone and four police officers pursued the alleged thief until he was captured several blocks away. The man was booked on suspicion of burglary.

Rathbone had signed a two-picture deal with Warner Brothers in 1936. The first project, *Confession* with Kay Francis, was an inferior remake of a German film, *Mazurka*. It was released in March, 1937.

The following month saw the U.S. release of a picture the actor had shot in England the previous summer. *Love from a Stranger,* distributed by United Artists, had Rathbone menacing Ann Harding in an excellent adaptation of Frank Vosper's suspense play.

In April, the Rathbones purchased a three-acre parcel of land in the San Fernando Valley for twelve thousand dollars. Their idea was to build a fifty-thousand-dollar home on the property, but the plan was never realized.

The month of August gave audiences the opportunity to see Basil support child star Bobby Breen in an RKO picture, *Make a Wish*. Music was by Oscar Straus, with lyrics by Louis Alter and Paul Francis Webster.

Tovarich was the second film under the Warner deal and it was released in November. Based on Robert E. Sherwood's adaptation of Jacques Deval's French play, the entertaining comedy starred Claudette Colbert and Charles Boyer. Rathbone's appearance as a Russian diplomat was short, though effective.

He then turned down a major role in *The Hurricane* (Raymond

Mr. and Mrs. Basil Rathbone, Nigel Bruce, and playwright Marc Connelly aboard the Normandie, **enroute to London in 1936.**

Massey got the assignment), in favor of the part of Ahmed, the wicked minister of state, in a weak Gary Cooper starrer, *The Adventures of Marco Polo,* for Samuel Goldwyn. Archie Mayo directed the dull adventure "epic."

Rathbone's next picture presented him with one of the choice roles of his career—the dastardly Sir Guy of Gisbourne. Filmed in Technicolor, Warner Brothers' production of *The Adventures of*

Tovarich.

With Olivia deHavilland on the set of The Adventures of Robin Hood.

Robin Hood boasted a first-rate cast, including Errol Flynn, Olivia deHavilland, Rathbone, Claude Rains, Ian Hunter, Eugene Pallette, Alan Hale, and Melville Cooper. There was no expense spared in this production about the legendary bandit of Sherwood Forest. Direction by Michael Curtiz and William Keighley was superb, as was the magnificent Oscar-winning score by Erich Wolfgang Korngold.

Miss deHavilland, who'd worked previously with him in *Captain Blood,* retains "a general impression of Mr. Rathbone's ebullience and kindness, and the charm and style with which he and his wife, Ouida, entertained. . . . Prior to the war, they gave quite marvelous parties at their house on Los Feliz Boulevard."

Indeed, the late thirties found the Rathbones constantly listed in the society columns of Los Angeles newspapers. As Huntz Hall recalls, "Basil gave the greatest parties this town would ever see. They were fun . . . inventive . . . the product of real showmanship."

Basil's closest friends were aware, however, that he was greatly distressed at the high cost of these social functions. Louis Hayward remembers chatting with the actor a few days after one lavish affair. Practically in tears, Rathbone confessed, "These parties of Ouida's are breaking me." He swore that he'd not allow her to plan any others, yet three weeks later invitations for a new gala event were in the mail.

Frank Lloyd's *If I Were King* was released by Paramount in September of 1938. Rathbone's off-beat portrayal of the hunchback king

On the set of If I Were King. **From left: Director Frank Lloyd, Lester Matthews, William Farnum, Ronald Colman, Rathbone, and Walter Kingsford.**

completely overshadowed Ronald Colman's interpretation of poet François Villon. He received his second Supporting Actor nomination for his performance, but, again, lost to Walter Brennan, who won, this time, for *Kentucky*.

The performer's final picture with Errol Flynn was an excellent remake of the 1930 Howard Hawks aviation classic, *Dawn Patrol*. As the guilt-ridden Major Brand, Rathbone gave a sensitive performance, which remains one of his finest. The December 1938, Warner Brothers release also featured David Niven and Donald Crisp in important roles and was directed by Edmund Goulding.

Rowland V. Lee, who had directed Rathbone in *Love from a Stranger*, now signed him to star in the title role of *Son of Frankenstein*, a sequel to Universal's two previous classics, *Frankenstein* and *Bride of Frankenstein*. Released in January of 1939, the excellent horror flick co-starred Boris Karloff, playing the Monster for the third time, and Bela Lugosi, as Ygor, the mad shepherd.

Aside from films, Basil was keeping busy doing radio shows. During 1938, he played three roles on Cecil B. DeMille's "Lux Radio Theatre" over CBS: In January, he starred with Grace Moore in *Enter Madame;* June had him doing *A Doll's House* with Joan Crawford; and, on October 31st, he was heard with Carole Lombard and Jeffrey Lynn in *That Certain Woman*. In later years, Rathbone confided to friends that he always regretted not having worked in pictures with DeMille, as "he was such a great showman."

1938 ended unhappily for the actor. On December 15th, the U.S. Treasury Department filed a thirty-eight-hundred-dollar tax lien against his film income.

According to the popular version of the story, Darryl Zanuck of Twentieth Century-Fox, actor/director Gregory Ratoff, and writer Gene Markey were at a Hollywood party when Ratoff said: "Somebody should turn Conan Doyle's Sherlock Holmes stories into a movie series."

The other two men liked the idea. After some discussion, Zanuck asked: "Who would play Holmes?"

"Who else but Basil Rathbone," replied Markey.

There was no way that he could have been aware of it at the time, but Markey's simple suggestion was to eventually alter the course of Rathbone's career—as well as his life.

Within a week of the party, Zanuck had signed Basil to play the London sleuth and veteran British character actor Nigel Bruce his associate, Dr. Watson. Rathbone always considered himself a logical choice for Holmes, as he felt he bore a striking resemblance to Frederic Dorr-Steele's portrait of the fictional character.

The initial film in the Fox series (and Rathbone's personal favorite) was a remake of Sir Arthur Conan Doyle's *The Hound of the Baskervilles*. Richard Greene, taking top-billing over Rathbone, played the young heir to the cursed Baskerville estate. Other cast members included Wendy Barrie, Lionel Atwill, John Carradine, and Mary Gordon, who played Mrs. Hudson, the landlady of Holmes's Baker Street address.

The finished picture had several faults. Most damaging was the fact that director Sidney Lanfield failed to create a proper mood for the classic mystery story. But the March 1939 release *did* do well enough at the box office to convince the studio to produce a sequel.

Next, Basil co-starred with Douglas Fairbanks, Jr., in another Rowland V. Lee project, *The Sun Never Sets*. The Universal production, dealing with two brothers in the British Colonial Service, offered Rathbone a fairly interesting role in a picture hampered with a ridiculous plot line. The film was a June release.

Also in June, Basil and Ouida left their house on Los Feliz and bought a home in Bel Air at 10728 Bellagio Road. The price was sixty-five thousand dollars. Four months later, they adopted an eight-month-old baby girl, Cynthia.

The Adventures of Sherlock Holmes went into theaters in August. Directed by Alfred Werker, the picture seemed to contain all the elements that were absent in its predecessor (i.e., a good, fast-paced script, rich production values, and, most important, suspense). The story, inspired by the old William Gillette play, had Holmes going up against Professor Moriarty, who, in turn, was after the crown

Rathbone as Holmes.

With Barbara O'Neil on location for The Sun Never Sets.

With Ouida and baby Cynthia.

jewels. George Zucco essayed the role of the arch-criminal, while Ida Lupino was the heroine of the piece.

Fox lost interest in the Holmes series after their second entry and decided to drop it. Rathbone couldn't have cared less, as other movie assignments were keeping him quite busy.

Universal signed Basil to star in a very good low budget drama, *Rio,* in which he played a crook serving time in a French penal colony. Able support was supplied by Victor McLaglen, Sigrid Gurie, and Robert Cummings.

Rowland V. Lee gave him the role of Richard III in Universal's *Tower of London,* a November release. The project was hurt by a weak screenplay; however, as the evil Duke of Gloucester, Rathbone gave a superb performance. The cast included Boris Karloff, Barbara O'Neil, Ian Hunter, and Vincent Price.

Radio was also occupying the actor's time during 1939. Aside from

Publicity shot from The Adventures of Sherlock Holmes.

Publicity shot from The Adventures of Sherlock Holmes.

guest appearances, such as one with Norma Shearer and Louis Hayward in *Smilin' Through*, a segment of the CBS "Gulf Oil Program," he signed to do his first series.

At NBC, Rathbone and Nigel Bruce were set to repeat their movie roles for the "Sherlock Holmes" radio show. The initial segment was heard on October 2nd and, although the show moved over to the Mutual network in 1943, the two British performers stayed with the

With hairdresser Helen Stoeffler on the set of Tower of London.

series for seven years—a total of two hundred seventy-five episodes.

Years later, in an interview, Rathbone recalled a difficult tongue twister he was once lumbered with: "My line was 'Watson, the board of directors is nothing but a horde of bores.' Unfortunately, that was not how it came out on the air."

War was declared in Europe during the summer of 1939 and, near the end of that year, Basil wrote to the War Office in London to offer his services. As might have been expected, he was refused because of his age. He was forty-seven.

Yet, both the actor and his wife did their part for the war effort. Basil was elected president of the Los Angeles chapter of British War Relief and, later, to the War Chest Executive Committee. He also helped entertain troops in the Southern California area and, along with Mrs. Rathbone, was regularly seen helping out at the Hollywood Canteen.

Ouida, on the other hand, contributed her talents to organize benefits for such worthy organizations as the RAF Benevolent Fund and the Red Cross. One such event at the Beverly Wilshire Hotel netted ten thousand dollars.

At the request of the British Consul, the couple served as unofficial host and hostess for such visiting dignitaries as Lord Halifax and Admiral Halsey, when they were in Los Angeles.

Rathbone did only two films in 1940. The first, released in August, was *Rhythm on the River,* a Bing Crosby vehicle for Paramount, which co-starred Mary Martin and had Basil playing a composer. The musical was a pleasant change of pace for the actor, but did nothing to enhance his image.

On August 5th, he appeared in Hollywood at the El Capitan Theater in a production of Noel Coward's *Tonight at Eight,* a collection of three one-act plays. Rathbone was seen with Gladys Cooper and Henry Stephenson in the second piece, *The Astonished Heart.* The other two plays were *We Were Dancing,* featuring Constance Bennett and Douglas Fairbanks, Jr., and *Red Peppers,* with Binnie Barnes, Reginald Gardiner, and Freddie Bartholomew. The project was produced for the benefit of British War Relief.

In November, Rathbone was seen in a Twentieth Century-Fox picture, *The Mark of Zorro* starring Tyrone Power and Linda Darnell. Direction was by Rouben Mamoulian. This swashbuckling tale, set in early California, had Basil playing his most ruthless screen villain—Captain Esteban Pasquale. Though flawed in story construction, the film still entertained audiences, with the final duel between Rathbone and Power being its major highlight.

Amid his 1940 radio activity, the actor was heard again on "Lux Radio Theatre," this time with Ida Lupino in *Wuthering Heights.*

Although four Rathbone films played in theaters the following year, none of them were above the programmer class. In fact, *The Mad Doctor,* a February 1941 release from Paramount, had been filmed two years previously by the studio, then held back because of post-production problems. Basil played a wife murderer in that minor effort.

His next picture, an April offering out of Universal, was even worse. *The Black Cat,* concerned with a series of murders in an eerie old mansion, took only its title from Edgar Allan Poe. An able, if wasted, supporting cast included Broderick Crawford, Hugh Herbert, Gale Sondergaard, and Alan Ladd.

International Lady had him representing Scotland Yard in a cliché-filled spy thriller, which top-lined George Brent and Ilona Massey, with direction by Tim Whelan. United Artists released the melodrama in October of 1941.

Cast as a traitor, Rathbone was his old evil self again in *Paris Calling,* a Universal film. The stars of the December release, dealing with the French Underground, were Elisabeth Bergner and Randolph Scott.

Publicity shot from International Lady.

It was his agent, Jules Stein of MCA, Inc., who convinced the Britisher that he should break precedent and sign a five-year contract with Metro-Goldwyn-Mayer. Stein believed that the world conflict would be a long one and wanted to assure his client of a steady income so that Basil, feeling financially secure, could pursue his war effort activities. The M.G.M. deal was signed on December 29, 1941.

His two initial pictures for Metro were inconsequential. The first, *Fingers at the Window*, was released in March of 1942. It starred Lew Ayres and Laraine Day and had Basil playing the mastermind behind a series of axe murders.

Crossroads gave him the role of a blackmailer. He supported a class-"A" cast, including William Powell, Hedy Lamarr, and Claire Trevor. The programmer was released in June.

During the early part of 1942, Universal acquired from the Conan Doyle estate the motion picture rights to twenty-two of the Sherlock Holmes stories. A sale price of three hundred thousand dollars gave the studio the prerogative of utilizing the stories intact or, simply,

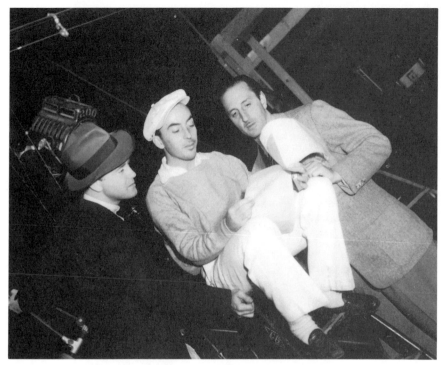

Lew Ayres, director Charles Lederer, and Rathbone on the set of
Fingers at the Window.

With Charles Chaplin at a 1942 Hollywood party.

borrowing elements from them. In addition, the filmmakers could devise original plots involving the Holmes/Watson characters.

Universal planned to produce a series of low budget features, based on the Doyle material, and hired Howard S. Benedict to serve as supervising producer of the project. Recalls Benedict: "All of the plots in the films were basically original, as we were unable to utilize more than an element or two from any of the Doyle stories. There just wasn't enough there to serve as an entire feature. For example, we borrowed the idea of the stick figures from 'The Adventure of the Dancing Men' and built a new story around it to make *Sherlock Holmes and the Secret Weapon*."

The natural choices for the leads in the series were, of course, Basil Rathbone and Nigel Bruce. They'd done the roles twice before on the screen and already had a strong following from their "Sherlock Holmes" radio series.

Director Jack Conway and Rathbone on the set of Crossroads. **Conway played a bit in the film.**

Rathbone's services were secured on loan-out from Metro-Goldwn-Mayer, the relevant agreement being signed on April 14, 1942. Bruce was also hired, as was Mary Gordon to repeat her role as the landlady, Mrs. Hudson, which she'd played at Fox.

Beginning with the second segment of the series, Dennis Hoey was set to play Inspector Lestrade of Scotland Yard on a semiregular basis. If he was unavailable for a particular episode, his part would be rewritten, so that another actor could represent the Yard.

Universal decided to modernize Sherlock Holmes for their series—setting the films during the then current World War. In the initial entries, the detective found himself up against Nazi agents.

Rathbone liked the up-dating idea, as he'd felt that the two pictures from Twentieth, both of which were set in the last century, had suffered by being too old-fashioned.

At Universal, Rathbone abandoned Holmes's calabash pipe and traded in the deerstalker hat for a fedora. Each of the series episodes were shot on a twelve to thirteen day schedule at a budget of one hundred thirty thousand dollars. They ran between sixty and seventy-four minutes in length.

Benedict recalls the series as a "very enjoyable project to work on," although there was one frustrating problem with Nigel Bruce: "The noise from a gunshot bothered Willy and, whenever he had to fire a pistol, we found him involuntarily closing his eyes. Sometimes, it would be several takes before we could get a useable one."

In general, the successful series was well-produced, with a total of twelve episodes being shot within a five-year period. After the first

With Evelyn Ankers and Nigel Bruce on the set of Sherlock Holmes and the Voice of Terror.

segment, which was directed by John Rawlins, Roy William Neill took over that assignment and, later, assumed the producer's function also. At that point, Benedict was given the title of *executive* producer.

The first segment of the series went into release in September of 1942. Titled *Sherlock Holmes and the Voice of Terror,* it had the sleuth thwarting a gang of German saboteurs. Of Rathbone's performance, the *New York Post* said: "He is an actor who appears to have been born and trained for this particular role."

Sherlock Holmes and the Secret Weapon was in theaters at the end of the year and was a much stronger entry than its predecessor. Professor Moriarty, in the person of Lionel Atwill, was Holmes's nemesis in a race to gain possession of a vital bombsight.

There were two further episodes the following year: *Sherlock Holmes in Washington,* a March release, and in September, *Sherlock Holmes Faces Death,* the first segment in which the detective was *not* fighting foreign agents. Holmes and Watson were also seen doing cameo bits in the Olsen and Johnson movie, *Crazy House,* going into theaters for an October playdate.

Rathbone took a short break from his "detective work" in 1943 to co-star as a vicious Gestapo chief in Metro's amusing spy thriller, *Above Suspicion,* with Joan Crawford and Fred MacMurray. Richard Thorpe, director of the project, recalls Basil as "one hundred percent professional and very capable. Unexpectedly, he had a great sense of humor."

His radio assignments during this general period were varied. Aside from the "Holmes" series, he was heard as Scrooge in a broadcast of *A Christmas Carol,* which featured daughter Cynthia, and on "Lux Radio Theatre," he played the title role in *The Phantom of the Opera,* with Nelson Eddy and Susanna Foster repeating their parts from the Universal remake of the Lon Chaney classic.

Three of the best *Sherlock Holmes* pictures were released in 1944. Appearing in January, *The Spider Woman* was the first episode to drop the detective's name from the title, a practice that was continued for the balance of the series. Academy Award winner Gale Sondergaard played a "female Moriarty" in the above-average mystery.

The Scarlet Claw, easily the most outstanding of the Universal productions, sent Holmes and Watson to the wilds of Canada to track down a phantom killer. It was released in April.

From the standpoint of quality, *The Pearl of Death,* an August release, ran a close second to *The Scarlet Claw.* An intriguing aspect of the detective film was the character of the Creeper, as played by Rondo Hatton, who was, in fact, a victim of acromegaly.

Rathbone did two other pictures in 1944. The first was *Bathing Beauty,* an "aqua-comedy," designed to display the talents of Esther Williams and Red Skelton. Produced for a May release by his "home" studio, Metro-Goldwyn-Mayer, the insignificant piece of film totally wasted Basil's talents and caused him to reassess his deal with the Culver City studio. As he told a close associate at the time: "I really don't mind Metro's selling my services for the Holmes pictures at a much larger fee than they're paying me. That's just good business. But, what *does* gripe me is the fact that, when I do a film for them, it's always a piece of junk like *Bathing Beauty*."

After giving his situation due consideration, the performer concluded that M.G.M.'s generous pension system was reason enough for *not* breaking his contract with that studio.

The second non-Holmes project in 1944 was Paramount's Technicolor epic, *Frenchman's Creek,* a September release, based on Daphne du Maurier's best-selling novel. The romantic swashbuckler was directed by Mitchell Leisen and starred Joan Fontaine.

By 1945, Rathbone was becoming bored with the role of Sherlock Holmes, and that year's three pedestrian entries in the series certainly betrayed his lack of interest. *The House of Fear, The Woman in Green,* and *Pursuit to Algiers* were released in March, June, and October, respectively. In every creative area of production, each suc-

With Ralph Forbes on the set of Frenchman's Creek.

ceeding segment seemed worse than the one before it. Incidentally, *The Woman in Green* presented Henry Daniell in the role of Holmes' arch enemy, Professor Moriarty.

On September 1, 1945, Rathbone served as master-of-ceremonies at the Hollywood Roosevelt Hotel for "A Tribute to Poland," sponsored under the joint auspices of Friends of Poland and the Polish-American Congress.

1944: With Joan Fontaine at the Hollywood Canteen.

Publicity shot from Heartbeat.

The eleventh *Sherlock Holmes* episode went into release the following February. Scripted by Frank Gruber, *Terror By Night* was
one of the series' better entries, the entire action being set on board
a train traveling from London to Edinburgh.

In April, Rathbone supported Ginger Rogers in a dull comedy,
Heartbeat, released through RKO-Radio Pictures and directed by Sam
Wood. Basil was effective as an instructor of student pickpockets.

There was one final segment in the Holmes series—*Dressed to Kill*.
Sloppily produced, the film also suffered from what seemed to be a
total indifference from both the actors and director. It was a May
release.

Rathbone had been wanting to get away from the Holmes character
for some time, so, since both his Mutual and Universal (through
M.G.M.) contracts expired during the summer of 1946, he seized
this opportunity to make his move. Ignoring the arguments of friends,

agents, and business associates, who considered him "insane" to take such actions, the actor refused to renew either his radio or motion picture deals, disposed of his Los Angeles home, and moved with his family back to New York. It was his hope to return to his first love—the theatre.

Among the reasons leading to Basil's decision was the fact that since he'd begun playing the Baker Street sleuth, his once varied career had become extremely limited and uninspiring. As he said in

a 1964 interview: "Once you have created a characterization, as I did with Holmes in *The Hound of the Baskervilles*, you can only *transpose* that character to different situations. That is, the creative process stops and you simply repeat yourself. Such was the case with the Universal series."

In time, Rathbone had grown to dislike the character of Sherlock Holmes. He felt the detective was too egotistical to make him sympathetic and his constant "put-down" of Watson was, in essence, the manifestation of a cruel streak.

On October 1, 1946, Basil and Eugenie Leontovich opened at New York's Plymouth Theater in *Obsession,* a revival of Louis Verneuil and Eugene Walter's two-character drama of murder, *Jealousy,* adapted by Jane Hinton. Reginald Denham staged the production. Of the actor's performance, Brooks Atkinson of the *New York Times* said: "On the whole, Mr. Rathbone has the better of it. The neatness of outline in his acting and the pleasant, clipped style he has in speaking are economical ways of playing an artificial drama." The play had only thirty-one performances in New York, then went on the road.

At the conclusion of the tour, Rathbone returned to Gotham to discover he was still being haunted by the spectre of Sherlock Holmes. Producers considered him too identified with the role and Basil found it difficult to find other stage or motion picture assignments. From the latter part of 1946 until fall of 1947, the actor's only significant work was as Inspector Burke in a radio series for the Mutual network, "Scotland Yard," which premiered in January 1947, and ran for the remainder of the season. John Crosby, in the *New York Herald Tribune,* said that the series offered "the discriminating mystery fan the services of Basil Rathbone, an extraordinarily well-trained actor."

Radio audiences also heard him during this period on such programs as "The Edgar Bergen and Charlie McCarthy Show," "Cavalcade of America," "The Fred Allen Show," "Theatre Guild of the Air," "The Jack Benny Show," and "The Burns and Allen Show."

Holmes was creating problems with the public also. Ouida recalls an incident in which her husband was being followed down the street by a group of children, begging, "Can we have your autograph, Mr. Holmes?"

Perturbed, Basil turned on the youngsters and demanded: "What is my *real* name?"

The fans were taken aback by the outburst, but one boy managed to reply, "Why, Sherlock Holmes, the detective."

With that, the actor said: "I will *not* give you my autograph until you say my *real* name." Then, he strode away.

Actually, the performer loved children dearly. His reaction to

Publicity shot with George Burns and Gracie Allen to promote a guest shot on the comedians' radio show.

these youngsters, although seemingly cruel, was, simply, his frustration speaking out.

It was Jed Harris who came to Rathbone's rescue. In the spring of 1947, the director sent Basil a play, *The Heiress* by Ruth and Augustus Goetz, suggested by Henry James's novel, *Washington Square*. Set in New York during the mid-1800s, the story dealt with a young lady's relationship with both her arrogant father and a fortune hunter. A Boston tryout of the show, bearing the same title as the novel, had flopped a few months earlier. However, Harris had seen that production and, realizing that it contained untapped potential, bought the rights and began rewriting.

The director offered Rathbone the role of the cruel Dr. Austin Sloper and Wendy Hiller the part of his spinster daughter, Catherine. The project was produced by Fred F. Finklehoffe, opening to excellent notices at the Biltmore Theater in New York on September 29, 1947. Other cast members included Peter Cookson as the suitor, Patricia Collinge, and Kate Raht. Of his performance, Atkinson of the *New York Times* said: "As Dr. Sloper, Catherine's keenly-inhuman parent, Mr. Rathbone has one of his most actable parts. He plays it perfectly with irony and arrogance."

About six weeks after the play opened, Rathbone slipped and fell in Central Park. A broken arm resulted and the actor, subsequently, did the show for many performances with his left arm in a sling.

The Heiress played for well over a year on Broadway, then went on tour. In March of 1948, Rathbone received the coveted Antoinette Perry Award for his performance in that production.

Basil always considered *The Heiress* to be the play that got him out of his Sherlock Holmes "rut" and reestablished him as a versatile character actor. Certainly, this was the case, but the Jed Harris production was also the last *major* success of the performer's career.

Publicity shot from The Heiress.

On May 30th, he was elected third vice president of Actors' Equity and, the next year, was named recording secretary of the same union.

Near the end of 1948, Rathbone was set by CBS to star on a new radio mystery series, "Tales of Fatima," which premiered on January 8, 1949.

Walt Disney signed the Britisher to serve as narrator for *The Wind in the Willows* segment of his animated cartoon feature, *Ichabod and Mr. Toad*. Similar chores were done by Bing Crosby on the second half of the picture, based on *The Legend of Sleepy Hollow*. The film was released in October of 1949.

Live television was an exciting new medium and Rathbone took advantage of his many opportunities to participate in it. 1950 saw him guesting at NBC on that nework's "Tele-Theatre," the *Queen of Spades* segment (3/6/50), and in, of all things, *Sherlock Holmes* (5/30/50), an unsold series pilot, done live, on the "NBC Show-case." At CBS, he guested in *The Kind Mr. Smith* - (12/28/50), an entry for "Airflyte Theatre."

There was a variety of other activity during the early 1950s. The actor tried vaudeville, playing such diverse cities as Miami and Montreal. His "act" consisted of dramatic readings from Shakespeare, Shelley, and the like. Said *Variety* of his 1950 Florida gig: "It's [the act] a bit over the average vaude fan's head, despite excellent pro-jection."

March 31, 1950: Basil appeared with the Philadelphia Orchestra to narrate the world premiere of Alexander Steinert's symphonic poem of Oscar Wilde's *The Nightingale and the Rose*. When the poem was later presented in New York, the *World-Telegram and Sun* said that the actor gave "one of the most gripping solo performances heard this season in Carnegie Hall."

There were other concert engagements: *Peter and the Wolf* for Leopold Stokowski and his Youth Orchestra; Schumann's *Manfred*, with both the Baltimore Symphony and the San Francisco Orchestra; and various productions of Honegger's *King David*.

1950 was also a busy theatre year for Rathbone. On February 8th, he opened at New York's City Center in a two week revival of *The Heiress*, a production that he co-directed with Jed Harris. The cast included Margaret Phillips as Catherine, Edna Best, and John Dall. Atkinson of the *New York Times* said: "Mr. Rathbone will be lucky if he ever has another part as suitable as the cold-minded and almost inhuman doctor. His performance was memorable when it was new in 1947, and it is every bit as good now—unctuous in manner, but immediately cruel, glib but monstrous, a perfectly designed piece of work."

George Schaefer, production executive for the presentation, which was staged by the New York City Theatre Company, recalls that, as

Rathbone and Gertrude Lawrence pose for photographers at a preview during the early 1950s.

he rehearsed, Rathbone constantly found new values to enrich his character. The actor would comment regularly: "My God, I did this show for so long and never saw this."

In June, Basil played Cassius again in a revival of Shakespeare's *Julius Caesar,* an arena production, staged by Dan Levin at the Hotel Edison in New York. The cast included Alfred Ryder, Joseph Holland, and Milton Selzer. The *New York Times* said of Rathbone's work: "Mr. Rathbone gives the part a mettlesome performance. It is lean and pithy, flashing with quick intelligence, and it is beautifully spoken. Mr. Rathbone has mastered the lines; they are brilliantly written by the king of our language, and Mr. Rathbone gives them the vitality of living speech."

Following the close of the play, he appeared as the attorney in several summer stock productions of Terence Rattigan's *The Winslow Boy.*

He was back on Broadway in October at the Lyceum Theater. The play was Aldous Huxley's short-lived *The Gioconda Smile,* staged and produced by Shepard Traube. Among the cast members of the psychological melodrama were Valerie Taylor, Marian Russell, and George Relph. The *New York Times* called Rathbone's acting "neat" and "accomplished."

Rathbone made more television appearances in 1951. CBS-TV's "Lux Video Theatre" starred Basil in a play entitled *Purple Fine Linen* (1/15/51). Then, he did a "Suspense" episode for the same network, an adaptation of Robert Louis Stevenson's *Dr. Jekyll and Mr. Hyde* (3/5/51). Over at NBC, the actor was seen on "Lights Out" in a segment entitled *Dead Man's Coat* (5/14/51).

That same year, he had his first fling on the lecture circuit, under the management of W. Colston Leigh. In his appearances, billed as *An Evening with Basil Rathbone,* he described his experiences on the stage and in films, and gave short dramatic readings. The performer's initial contract was for six weeks, with four lectures per week.

He was also signed for another Broadway show, *Music in the Air,* but, due to an inadequate rehearsal schedule, withdrew from the production on August 15, 1951.

February 1, 1952 found Rathbone opening on Broadway at the Coronet Theatre in S. N. Behrman's *Jane,* an adaptation of Somerset Maugham's story. The Theatre Guild production was staged by Cyril Ritchard and co-starred Edna Best, Howard St. John, Philip Friend, and Irene Browne. The comedy was a moderate success, playing a total of one hundred performances.

Rathbone's role was patterned after Maugham himself. Said Atkinson in the *New York Times:* "Mr. Rathbone's writer is one of his top performances. Although Willie's tongue is malicious, he enjoys the life he is drifting through and his instincts are generous. Since Mr. Rathbone is a careful workman, he speaks his lines adroitly."

His schedule permitting, Basil continued to keep busy in television, often journeying to Canada to take part in programs for the CBC. In the United States, his 1952 television activity included another guest shot on the "Lux Video Theatre," *Masquerade* (5/5/52), and a hosting assignment for a CBS summer replacement series, "Your Lucky Clue." *Variety* termed the panel show a "dog," blaming failure on "the weak moderating job turned in by Basil Rathbone and the lifeless work of the panel."

There was further video activity in 1953. The actor starred in two plays for the syndicated "Broadway Television Theatre," *Criminal at Large* by Edgar Wallace (2/2/53 in New York) and as Benvenuto Cellini in *The Firebrand* by Edwin Justus Mayer (3/2/53 in New York). He was back on "Suspense" (5/26/53) in a Sherlock Holmes mystery, *The Adventure of the Black Baronet,* based on a story by Sir Arthur Conan Doyle's son, Adrian, and John Dickinson Carr. Another CBS series, "Danger," retained his services for a play by Marie Baumer, entitled *The Educated Heart* (11/17/53) and, over at ABC-TV, he did a musical adaptation of James Thurber's fantasy, *The Thirteen Chairs* (12/29/59) on the "Motorola Television Hour." The cast for this production included Sir Cedric Hardwicke, John Raitt, Roberta Peters, and Russel Nype.

April 15, 1953: Rathbone appeared, along with five other players, at the Brooklyn Academy of Music in *An Evening with Will Shakespeare,* which consisted of readings from the Poet's work.

Toward the end of 1951, Basil had suggested to his wife that she write for him a Sherlock Holmes play. Excluding two minor television dramas, he'd been away from the character for five years and felt that he could now return to it *briefly*—without recreating the problems that had forced him to abandon the role in 1946.

Ouida studied all of the Conan Doyle stories, finally deciding to utilize material from five of them for her play. She wrote the melodrama while her husband was away doing his *An Evening With Basil Rathbone,* which had become quite popular with audiences, and incorporated, whenever possible, Doyle's original dialogue. Completed late in 1952, the manuscript was shown to Adrian Conan Doyle, who gave it his "blessing."

Bill Doll liked the play and decided to produce it, under the direction of Reginald Denham. Unfortunately, Nigel Bruce was recovering from a heart attack and was unable to play Watson in the production, so that role was inherited by Jack Raine. Thomas Gomez was signed as Professor Moriarty.

After a three-week tryout in Boston, the melodrama opened in New York at the Century Theater on October 30, 1953. Of *Sherlock Holmes,* the *New York Times* said: "Mrs. Rathbone's salute to the celebrated detective is cumbersome and uneven. Holmes, the great logician, would regret its untidiness."

Regarding Basil's performance, the same paper reported: "Although Basil Rathbone is a very able actor and, although he has played Sherlock Holmes repeatedly, superannuated Irregulars find his portrait too emotional."

The production closed after three performances.

Hollywood beckoned again in late 1953 and Rathbone traveled to the West Coast to serve as Bob Hope's straight man in a formula comedy from Paramount, *Casanova's Big Night.* The Technicolor feature was released in March of 1954.

That same year, the British actor made some interesting television

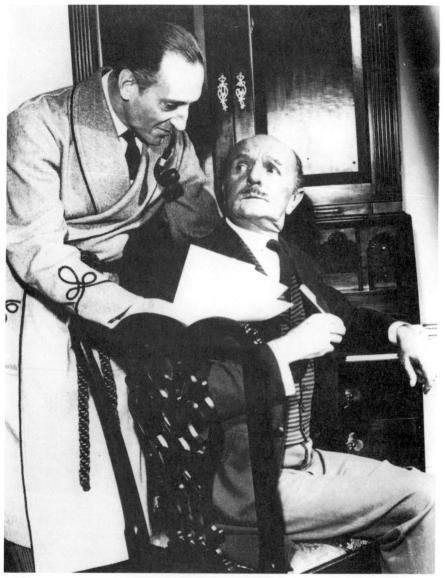

With Jack Raine in the stage production of Sherlock Holmes.

appearances for CBS. On August 16th, he was seen in *The House of Gair,* a live presentation of "Studio One: Summer Theatre." Allen Reisner, who directed the play, recalls that "Basil was quite nervous during rehearsals and was having trouble remembering lines. However, when he went on the air, he was fine."

He also did the part of a jewel thief in the *Volturio Investigates* segment of "Schlitz Playhouse of Stars" (12/3/54) and of greater

With John Carradine on the set of Casanova's Big Night.

interest, essayed the role of Marley's Ghost in a musical adaptation
of Dickens's *A Christmas Carol,* presented by "Shower of Stars" on
December 23rd. Fredric March played Scrooge in the production,
which boasted a libretto by Maxwell Anderson and score by Bernard
Herrman.

Rathbone did another television musical in 1955. *Svengali and the
Blonde,* a NBC special, co-starred him with Carol Channing in an
adaptation of George du Maurier's novel, *Trilby.* Producer/director
Alan Handley was co-author with Charles Gaynor, who did both
words and music. Ethel Barrymore narrated the offering, airing on
July 30th. According to *Variety:* "Basil Rathbone as Svengali played
it with fiendish delight, although accusatively a scenery chewer."

Video viewers also saw him guest on "The Eddie Cantor Show"
in a skit entitled *Always the Butler* (5/23/55), and as co-host with
Burl Ives for a CBS Thanksgiving Day special.

Earlier that year, Paramount had called Rathbone back to Hollywood for a co-starring role with Humphrey Bogart, Aldo Ray, Peter
Ustinov, and Joan Bennett in *We're No Angels,* an adaptation of a
French comedy by Albert Husson about three convicts helping a
kindly shopkeeper and his family rid themselves of nasty relatives.

Released in June, the picture was a commercial, if not artistic, success.

While he was working at the studio, the actor submitted two short stories he'd written ("The Death of a Church" and "The Gentleman's Gentleman") to the story department for consideration as possible future projects for Paramount. The response was a polite refusal.

Basil spent the summer of 1955 doing *The Winslow Boy* in stock, then, in October, joined with Helen Gahagan Douglas, wife of actor Melvyn Douglas, in a program of readings and dramatic interpretations, which they premiered at the Brooklyn Academy of Music, then followed with a tour. The material for the production, entitled *One Plus One,* was drawn from the short stories and poems of Chekhov, George Moore, DeMaupassant, Dickinson, and Shakespeare.

Rathbone filmed a second picture for Paramount in 1955, but it was not released to theaters until January of the following year.

Publicity shot from Svengali and the Blonde.

The Court Jester, a charming musical/comedy starring Danny Kaye, had Basil spoofing the roles he'd done in such classics as *The Adventures of Robin Hood* and *The Mark of Zorro.*

On February 1, 1956, he was seen with Dennis O'Keefe and Neil Hamilton in Palmer Thompson's suspense drama, *Five Minutes to Live,* a presentation of "Kraft Theatre" (NBC-TV). Then, in May,

Publicity shot from The Abduction from the Seraglio.

On the set of The Black Sleep. **From left: Rathbone, Bela Lugosi, director Reginald LeBorg, and Herbert Rudley.**

Basil appeared on stage to narrate the Mozart opera, *The Abduction from the Seraglio,* produced by the American Shakespeare Festival at Stratford, Connecticut.

Movie audiences saw him again in June. The film was *The Black Sleep,* an average horror "epic" from United Artists. The cast, in which Rathbone was top-billed, featured Akim Tamiroff, Lon Chaney, Jr., Bela Lugosi, and John Carradine.

July found Basil playing Oberon in a production of *A Midsummer Night's Dream* at the Empire State Music Festival in Ellenville, New York. Cast members included comic Red Buttons as Bottom and Nancy Wickwire as Titania. The traditional Mendelssohn score was abandoned for this interpretation of Shakespeare's play, in favor of a fresh one by German composer Carl Orff. Leopold Stokowski served as conductor.

Red Buttons remembers Rathbone as "a wonderful, wonderful guy and a lot of fun. He loved life and loved to live. Basil was very kind to me, giving me much help and encouragement, since I'd never done Shakespeare before. I was crazy about him."

Rathbone concluded 1956 with a first-rate television role. On December 23rd, he starred as Scrooge in *The Stingiest Man in Town,* a musical adaptation of Dickens' *A Christmas Carol.* The show, a ninety-minute presentation on NBC's "Alcoa Hour," had book and lyrics by Janice Torre, with music composed by Fred Spielman. The cast included Vic Damone, Johnny Desmond, and Patrice Munsel. A highlight of the production was Basil's singing two numbers, "Humbug" (with Desmond) and "The Christmas Spirit."

Variety said: "Basil Rathbone had a role he could really sink his teeth into and did with complete gusto. He was even given songs to accentuate his avarice as the despicable Scrooge."

He was back on the "tube" early the next year in *The Lark* (2/10/57), adapted from Jean Anouilh's play about Joan of Arc. A presentation of NBC's "Hallmark Hall of Fame," the drama featured an impressive cast, including Julie Harris, Boris Karloff, and Eli Wallach. Rathbone played the Inquisitor.

George Schaefer, who directed the prestige production, recalls that, at one point in the play (done live), "Basil forgot his lines. There was a pregnant and dramatic pause before he continued."

Rathbone was then set to co-star with Geraldine Fitzgerald in *Hide and Seek,* a play by Stanley Mann and Roger MacDougall, which was staged by Reginald Denham at the Ethel Barrymore Theater. Opening on April 2, 1957, the dull drama, in which Basil played Sir Roger Johnson, dealt with the moral responsibility of nuclear scientists. It closed after seven performances.

That July, the actor played Sir Wilfred Robarts, Q.C., in a summer stock production of Agatha Christie's courtroom mystery, *Witness for the Prosecution,* presented by Theatre-By-The-Sea in Mantunuck, Rhode Island.

On November 20, 1957, he was seen as the Duke in *Huck Finn,* a musical version of the Mark Twain classic, on CBS-TV's "United States Steel Hour." Also in the cast were Jimmy Boyd in the title role, Jack Carson, and Florence Henderson. With Carson, Basil sang a number, entitled "The Boasting Song." In its review, *Variety* said: "Surprisingly, Rathbone, noted for his fine diction, was sometimes hard to understand, a combination of an assumed Southern accent and some poor mike pickups. However, he deftly captured the rascality of the Duke."

He did another play for "Kraft Theatre" on December 11th. George Dyslin's *Heroes Walk on Sand* was an interesting drama, set in a revolution-torn European country, which co-starred Elliott Nugent, Walter Abel, and Ann Harding. Rathbone's role was that of General Zomback.

There were two more television musicals in February of 1958. On the 9th, he did the role of Dr. Boekman in a "Hallmark Hall of Fame" production, *Hans Brinker,* starring Tab Hunter and Peggy King. The ninety-minute presentation was based on the Mary Mapes Dodge novel.

Then, on February 21st, he appeared as the Emperor in the CBS
"Dupont Show of the Month" production of *Aladdin,* with script by
S. J. Perelman and songs by Cole Porter. The cast included Sal Mineo
in the title role, Cyril Ritchard, Anna Maria Alberghetti, and Dennis
King. Ralph Nelson directed. Rathbone sang a pleasant Porter tune,
"Wouldn't It Be Fun," which was, incidentally, the last song the
composer ever wrote.

Variety, calling the production "ordinary," said of the Britisher:
"Basil Rathbone, as the emperor, was a victim of bad direction."

Writer/director William Spier signed Basil to headline *Midnight
at 8,* a new show being set for an extensive road tour during the
fall of 1958. Spier's plan was to dramatize classic tales of horror by
such authors as Edgar Allan Poe and Conan Doyle. Unfortunately, the
play closed during tryouts, when serious problems developed with
the electronic special effects equipment, the use of which was necessary to the success of the production.

Rathbone was back on movie screens in November. The film
was John Ford's excellent adaptation of Edwin O'Connor's novel,
The Last Hurrah, a vehicle for Spencer Tracy, whose part was based
on Boston's legendary mayor, James M. Curley. Although his role
as the influential banker was a short one, Basil's performance was
memorable. The Columbia release was the last *important* film in which
the actor would appear.

Between film, television, and New York stage assignments, Rathbone always seemed to keep himself working. He enjoyed doing summer stock—*The Winslow Boy,* Rattigan's *Separate Tables, Witness
for the Prosecution,* and Leslie Stevens's *The Marriage-Go-Round*
being his favorite vehicles. In fact, during the early part of the 1960s,
he made an extensive tour of Australia, doing the Stevens comedy
in that continent's major cities.

When he wasn't performing in a play, the actor filled his time
by visiting colleges, clubs, as well as other organizations, and performing his one-man show, *An Evening With Basil Rathbone*—at an
average fee of fifteen hundred dollars per appearance.

He would begin his program with a number of personal and
professional reminiscences, after which he would recite a well-selected
series of poems. These included such pieces as: "Annabelle Lee" by
Edgar Allan Poe; "Hands" by Dylan Thomas; "Bredon Hill" by A.
E. Housman; "Ode to the West Wind" by Shelley; "A Lady Thinks
She is Thirty" by Ogden Nash; Shakespeare's "116th Sonnet"; and so
forth. Following intermission, he would do selections from *Hamlet,
Macbeth, Romeo and Juliet,* and, in conclusion, Prospero's soliloquy
from *The Tempest.* All in all, it was a well-balanced and pleasing bill.

An interviewer once asked Basil why actors like himself were doing similar solo appearances. His reply: "The reason so many actors

are touring the country with one-man shows is that otherwise we would be doing the old act of starving in a garret."

It was May of 1959. Basil was making preparations to tour the summer theater circuit in a tryout of Ouida's new play, *Dark Angel,* when he received an offer from producer Alfred deLiagre, Jr., to replace Raymond Massey as Mr. Zuss in the Broadway production of

Publicity shot for his one-man show, An Evening with Basil Rathbone.

With Frederic Worlock in J.B.

Archibald MacLeish's Pulitzer Prize-winning play, *J.B.* Under the direction of Elia Kazan, the show had opened to excellent notices the previous December at the A.N.T.A. Theater.

Rathbone was most anxious to participate in this symbolic treatment of the Book of Job—but *not* in the role of Zuss. The part that, in fact, fascinated the actor was Mr. Nickles, the devil's advocate, then being portrayed by Christopher Plummer. However, since the younger performer was not planning to stay with the production when it went on tour the following fall, Basil decided to fill the void left by Massey's departure and accept the role of Mr. Zuss—in the hope that he could capture the more desirable part after Plummer vacated it.

He played Zuss on Broadway for approximately ten weeks. Then, after reading Nickles for deLiagre, Kazan, and MacLeish, he was "promoted" to the role for the tour, with Frederic Worlock replacing him as Zuss.

The road company, which played to excellent houses, was in Cleveland during late December of 1959, when a heckler began replying to Rathbone's lines. To both the surprise and appreciation of the audience, Basil stopped the performance until the man could be removed.

On January 19th in Columbus, Ohio, the actor collapsed following a performance of *J.B.* and was rushed to Mount Carmel Hospital, his ailment being diagnosed as "extreme fatigue." Fortunately, he was able to rejoin the play the next week in St. Paul, Minnesota.

Later that year, in a newspaper interview, Rathbone commented on the state of the theatre in the United States. He did not approve of the type of plays that were being offered at that time, calling them "downbeat stuff . . . a product of the ashcan." He said of the authors: "I've become tired to death of the angry young man who doesn't propose to do anything about the whirl of things, but just sit back and holler."

Basil spent the summer of 1961 in Rome, playing the role of Caiaphas in an Italian/French co-production, *Pontius Pilate.* The dull spectacle, directed by Irving Rapper, starred Jean Marais, Jeanne Crain, and John Drew Barrymore. It was not released in the United States until 1964.

November 30, 1961: Rathbone was seen as Disraeli in Laurence Housman's *Victoria Regina,* another presentation of NBC's "Hallmark Hall of Fame." The stars were Julie Harris as Queen Victoria, James Donald as Albert, Isabel Jeans, Pamela Brown, and Barry Jones.

Basil's part consisted of only one scene, but he made the most of it. In a television interview a few years later, he revealed that it was his favorite role: "I got a tremendous thrill when I saw myself in makeup. It was one of the few occasions in my career where I looked the same way I felt."

Director George Schaefer recalls that, at the time of the telecast, the performer commented: "I get more nervous waiting around to do this eight-minute scene than if I were in an entire show."

Rathbone was seen in three theatrical features during 1962. *The Magic Sword* was a juvenile "spectacle" dealing with knighthood and dragons in "merry old England." Basil was top-billed in the part of an evil sorcerer for this April release.

The following month, he supported Vincent Price in *Tales of Terror,* one of Roger Corman's horror films for American International. Rathbone appeared in the last of three segments, which were based on the stories of Edgar Allan Poe.

Finally, in October, he was seen with Mary Murphy in *Two Be-*

fore Zero, a forgettable documentary dealing with the rise of communism.

1962 was also the year that Rathbone's autobiography, *In and Out of Character,* was published by Doubleday. In a 1963 interview with Don Alpert of the *Los Angeles Times,* he said of the book: "It is *not* an autobiography. It's reminiscences. When I went to Doubleday,

As Disraeli in the "Hallmark Hall of Fame" production of Victoria Regina.

I didn't want to write a book. I said I don't have anything nasty to say about people. I rather like them, you know.

"There is an awful lot you can write about people without being depreciating. I have a dear friend who told me she loved the book, but 'Darling, don't you hate anybody?' "

Although the reviews and sales on the book were nothing to get excited about, the volume *did* contribute to an increased demand by colleges for the actor's one-man show, which he now subtitled *In and Out of Character* also. As he remarked in the aforementioned *Los Angeles Times* interview: "One of the most enjoyable things is to take the show to colleges and universities. This is the most fabulous audience you can play to. They're very critical. They're way ahead of you. There's no such thing as a highbrow when you go to a college. You better make sense, fella."

Adding to the renewed public interest in Rathbone at this point in his career was the fact that the Universal *Sherlock Holmes* series was enjoying a tremendous popularity in the syndicated television market. Local stations would constantly repeat the twelve films to an ever-increasing audience. Indeed, Rathbone even shot a series of introductions to the pictures, which were played along with them on various television stations around the country. (The star's continued popularity today can also be attributed to these films, which are still shown regularly on television. Through these celluloid annals, a legion of Sherlock Holmes fans around the world have come to accept Rathbone as the definitive personification of their detective hero.)

The actor was no stranger to the recording industry in 1963. He'd previously narrated a highly successful recording of *Peter and the Wolf* with Leopold Stokowski conducting, as well as a long-playing album dealing with the great themes in poetry. Now, during the final few years of his life, he was contracted by Caedmon Records to cut several albums in which he would read some of the classic stories and poems from world literature. Among the authors Rathbone drew his selections from were Edgar Allan Poe, Oscar Wilde, Alfred Tennyson, Nathaniel Hawthorne, Rudyard Kipling, George Eliot, and, of course, the Sherlock Holmes stories by Conan Doyle.

Also at this time, Basil was being heard regularly on the NBC radio show "Monitor"—reading poetry, both classical and contemporary.

In April of 1963, President John F. Kennedy invited Rathbone to the White House to give a dramatic reading in a program honoring the Grand Duchess Charlotte of Luxembourg.

Then, near the end of June, he appeared in Gotham in a dramatic reading, *Shakespeare in Music,* which had speeches from the

Bard's plays interspersed among operatic arias and orchestral pieces based on the same plays. The *New York Times* thought he performed in a "pompous and self-indulgent manner."

On November 14th, in conjunction with a performance of his one-man show, the Women's Division of the Culver City Chamber of Commerce honored the Britisher for his fifty-year career in show business.

Rathbone's only film in 1963 was American International's entertaining black comedy, *The Comedy of Terrors,* which teamed him with old friends Vincent Price, Peter Lorre, and Boris Karloff. It was a December release.

With the exception of doing his *An Evening with Basil Rathbone,* 1964 was fairly uneventful for the star. However, the following year, television audiences saw him do the *Who Killed Hamlet?* episode of Gene Barry's detective series, "Burke's Law," airing over ABC on April 7th, 1965, and a two-part "Dr. Kildare," entitled *Perfect Is Hard To Be* (12/27/65 and 12/28/65), for NBC.

He and Huntz Hall were signed in mid-July of 1965 by movie producer Steve Gold of Blue Sky Productions to star in a rock version of *Dr. Jekyll and Mr. Hyde.* Entitled *Dr. Rock and Mr. Roll,* the picture was never made, as the financing for the project ultimately fell through.

Nevertheless, there were other film assignments that *did* proceed as planned. Producer Roger Corman hired Rathbone for *Queen of Blood,* a science-fiction entry that utilized considerable footage from a Russian-made picture. During the same three days the actor worked on *Queen,* Corman had him shoot some scenes for a second feature, *Voyage to a Prehistoric Planet.* American International released both "epics." *Queen of Blood* went into theaters in March of 1966, but the other film has only been seen on syndicated television.

AIP then set Basil for *Ghost in the Invisible Bikini,* an entry in that studio's *Beach Party* series. The cast of the April 1966 release included Boris Karloff and Patsy Kelly.

On June 16th, Rathbone served as narrator for an ABC-TV documentary special, "The Baffling World of ESP."

He was back on the same network two months later in an airing of an unsold television pilot, "The Pirates of Flounder Bay," which had been shot at Metro-Goldwyn-Mayer with a cast that included William Cort, Keenan Wynn, Jack Soo, and Bridget Hanley.

Miss Hanley, who was later to star in another ABC-TV series, "Here Come the Brides," recalls an incident: "We'd just returned from lunch and were filming a banquet scene. It was Mr. Rathbone's line. He opened his mouth to speak, but instead of words, all that came forth was a very loud belch. Needless to say, such a sound coming from a distinguished gentleman like Mr. Rathbone broke up the entire cast and crew. You might say that he burped in a grand manner."

Rathbone had been writing to George Schaefer, requesting that the producer/director of "Hallmark Hall of Fame" consider him for leading roles in two upcoming projects in that series, *Anastasia* and *The Admirable Crichton*. Although his age prevented the actor from being cast in those particular parts, Schaefer *did* utilize Basil's services again on the NBC-TV series.

Set in seventeenth-century England, Jerome Ross' *Soldier in Love* aired on April 26, 1967, with a cast that included Jean Simmons, Claire Bloom, and Keith Mitchell. *Variety* commented: "Basil Rathbone is good in a small, but effective, part as the Duke of York. . . ."

Around the time he did this project, Rathbone gave an interview, in which he discussed one of his "pet peeves": "I'm utterly opposed to actors who are directors and performers as well. I say: one thing at a time. Why should Rubenstein conduct? Why should Stokowski play the piano?"

Bridget Hanley reacts to Rathbone's "sophisticated" belch while filming "The Pirates of Flounder Bay," a television pilot.

Maxine Taylor, Basil Rathbone, Claire Bloom, and Keith Mitchell in the "Hallmark Hall of Fame" production of Soldier in Love.

There were two final motion pictures.

Early in 1967, Rathbone was summoned to Mexico City by movie director Ismael Rodriguez to star with John Carradine and Cameron Mitchell in a black comedy/fantasy, *Autopsy of a Ghost*. The film, which offered a story reminiscent of Rostand's *The Last Night of Don Juan,* had only a limited release in the United States and, then, only in a Spanish-language version.

Hillbillys in a Haunted House was one of those exploitation pictures that an actor does *"strictly* for the money." Filmed in June, the cast of the Woolner Brothers project included John Carradine, Lon Chaney, Jr., and a host of country-western singing stars.

A month later, Basil Rathbone was dead.

Following a series of appearances in his one-man show, he'd returned to New York "looking very tired." At Ouida's suggestion, the actor went to see his doctor, who said there was nothing to be concerned about.

Mrs. Rathbone recalls the incidents of the next day: "Basil was

Rathbone during the early 1960s.

very sad, as an old friend of his had died. We were in the living room
of our apartment discussing it, when he suddenly said, 'You know,
I'm not afraid to die, but I just wish it didn't have to be.'

"We talked for a few more minutes and he seemed to cheer up
a bit. Then, he went into his den, because he wanted to play a record
he'd just purchased.

"About five minutes later, I went into the room to ask him something . . . and he was 'gone.'"

According to the obituaries, the cause of death was a heart attack. The date—July 21, 1967. He was seventy-five years old.

Funeral services were held at St. James Episcopal Church. Among the notables in attendance were Cyril Ritchard, Cathleen Nesbitt, and Sol Hurok. Cornelia Otis Skinner recited two sonnets that Basil often read aloud to his wife: Elizabeth Browning's "How Do I Love Thee?" and the Rupert Brooke poem, "If I should die, think only this of me, that there's some corner of a foreign field that is forever England."

Newspapers reported that the actor left an estate valued between ten and twenty thousand dollars, with assets divided equally between his wife and son, Rodion.

Living with little more than her memories, Ouida Rathbone's last years were not easy ones. Daughter Cynthia died in 1969 of an undisclosed illness and, if that were not enough, the widow seemed constantly pressed for finances. At one point her more affluent Hollywood friends are said to have taken up a collection on her behalf.

On November 29, 1974, she died in New York's Roosevelt Hospital from complications suffered from a broken hip. Her age was listed as eighty-eight.

* * * * * * * * * * * *

The inner quality of Basil Rathbone might best be reflected by the instructions in his will: "I wish to be buried beside my wife— so close that, if it were possible, we might hold each other's hand. . . .

"I wish to be buried above ground, as I look upon death as a gateway to an ascension and an elevation—not a descent."

III

The Films of Basil Rathbone*

INNOCENT

(1921)

A Stoll Film Production. Directed by Maurice Elvey. From a novel by Marie Corelli. Scenario: William J. Elliott. Camera: Germaine Burger. Released: March 1921. 5,933 feet.

CAST: *Innocence*: Madge Stuart; *Amadis de Jocelyn*: Basil Rathbone; *Robin*: Lawrence Anderson; *Hugo de Jocelyn*: Edward O'Neill; *Ned Landon*: Frank Dane; *Armitage*: W. Cronin Wilson; *Lady Maude*: Ruth MacKay; *Miss Leigh*: Mme. d'Esterre.

THE FILM: Basil Rathbone was first seen by movie audiences in a well-received poetic drama from director Maurice Elvey. Critics felt the story was somewhat artificial, although they had nothing but praise for the picture's beautiful rustic exteriors and remarkable camera-work, as well as the dramatic performances.

Innocence (Madge Stuart) is an orphan, who leaves her country home after the death of her foster-father. Traveling to the city, she makes a living as a novelist and, subsequently, has an affair with painter Amadis de Jocelyn (Rathbone).

The artist ultimately discards Innocence and she returns to the farm. Enroute, she is caught in a storm and dies.

Rathbone garnered favorable notices for his portrayal of the selfish lover.

* Contrary to previously published information, Basil Rathbone did *not* appear in the following motion pictures: *The Loves of Mary, Queen of Scots; The Love of Sunya; Barnum Was Right; Just Smith;* and *Dr. Rock and Mr. Roll.*

CRITICAL COMMENT:

"Basil Rathbone makes a romantic figure as the perfidious painter."
The Bioscope

Innocent: **With Madge Stuart.**

THE FRUITFUL VINE

(1921)

A Stoll Film Production. Directed by Maurice Elvey. From a novel by Robert Hichens. Scenario: Leslie Howard Gordon. Camera: Germaine Burger. Art Director: Walter Murton. Editor: H. Leslie Brittain. Released: September 1921. 7,100 feet.

CAST: *Don Cesare Carelli*: Basil Rathbone; *Dolores Cannynge*: Valya; *Sir Theodore Cannynge*: Robert English; *Edna Denzil*: Mary Dibley; *Francis Denzil*: Teddy Arundell; *Dr. Mervynn Ides*: Fred Raynham; *Lady Sarah Ides*: Irene Rooke; *Princess Mancelli*: Paulette del Baye; *Theo Denzil*: Peter Dear.

THE FILM: Generally credited as being Rathbone's film debut, *The Fruitful Vine* was, in fact, released several months after *Innocent*, also made in 1921. Most critics praised the picture's production values, but felt the story left much to be desired.

Wishing to bear her elderly husband (Robert English) an heir, Dolores Cannynge (Valya) gives herself to Don Cesare Carelli (Rathbone). She later dies during childbirth, unaware that her husband knows the truth. The picture concludes with Carelli and Cannynge in a bitter struggle for the infant.

Rathbone's performance in this silent production did not impress the critics.

CRITICAL COMMENT:
"Few of the actors are sufficiently emotional to appeal very deeply. They are mostly too cold and restrained, and are overshadowed by the settings."

Kinematograph Weekly

The Fruitful Vine: **With Valya.**

THE SCHOOL FOR SCANDAL

(1923)

A BP Production. Produced and directed by Bertram Phillips. From the play by Richard Brinsley Sheridan. Scenario: Frank Miller. Released: August 1923. 6,350 feet.

CAST: *Lady Teazle*: Queenie Thomas; *Sir Peter Teazle*: Frank Stanmore: *Joseph Surface*: Basil Rathbone; *Charles Surface*: John Stuart; *Sir Oliver Surface*: Sydney Paxton; *Moses*: A. G. Poulton; *Lady Sneerwell*: Elsie French; *Mrs. Candour*: Mary Brough, *Trip*: Jack Miller; *Maria*: Billie Shotter.

THE FILM: This silent version of Richard Brinsley Sheridan's comedy of manners, set in 1777 London, had Rathbone essaying the role of Joseph Surface, the young man who schemes to marry Maria (Billie Shotter), a wealthy heiress, for her fortune. To mask his designs, Joseph carries on a flirtation with Lady Teazle (Queenie Thomas), wife of Maria's guardian.

Lady Teazle visits Joseph and is surprised by her husband, Sir Peter (Frank Stanmore). Hidden behind a screen, the lady learns Joseph's true character and receives proof of her husband's love.

Charles Surface (John Stuart), Joseph's brother and suitor to Maria, arrives. He discovers Lady Teazle, who, in turn, exposes Joseph.

Critics enjoyed this production of *The School for Scandal,* especially praising the film's performances and settings.

CRITICAL COMMENT:
". . . the company engaged is no doubt wise in not being bound down by stage tradition, and in presenting the different characters by those methods best suited for the provision of popular entertainment."

The Bioscope

TROUPING WITH ELLEN

(1924)

An Eastern Production through Producers Distributing Corporation. Directed by T. Hayes Hunter. Screen Dramatization: Gerald C. Duffy. Photography: J. Roy Hunt. Released: October 1924. 70 minutes.

CAST: *Ellen Llewellyn*: Helene Chadwick; *Lil*: Mary Thurman; *Andy Owens*: Gaston Glass; *Tony Winterslip*: Basil Rathbone; *"The Old Man"*: Riley Hatch; *Mabel Llewellyn*: Zena Keefe; *Mrs. Llewellyn*: Kate Blanke; *Mr. Llewellyn*: (Frederick) Tyrone Power.

THE FILM: The British actor made his American movie debut in this silent drama. Known in England as *Pity the Chorus Girl*, the picture starred Helene Chadwick and Gaston Glass.

Rathbone played the aristocratic and wealthy Tony Winterslip, who proposes to Ellen (Chadwick), a chorus girl. She refuses him because he is unaspiring and dependent on his wealth. Instead, she marries her boy friend, Andy Owens (Glass), a composer.

Rathbone received good reviews for his performance.

CRITICAL COMMENT:
". . . his wealthy rival is well-played by Basil Rathbone. . . ."
Variety

THE MASKED BRIDE

(1925)

A Metro-Goldwyn-Mayer Picture. Directed by Christy Cabanne. Scenario: Carey Wilson. Story: Leon Abrams. Photography: Oliver Marsh. Art Directors: Cedric Gibbons and Ben Carre. Film Editor: Frank E. Hull. Released: November 1925. 68 minutes.

CAST: *Gaby*: Mae Murray; *Bruce Gordon*: Francis X. Bushman; *Prefect of Police*: Roy D'Arcy; *Antoine*: Basil Rathbone; *Miss Gordon*: Pauline Neff; *Vibout*: Fred Warren.

THE FILM: Rathbone's first *important* picture was a vehicle for silent film star Mae Murray. Metro-Goldwyn-Mayer had originally assigned Josef von Sternberg to direct the film, but after two weeks of shooting, the Austrian became bored with the project and, in protest, began shooting the rafters of the sound stage—instead of the actors. He was replaced by Christy Cabanne.

The story tells of Gaby (Murray), a French cabaret dancer and consort of an apache, Antoine (Rathbone). She falls in love with Bruce Gordon (Francis X. Bushman), an American millionaire, in Paris researching crime. Antoine forces her to steal a five-million-franc necklace from the American and threatens to kill him if she refuses. Gaby is arrested by the Prefect of Police (Roy D'Arcy), but is forgiven by Gordon, who proceeds with their wedding plans.

Critics were generally impressed with Rathbone's work in this entertaining, if improbable, melodrama. Miss Murray also received excellent notices for her "charming" performance.

CRITICAL COMMENT:

"The role of Antoine is acted by Basil Rathbone, who gives a most commendable performance."

New York Times

"Basil Rathbone is the heavy, the dancing partner of Miss Murray, and handled himself to advantage in a role that was far from being sympathetic."

Variety

The Masked Bride: **With Mae Murray.**

The Masked Bride: **With Mae Murray.**

The Masked Bride: **With Mae Murray.**

THE GREAT DECEPTION

(1926)

A Robert Kane Production released by First National. Directed by
Howard Higgin. From a novel, *The Yellow Dove*, by George Gibbs.
Scenario: Paul Bern. Photography: Ernest Haller. Released: August
1926. 61 minutes.

CAST: *Cyril Mansfield*: Ben Lyon; *Lois*: Aileen Pringle; *Rizzio*:
Basil Rathbone; *Handy*: Sam Hardy; *Mrs. Mansfield*: Charlotte
Walker; *Lady Jane*: Amelia Summerville; *General von Franken-
hauser*: Hubert Wilke; *von Markow*: Lucian Prival; *Burton*: Lucius
Henderson; *Maxwell*: Mark Gonzales.

THE FILM: *The Great Deception* was an exciting, but somewhat
implausible, tale of espionage during World War I.

Cyril Mansfield (Ben Lyon) works in England for the German
Secret Service, yet is, in fact, loyal to British Intelligence. A German

The Great Deception: **With Aileen Pringle and Ben Lyon.**

agent, Rizzio (Rathbone), suspects Cyril's disloyalty to the Father-
land and abducts his girl friend, Lois (Aileen Pringle). She innocently
betrays her lover and the pair are condemned to death. Luckily, they
are able to escape before the sentence is carried out.

Rathbone was impressive in this silent melodrama, which received
generally mixed reviews.

CRITICAL COMMENT:
"Basil Rathbone plays the role of a German agent, known as
Rizzio, in a convincing fashion."

New York Times

THE LAST OF MRS. CHEYNEY

(1929)

A Metro-Goldwyn-Mayer Picture. Supervised by Irving Thalberg. Directed by Sidney Franklin. From the play by Frederick Lonsdale. Continuity: Hans Kraly and Claudine West. Photography: William Daniels. Art Director: Cedric Gibbons. Film Editor: Conrad A. Nervig. Recording Engineers: G. A. Burns and Douglas Shearer. Wardrobe: Adrian. Released: July 1929. 94 minutes.

CAST: *Mrs. Cheyney*: Norma Shearer; *Lord Arthur Dilling*: Basil Rathbone; *Charles*: George Barraud; *Lord Elton*: Herbert Bunston; *Lady Maria*: Hedda Hopper; *Joan*: Moon Carroll; *Mrs. Wynton*: Madeline Seymour; *Willie Wynton*: Cyril Chadwick; *Mrs. Webley*: Maude Turner Gordon; *William*: Finch Smiles; *George*: George K. Arthur.

THE FILM: Movie audiences first heard Rathbone speak in Metro-Goldwyn-Mayer's adaptation of Frederick Lonsdale's successful comedy,

The Last of Mrs. Cheyney: **With Norma Shearer.**

The Last of Mrs. Cheyney: **Basil Rathbone, Player, and Norma Shearer.**

The Last of Mrs. Cheyney, which had starred Ina Claire and Roland
Young on the New York stage.

In general, the critics approved of the early sound feature, praising
both Rathbone and star Norma Shearer, as well as director Sidney
Franklin.

The production rehearsed for three weeks before it began a
shooting schedule that ran the same length of time.

Adventuress Fay Cheyney (Shearer) poses as a wealthy widow at
a Monte Carlo hotel. Aided by Charles (George Barraud), she plans
to steal an expensive necklace, but has second thoughts after she falls
in love with the intended victim's nephew, Lord Arthur Dilling
(Rathbone). Ultimately, Fay takes the necklace during a house party.
Dilling catches the lady jewel thief in the act and promises not to ex-
pose her if she will let him have his way with her.

Refusing to be blackmailed, Mrs. Cheyney confesses her crime to
the other guests. They are about to call the police when Lord Elton
(Herbert Bunston) informs them that Fay has a love letter he wrote,
which could prove an embarrassment to everyone present. The aristo-
crats buy her off, but Fay is a woman of principle and destroys both

the letter and the check. Grateful, the guests welcome her back into their group.

Norma Shearer reflects: "It was a joy to act with Mr. Rathbone and I remember him most affectionately as a charmer, both on and off the screen. His beautiful voice, noble features, and distinguished bearing made him one of the great gentlemen of his time."

Metro remade *The Last of Mrs. Cheyney* in 1937 with Joan Crawford, William Powell, and Robert Montgomery essaying the roles of Fay, Charles, and Dilling, respectively. A second remake in 1951 was called *The Law and the Lady* and starred Greer Garson, Michael Wilding, and Fernando Lamas.

CRITICAL COMMENT:

"Basil Rathbone fills the part of Lord Arthur Dilling, which was acted in the play by Roland Young. Mr. Rathbone is capital, making allowances, of course, for the temperamental reproducing device. His lines won favor with the spectators yesterday, and the poise with which he conducts himself suits the part."

New York Times

THE BISHOP MURDER CASE

(1930)

A Metro-Goldwyn-Mayer Picture. Directed by Nick Grinde and David Burton. From the story by S. S. Van Dine. Screenplay: Lenore J. Coffee. Photography: Roy Overbaugh. Art Director: Cedric Gibbons. Film Editor: William Le Vanway. Released: February 1930. 91 minutes.

CAST: *Philo Vance*: Basil Rathbone; *Belle Dillard*: Leila Hyams; *Sigurd Arnesson*: Roland Young; *Prof. Bertrand Dillard*: Alec B. Francis; *Adolph Drukker*: George Marion; *Mrs. Otto Drukker*: Zelda Sears; *John E. Sprigg*: Carroll Nye; *John Pardee*: Charles Quartermaine; *Ernest Heath*: James Donlan; *Pyne*: Sydney Bracey; *John F.-X. Markham*: Clarence Geldert; *Raymond Sperling*: Delmer Daves.

THE FILM: William Powell became the screen's first Philo Vance

The Bishop Murder Case: **Charles Quartermaine, Basil Rathbone, and Clarence Geldert.**

The Bishop Murder Case: **With Roland Young, Clarence Geldert, and Charles Quartermaine.**

in the 1929 Paramount film, *The Canary Murder Case.* A year later, Rathbone essayed the role of S. S. Van Dine's gentleman sleuth in a Metro-Goldwyn-Mayer production, *The Bishop Murder Case.*

The story revolves around a series of murders, which take place at the home of Professor Bertrand Dillard (Alec B. Francis). The killer sends notes in children's rhymes and signs them "The Bishop." Philo Vance takes on the investigation, ultimately proving that the Professor is, in fact, the guilty party.

Rathbone was a bit too formal as Vance and failed to capture the relaxed, man-about-town quality inherent in the character. The picture itself, however, was a good mystery film with an interesting plot, and had a surprisingly mobile camera for such an early talking picture.

Other actors who have played Philo Vance on film include: Warren William, Paul Lukas, Edmund Lowe, Wilfred Hyde-White, Grant Richards, James Stephenson, William Wright, and Alan Curtis.

CRITICAL COMMENT:
    "Rathbone makes a handsome, intelligent Vance, not given to undue keen eye expression. Voice is not strong but diction is clear."
                                                                        Variety

"Mr. Rathbone vies easily with William Powell as an interpreter of Philo Vance. So far as to which of the two is preferable in the role is a matter to be decided by the imaginative Mr. Van Dine."

New York Times

A NOTORIOUS AFFAIR

(1930)

A First National Picture. Directed by Lloyd Bacon. From a play, *Fame,* by Audrey Carter and Waverly Carter. Adaptation/Dialogue: J. Grubb Alexander. Photography: Ernest Haller. Set Design: Anton Grot. Film Editor: Frank Ware. Released: April 1930. 67 minutes.

CAST: *Patricia Hanley Gherardi*: Billie Dove; *Paul Gherardi*: Basil Rathbone; *Countess Balakireff*: Kay Francis; *Sir Thomas Hanley*: Montagu Love; *Dr. Allen Pomroy*: Kenneth Thompson. *Also*: Philip Strange, Gino Corrado, and Elinor Vandivere.

THE FILM: Rathbone was not at his best in this screen adaptation of a play, *Fame,* by Audrey Carter and Waverly Carter. His foreign accent was inconsistant and, at times, he delivered his speeches too broadly. However, compared to the rest of the cast, his notices were excellent.

A Notorious Affair: **With Kay Francis.**

A Notorious Affair: **With Billie Dove.**

A Notorious Affair (working title: *Faithful*) is the story of Patricia Hanley (Billie Dove), who sacrifices her social position to marry a struggling violinist, Paul Gherardi (Rathbone). Through the help of Countess Balakireff (Kay Francis), Paul becomes an important concert artist. He subsequently runs off with the femme fatale. Patricia, in turn, renews an acquaintence with an old flame, Dr. Allen Pomroy (Kenneth Thompson).

When Paul suffers a paralytic attack due to his overwork, Patricia returns to her husband and, following an operation, nurses him back to health. Paul's affair with the Countess has ended and, after Patricia gives up Pomroy, the couple are reunited.

Rathbone almost seems to be commenting on his own performance in the film when, near the conclusion, as he explains his previously nasty attitude to his wife, he says: "I wanted just to hold you, but only succeeded in making myself more melodramatic."

CRITICAL COMMENT:

"The rest of the photoplay runs along smoothly enough, with Mr. Rathbone corralling the majority of the performing honors."

New York Times

THE LADY OF SCANDAL

(1930)

A Metro-Goldwyn-Mayer Picture. Directed by Sidney Franklin. From a play, *The High Road,* by Frederick Lonsdale. Scenario: Hans Kraly. Dialogue: Claudine West and Edwin Justus Mayer. Photography: Oliver T. Marsh and Arthur Miller. Art Director: Cedric Gibbons. Film Editor: Margaret Booth. Gowns: Adrian. Released: June 1930. 67 minutes.

CAST: *Elsie*: Ruth Chatterton; *Edward*: Basil Rathbone; *John*: Ralph Forbes; *Lady Trench*: Nance O'Neil; *Lord Trench*: Frederick Kerr; *Lord Crayle*: Herbert Bunston; *Sir Reginald*: Cyril Chadwick; *Lady Minster*: Effie Ellsler; *Hilary*: Robert Bolder; *Alice*: Moon Carroll; *Ernest*: Mackenzie Ward; *Morton*: Edgar Norton.

The Lady of Scandal.

The Lady of Scandal: **With Ruth Chatterton.**

THE FILM: Metro-Goldwyn-Mayer's romantic comedy/drama was based on a play, *The High Road* by Frederick Lonsdale, which had starred Edna Best and Herbert Marshall on the stage.

Rathbone's role was sympathetic. He was Edward, the Duke of Warrington, a man in love with two women.

Elsie Hilary (Ruth Chatterton), the central character of the film, is a popular English musical-comedy actress, who falls in love with John Crayle (Ralph Forbes), a nobleman. He takes her to his estate to meet his disapproving relatives. However, the family is soon enchanted by Elsie and their attitude toward her changes.

A secret romance develops between Elsie and Edward, John's cousin. The actress learns from Sir Reginald (Cyril Chadwick), a member of the Crayle family, that Edward had been having an affair with the young wife of an elderly baronet. When she confronts her lover with this knowledge, he promises to give up the other woman.

John realizes that he and Elsie are not suited for each other and their betrothal is terminated. In the meantime, the elderly baronet has died, leaving Edward's other love a widow. Elsie insists that Edward go to her.

The actress decides that life among the upper social classes of

Britain is not for her and returns to the stage. She informs the family that, should they ever wish to see her again, they will have to purchase a ticket.

The film was well received by the press.

CRITICAL COMMENT:
    "Basil Rathbone gives an expert performance as the Duke."
                                                    New York Times

THIS MAD WORLD

(1930)

A Metro-Goldwyn-Mayer Picture. Directed by William DeMille. From a play by Francois Curel. Dialogue: Clara Beranger and Arthur Caesar. Adaptation: Clara Beranger. Photography: Peverell Marley and Hal Rosson. Art Director: Cedric Gibbons. Film Editor: Anne Bauchens. Sound Engineers: J. K. Brock and Douglas Shearer. Gowns: Adrian. Released: July 1930. 70 minutes.

CAST: *Victoria*: Kay Johnson; *Paul*: Basil Rathbone; *Pauline*: Louise Dresser; *Anna*: Veda Buckland; *Emile*: Louis Natheaux.

THE FILM: This well-acted romantic melodrama of World War I was a disappointment. Although Rathbone turned in an above-par performance as the film's hero, as did Kay Johnson playing opposite him, they were hindered by a pedestrian script, which marred the entire project.

This Mad World: **With Kay Johnson.**

This Mad World: **With Kay Johnson.**

The setting is France—behind the German lines. Paul (Rathbone) is a French spy. While on a secret mission, he visits his mother, Pauline (Louise Dresser), and meets a guest at her inn, Victoria (Johnson), who is the wife of a German general.

The spy and the lady are attracted to each other and she prevents his arrest by the German troops. However, when she subsequently learns that Paul is responsible for the death of her nephew, Victoria betrays him, then, in anguish, commits suicide. Paul is executed by a firing squad.

This Mad World was a slow-moving and familiar production, which made little impression on either critics or audience.

CRITICAL COMMENT:

"Basil Rathbone plays the spy with plenty of dash."

Film Daily

THE FLIRTING WIDOW

(1930)

A First National Picture. Directed by William Seiter. From a play, *Green Stockings,* by Alfred Edward Woodley Mason. Scenario/Dialogue: John F. Goodrich. Photography: Sid Hickox. Film Editor: John F. Goodrich. Released: August 1930. 74 minutes.

CAST: *Celia*: Dorothy Mackaill; *Colonel Smith*: Basil Rathbone; *Evelyn*: Leila Hyams; *James Raleigh*: William Austin; *Faraday*: Claude Gillingwater; *Aunt Ida*: Emily Fitzroy; *Phyllis*: Flora Bramley; *Bobby*: Anthony Bushell; *Martin*: Wilfred Noy.

THE FILM: Based on a play by Alfred Edward Woodley Mason, this light comedy had only the performances of Rathbone and Dorothy Mackaill to recommend it. Director William Seiter did nothing more than film a stage play—and a mediocre one at that.

Sir William Faraday (Claude Gillingwater) will not allow his

The Flirting Widow: **With Dorothy Mackaill.**

The Flirting Widow: **With Dorothy Mackaill.**

daughter, Phyllis (Flora Bramley), to marry until Celia (Mackaill), his eldest girl, is wed. To help her sister, Celia announces that she is engaged to a Colonel John Smith. The imaginary military man is suppose to be stationed in Arabia. The family is delighted and Faraday gives his consent for Phyllis to wed Bobby Tarver (Anthony Bushell).

Problems arise when, at her sister's insistence, Celia writes a love letter to her "fiancé," which is accidentally posted and, subsequently, received in Arabia by a *real* Colonel Smith (Rathbone).

Following Phyllis's wedding, Celia publishes a notice in the paper that her "fiancé" has been killed. Almost immediately thereafter, the real Colonel, home on leave, visits the Faraday estate under the guise of being a friend of the deceased. After making Celia very uncomfortable, Smith realizes that he loves her and reveals his true identity.

Rathbone, showing a fine flair for comedy, and Miss Mackaill contributed some very funny scenes in what was otherwise a dull picture.

CRITICAL COMMENT:

"Mr. Rathbone, as usual his competent self, appears to great advantage as the Colonel, and Miss Mackaill manages to pull through the ordeal as the innocent victim of the Colonel's scheming."

New York Times

A LADY SURRENDERS

(1930)

A Universal Picture. Directed by John M. Stahl. Produced by Carl Laemmle, Jr. From the novel, *Sincerity,* by John Erskine. Continuity: Gladys Lehman. Dialogue: Arthur Richman. Photography: Jackson Rose. Sets: Walter Kessler. Film Editors: Maurice Pivar and Wi am L. Cahn. Released: September 1930. 95 minutes.

CAST: *Mary*: Genevieve Tobin; *Isabel*: Rose Hobart; *Winthrop*: Conrad Nagel; *Carl Vaudry*: Basil Rathbone; *Sonia*: Carmel Myers; *Lawton*: Franklin Pangborn; *Mrs. Lynchfield*: Vivian Oakland.

THE FILM: *A Lady Surrenders* was a pleasant drawing-room comedy, which entertained its audiences, but left them with no lasting impression.

The screenplay tells of Winthrop Beauvel (Conrad Nagel) and his bored wife, Isabel (Rose Hobart). Isabel mistakenly accuses her husband of being unfaithful to her and sails to Europe to obtain a

A Lady Surrenders: **With Rose Hobart.**

A Lady Surrenders: **With Rose Hobart.**

divorce. On board the ship, she is romanced by Carl Vaudry (Rathbone), who eventually jilts her.

Isabel decides not to get the divorce. When she returns home, however, she discovers that Winthrop, thinking himself free, has married Mary (Genevieve Tobin).

Following a stormy meeting between the two women, Mary attempts suicide. Isabel realizes her competitor's seriousness and agrees to surrender Winthrop.

Rathbone, as well as the rest of the cast, got reasonably good reviews for their work in this program picture.

CRITICAL COMMENT:

"Basil Rathbone, who really is an Englishman, is the only one of the film's featured quartet with a reason to talk like that, because he plays a European."

Variety

SIN TAKES A HOLIDAY

(1930)

A Pathé Picture. Directed by Paul Stein. Produced by E. B. Derr. From a story by Robert Milton and Dorothy Cairns. Screenplay: Horace Jackson. Photography: John Mescall. Art Director: Carroll Clark. Film Editor: Daniel Mandell. Released: November 1930. 81 minutes.

CAST: *Sylvia*: Constance Bennett; *Gaylord Stanton*: Kenneth Mac-Kenna; *Durant*: Basil Rathbone; *Grace*: Rita LaRoy; *Richards*: Louis John Bartels; *Sheridan*: John Roche; *Anna*: ZaSu Pitts; *Miss Munson*: Kendall Lee; *Ruth*: Murrell Finley; *Miss Graham*: Helen Johnson.

THE FILM: Constance Bennett and Kenneth MacKenna were the stars of this domestic comedy, in which Rathbone essayed a secondary role.

The story dealt with Gaylord Stanton (MacKenna), an attorney,

Sin Takes a Holiday: **With Constance Bennett.**

Sin Takes a Holiday: **With Constance Bennett.**

who is named as corespondent in a divorce case. He had been having an affair with Grace Lanier (Rita LaRoy).

Knowing that Grace will want to marry him when she is free, Stanton makes a business arrangement with his flippant secretary, Sylvia (Bennett), whereby they will marry in name only. Sylvia may go where she wishes and is to receive a salary of five thousand dollars per year.

Sylvia journeys to Paris, where she meets and is romanced by

Durant (Rathbone). In the meantime, Stanton informs Grace that he is married, his wife being an invalid in a sanitarium.

Durant begs Sylvia to get a divorce and marry him. Confused, as she is really in love with her husband, Sylvia returns home to confront him. When he sees her after the long separation, Stanton realizes that he *does* love his wife and they are reunited.

Rathbone received good reviews for his work in the picture, which got generally luke-warm notices from the critics.

CRITICAL COMMENT:
"Rathbone is capital as Durant."

New York Times

A WOMAN COMMANDS

(1932)

An RKO Pathé Production. Directed by Paul L. Stein. Produced by Charles R. Rogers. From a screen story by Thilde Forster. Associate Producer: Harry Joe Brown. Camera: Hal Mohr. Music: Nacio Herb Brown. Sound: Earl Wocott. Released: January 1932. 85 minutes.

CAST: *Mme. Maria Draga*: Pola Negri; *King Alexander*: Roland Young; *Captain Alex Pasitsch*: Basil Rathbone; *Colonel Stradimiro-vitsch*: H. B. Warner; *Iwan*: Anthony Bushell; *The Prime Minister*: Reginald Owen; *Mascha*: May Boley; *The General*: Frank Reicher; *Chedo*: George Baxter; *Crown Prince Milan*: Cleo Louise Borden.

A Woman Commands: **With Pola Negri.**

A Woman Commands: **With Pola Negri.**

THE FILM: Pola Negri's first talking picture was to have co-starred Laurence Olivier in the role of Captain Alex Pasitsch. Shortly before the start of principal photography, however, the actor became ill and was forced to withdraw.

Although she had some reservations that he might be "too stiff" to play her dashing lover, Miss Negri agreed that Basil Rathbone could be a satisfactory replacement and tested with him. Based on that footage, the performer was cast.

Unfortunately, the actress's fears were borne out in the completed film. Most critics found Rathbone to be the one weak performance in the otherwise entertaining, if unimportant, picture.

Thilde Forster's screenplay, set in a small European country, tells of Maria Draga (Negri), a beautiful cabaret entertainer, who is being romanced by both the impulsive King Alexander (Roland Young) and Captain Alex Pasitsch (Rathbone). The officer has squandered a considerable amount of money on Maria and is upset when she refuses to accompany him to his lonely outpost.

Eventually, Maria weds Alexander, an act that makes enemies for the monarch in the royal court. It is a happy marriage until the king is killed by a revolutionist's bomb. The film ends with Maria being reunited with Pasitsch.

As the happy-go-lucky ruler, Roland Young garnered the best notices in the production.

CRITICAL COMMENT:

"Basil Rathbone plays a stenciled guardsman lover with unusual inflexibility."

Variety

ONE PRECIOUS YEAR

(1933)

A B. & D./Paramount (British) Production. Directed by Henry Edwards. From a play, *Driven,* by Temple Thurston. Screenplay: E. Temple Thurston. Released: February 1933. 76 minutes.

CAST: *Dierdre Carton*: Anne Grey; *Derek Nagel*: Basil Rathbone; *Stephen Carton*: Owen Nares; *Julia Skene*: Flora Robson; *Sir Richard Pakenham*: Ben Webster; *Mr. Telford*: Evelyn Roberts; *Sir John Rome*: H. G. Stoker; *Dr. Hibbert*: Robert Horton.

THE FILM: This interesting, if talky, British drama cast Rathbone as Derek Nagel, a handsome cad, who has an affair with Dierdre (Anne Grey), the neglected wife of Stephen Carton (Owen Nares), a Foreign Office official. Dierdre has been informed by her physician that she has only one year to live.

Eventually, Nagel "drops" the married woman—about the same time that her husband learns of the relationship. Stephen forgives her indiscretion and the film ends happily—with the doctor announcing that a cure has been discovered for Dierdre's disease.

Although well-acted, the picture was easily forgettable.

CRITICAL COMMENT:
"There is a high standard of acting throughout."
Picturegoer Weekly

AFTER THE BALL

(1933)

A Gaumont-British Production. Released in the United States by Fox. Directed by Milton Rosmer. Adapted from a German film, *Opera Ball,* by H. M. Harwood. Scenario: J. O. C. Orton. Camera: Percy Strong. Music: Otto Stransky. Lyrics: Clifford Grey. Released: March 1933. 70 minutes.

CAST: Elissa Strange: Esther Ralston; *Jack Harrowby*: Basil Rathbone; *Larita*: Marie Burke; *Victorine*: Jean Adrienne; *Peter Strange*: George Curzon; *Albuera*: Clifford Heatherley.

THE FILM: Directed by Milton Rosmer, this Fox release of a Gaumont-British production was a dull remake of a successful German talkie, *Opera Ball*. Rathbone co-starred in the film with Esther Ralston.

After the Ball: **With Esther Ralston.**

After the Ball.

The story takes place during a meeting of world diplomats in Geneva. The debates are becoming lengthy and the wives of the treaty-makers are bored.

Elissa Strange (Ralston), wife of the British representative, attends the grand mask ball with her maid, since her husband, Peter (George Curzon), is bogged down in a meeting. At the affair, she meets Jack Harrowby (Rathbone), a friend of Peter's, but a stranger to her, and they carry on a firtation. He follows her home.

Complications arise when a State Seal disappears and, subsequently, turns up in Elissa's garden. However, in a surprise finish, all ends well.

Notices for the two leading players were good.

CRITICAL COMMENT:
"Basil Rathbone is a model of amorous gallantry."
New York Times

LOYALTIES

(1933)

An Associated Talking Picture. Directed by Basil Dean. From the play by John Galsworthy. Screenplay: W. P. Lipscomb. Photography: Robert Martin. Art Director: Edward Carrick. Sound: Eric Williams. Released: May 1933. 75 minutes.

CAST: *Ferdinand de Levis*: Basil Rathbone; *Margaret Orme*: Heather Thatcher; *Capt. Ronald Dancy, D.S.O.*: Miles Mander; *Mabel Dancy*: Joan Wyndham; *Major Colford*: Philip Strange; *General Canynge*: Alan Napier; *Charles Winsor*: Algernon West; *Lady Adela Winsor*: Cecily Byrne; *Lord St. Erth*: Athole Stewart; *Sir Frederic Blair*: Patric Curwen; *Lord Chief Justice*: Marcus Barron; *Gillman*: Ben Field; *Inspector Jones*: Griffith Humphreys; *Augustus Borring*: Patrick Waddington. *Also*: L. Hanray, Arnold Lucy, and Robert Mawdesley.

THE FILM: Rathbone considered his performance as a modern-day Shylock in this British adaptation of John Galsworthy's *Loyalties* to

Loyalties: **With Algernon West, Athole Stewart, and Alan Napier.**

Loyalties: **Patrick Waddington, Miles Mander, Philip Strange, and Basil Rathbone.**

be one of the most satisfying of his career. The play, dealing with anti-Semitism among London's upper social classes, had starred James Dale in a 1922 New York stage production.

It was an engrossing film, garnering first-rate notices for director Basil Dean and the cast, headed by Rathbone.

Ferdinand de Levis (Rathbone) is a proud and wealthy Jew, eager to gain social position. At a party, a large sum of money is stolen from his wallet. Although he suspects Dancy (Miles Mander) of the theft, his hosts appeal to de Levis not to call in the police, as that is not the "gentlemanly" thing to do.

After he has been blackballed by a British club, de Levis, tired of being tolerated for his wealth alone, accuses Dancy in public of being a thief and the latter is forced to sue him for slander. The Jew triumphs in court, but it is an "empty" victory.

Actor Alan Napier recalls that Rathbone was a sincere person, who wanted to be liked, and always endeavored to accomplish this: "He enjoyed sitting around the set . . . telling stories and being the center of attention.

"I knew Basil for years and I was constantly surprised at how young he always seemed in relationship to his age. . . . He was a very gracious man."

Basil Dean's second assistant director on the picture was Carol Reed, later responsible for such cinema classics as *The Third Man, The Fallen Idol,* and *Oliver!*

CRITICAL COMMENT:

"Basil Rathbone contributes an excellent performance as Ferdinand de Levis, the Shylock in modern dress of the Galsworthy work. . . . Mr. Dean, Mr. Rathbone and the rest have more than caught the spirit of the play. In their hands, the transcription has been so well contrived that the work seems to have been made expressly for the screen, rather than for the stage."

New York Times

DAVID COPPERFIELD

(1935)

A Metro-Goldwyn-Mayer Picture. Directed by George Cukor. Produced by David O. Selznick. From the novel by Charles Dickens. Adaptation: Hugh Walpole. Screenplay: Howard Estabrook. Art Director: Cedric Gibbons. Photography: Oliver T. Marsh. Film Editor: Robert J. Kern. Sound: Douglas Shearer. Released: January 1935. 133 minutes.

CAST: Mr. Micawber: W. C. Fields; Dan Peggotty: Lionel Barrymore; Dora: Maureen O'Sullivan; Agnes: Madge Evans; Aunt Betsey: Edna May Oliver; Mr. Wickfield: Lewis Stone; David, the man: Frank Lawton; David, the child: Freddie Bartholomew; Mrs. Copperfield: Elizabeth Allan; Uriah Heep: Roland Young; Mr. Murdstone: Basil Rathbone; Clickett: Elsa Lanchester; Mrs. Micawber: Jean Cadell; Nurse Peggotty: Jessie Ralph; Mr. Dick: Lennox Pawle; Jane Murdstone: Violet Kemble Cooper; Mrs. Gummidge: Una O'Connor; Ham: John Buckler; Steerforth: Hugh Williams; Limmiter: Ivan Simpson.

David Copperfield: **With Elizabeth Allan.**

David Copperfield: **With Elizabeth Allan, Freddie Bartholomew, and Violet Kemble Cooper.**

Also: Herbert Mundin, Fay Chaldecott, Florine McKinney, Harry Beresford, Hugh Walpole, and Arthur Treacher.

THE FILM: *David Copperfield* changed the course of Basil Rathbone's career. Hollywood "discovered" the British actor after he played the loathsome Mr. Murdstone in David O. Selznick's superb film version of the immortal Charles Dickens novel and, subsequently, made him the screen's number one villain.

Director George Cukor remembers working with Rathbone on the picture: "I told Basil just one thing . . . be cold. That was my only direction. It was a hard part for him to do because such cruelty was against his very nature.

"In the scene where he had to beat Freddie Bartholomew, I instructed him to really whack the boy. Little Freddie was well-padded and didn't feel a thing, but, after the scene was finished, Basil came to me and confessed that he'd become sick to his stomach because he had to beat a child."

Although it incorporated a great number of episodes from the book, Selznick's production moved swiftly—thanks to a well-constructed screenplay and the meticulous direction of Mr. Cukor.

The producer assembled an able cast to bring the Dickens characters to life. W. C. Fields, who replaced Charles Laughton after the British actor quit over "artistic differences," was an excellent Micawber and Roland Young was perfection as the slimy Uriah Heep. Lionel Barrymore, Edna May Oliver, Maureen O'Sullivan, Lennox Pawle, Lewis Stone, and Jessie Ralph—each were magnificent in their individual roles, as were Freddie Bartholomew as David, the boy, and Frank Lawton as David, the man.

David Copperfield is born six months after the death of his father. His mother, Clara (Elizabeth Allan), remarries. David's new step-father is the cruel Mr. Murdstone. After his mother dies in childbirth, Murdstone sends David to work in his export warehouse.

In London, David stays with Mr. Micawber, a pauper with aristocratic aspirations, who eventually goes to debtor's prison. David runs away to Dover to live with his Great Aunt Betsey (Oliver) and her friend, Mr. Dick (Pawle). Murdstone and his sister (Violet Kemble-Cooper) attempt to reclaim the lad, but Aunt Betsey sends them away.

David returns to school and, following graduation, decides to become a writer. While a student, he had lived with Mr. Wickfield (Stone) and his daughter, Agnes (Madge Evans). Unaware that Miss Wickfield loves him, David proposes to Dora Spenlow (O'Sullivan), a sickly and very childish girl. Dora dies, ending their relatively short marriage.

Mr. Wickfield has been victimized by a business associate, Uriah Heep. David, with the aid of Micawber, exposes Heep, thereby helping Wickfield to regain his self-respect. Finally, David realizes that he loves Agnes and asks her to become his wife.

Rathbone was properly hateful as the sadistic Murdstone, who "broke" his wife by tormenting her son. There is no flicker of warmth in the man. So that Clara will demean herself to him, he announces after their marriage: "My own feeling toward you chills." His tyrannical methods work. The inexperienced girl, not wishing to offend, lets her husband have his way with David. Murdstone remains one of Rathbone's most memorable screen characterizations.

David Copperfield was remade in 1970 with James Donald playing Murdstone.

CRITICAL COMMENT:

"Rathbone is not as happily cast as the others. It really is the toughest assignment in the entire cast, but he does what can be done with the bit."

Variety

ANNA KARENINA

(1935)

A Metro-Goldwyn-Mayer Picture. Directed by Clarence Brown. Produced by David O. Selznick. From Count Leo Tolstoy's novel. Screenplay: Clemence Dane and Salka Viertel. Adaptation and Dialogue: S. N. Behrman. Collaborator: Erich von Stroheim. Art Director: Cedric Gibbons. Costumes: Adrian. Music: Herbert Stothart. Photography: William Daniels. Sound: Douglas Shearer. Editor: Robert J. Kern. Released: August 1935. 95 minutes.

CAST: *Anna Karenina*: Greta Garbo; *Count Alexei Vronsky*: Fredric March; *Kitty*: Maureen O'Sullivan; *Countess Vronsky*: May Robson; *Sergei*: Freddie Bartholomew; *Karenin*: Basil Rathbone; *Stiva*: Reginald Owen; *Yashvin*: Reginald Denny; *Dolly*: Phoebe Foster; *Levin*: Gyles Isham; *Grisha*: Buster Phelps; *Mahotin*: Mischa Auer. *Also*: Ella Ethridge, Joan Marsh, Sidney Bracey, Cora Sue Collins, Harry Allen, and Sarah Padden.

Anna Karenina: **With Greta Garbo.**

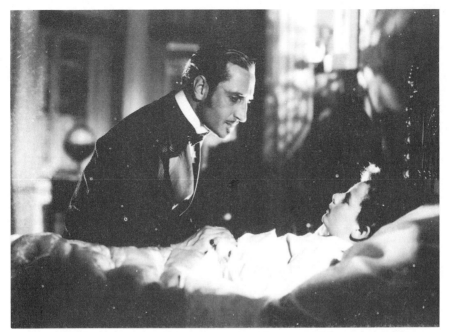

Anna Karenina: **With Freddie Bartholomew.**

Anna Karenina: **With Greta Garbo and Fredric March.**

THE FILM: Greta Garbo first played Anna Karenina in 1927. *Love*, the silent version of Tolstoy's novel, also had John Gilbert and Brandon Hurst in the cast, essaying the roles done by Fredric March and Rathbone in the 1935 film.

David O. Selznick's remake was a sumptuous production and Clarence Brown's direction brought out all possible values. Brown, incidentally, had replaced George Cukor, who had withdrawn from the project prior to the start of principal photography.

Performances were excellent, with Miss Garbo delivering a haunting interpretation of a difficult role.

The story is set in nineteenth-century Russia. On a visit to see her brother in Moscow, Anna Karenina (Garbo) meets Count Vronsky (March) and they fall in love. Anna is married to a wealthy bureaucrat, Karenin (Rathbone). They have a son, Sergei (Freddie Bartholomew).

After she returns home, the affair continues. Eventually, Anna asks Karenin for a divorce. He refuses her, threatening that she will lose all claim to their son if she goes off with Vronsky. Desperately in love with the Count, who has resigned his army commission, Anna departs with him for Venice.

At first, the lovers are happy together. However, Vronsky later becomes restless and, in the wake of an argument with Anna, he returns to military life.

Anna goes to the train station to make peace with Vronsky, but hesitates when she sees him with another girl. Realizing that she has lost both her lover and son, she throws herself beneath the wheels of a train.

Rathbone's role of the seemingly heartless Karenin was not an easy one. The actor had to endow the character with certain humanistic qualities, which weren't immediately apparent in his dialogue. A perfect example is the scene in which he watches Anna playing with Sergei. We sense that Karenin wishes he could have a similar tender relationship with his son, but recognizes that he lacks the necessary innate warmth. Instead, he feels like an outsider—and can only excuse himself.

It was a sensitive portrayal.

In the July 1936 issue of *Motion Picture Magazine*, Rathbone discussed his impressions of Garbo: "During the filming of the picture, I watched her and learned what I think is the secret of good screen acting—play your part with the least possible physical movement, and the greatest possible mental projection. . . . Garbo has this power of mental projection to a superb degree."

Anna Karenina was remade again in 1948 by Twentieth Century-Fox, with Vivien Leigh, Kieron Moore, and Ralph Richardson in the leading roles.

CRITICAL COMMENT:

"Basil Rathbone is excellent as the husband."

New York Times

THE LAST DAYS OF POMPEII

(1935)

An RKO Radio Release of a Merian C. Cooper Production. Directed by Ernest B. Schoedsack. From a story by James A. Creelman and Melville Baker. Adaptation: Ruth Rose and Boris Ingster. Camera: Eddie Linden, Jr., and Ray Hunt. Special Effects: Vernon Walker and Harry Redmond. Editor: Archie Marschek. Music: Roy Webb. Released: October 1935. 90 minutes.

CAST: *Marcus*: Preston Foster; *Burbix*: Alan Hale; *Pontius*: Basil Rathbone; *Flavius (as a man)*: John Wood; *Prefect*: Louis Calhern; *Flavius (as a boy)*: David Holt; *Clodia*: Dorothy Wilson; *Leaster*: Wyrley Birch; *Julia*: Gloria Shea; *Gaius*: Frank Conroy; *Cleon*: William V. Mong; *Calvus*: Edward Van Sloan.

THE FILM: Rathbone's portrayal of Pontius Pilate was the best thing about this Merian C. Cooper production, which may have impressed audiences in 1935, but has not withstood the test of time.

The Last Days of Pompeii: **With Preston Foster and David Holt.**

Borrowing only the title from the well known Bulwer-Lytton book, writers James Ashmore Creelman and Melville Baker wrote an original story that became the basis for Ruth Rose's screenplay.

Marcus (Preston Foster), a blacksmith in Pompeii, enters the arena as a gladiator. The deaths of his wife and baby under the wheels of a nobleman's chariot has made him decide that only wealth mat-

The Last Days of Pompeii: **As Pontius Pilate.**

ters in the world. He proceeds to become the champion competitor of Pompeii.

Marcus adopts Flavius (David Holt), the son of a gladiator he has killed in the arena, and soon grows to love the boy as his own. He wants Flavius to have only the finest things. After he is wounded in the "games," Marcus turns to slave trading in order to earn money.

A Wise Woman (Zeffie Tilbury) tells Marcus to take Flavius to see the "greatest man in Judea," who he assumes to be Pontius Pilate. They make the journey and are granted an audience with the governor. Pilate likes Marcus and proposes a plan, whereby the former gladiator will steal horses and gold from a neighboring tribe.

The raid is a success. Marcus's happiness is marred, however, when Flavius is injured in a fall from a horse. He takes the boy to a great prophet and Flavius is restored to health.

Before he departs Judea, Marcus reports to Pilate. The aristocrat is troubled because he has just sentenced the "King of the Jews" to die on the cross. As he leaves the city, Marcus learns that the condemned prophet is the same one that had helped Flavius, but he refuses to lay down his life to save the man from the mob.

Years pass. The wealthy Marcus has become head of the arena. Flavius (John Wood), now grown, disapproves of his father's work and assists a group of slaves in escaping their ultimate slaughter by the gladiators.

When Flavius is recaptured along with the slaves and sent to the arena to die, Marcus tries to stop the games. Mount Vesuvius erupts, causing tremendous earthquakes, which destroy Pompeii. Marcus sacrifices his life so that Flavius and a group of slaves can escape the catastrophe.

As the former gladiator dies, the prophet he turned his back on years before—Jesus Christ—appears and blesses him.

Initially, Rathbone had refused to consider playing the role of Pilate because the part called for only a week's filming on the project. Nevertheless, as a favor to his agent, the actor finally read the script. Realizing he had been mistaken to refuse it, he called the agent and told him to get him the role at any price. He later recalled his reason: "The part was me and I was the part. . . . It was magnificently written with economy of words—truely a sublime characterization."

Rathbone's interpretation of Pilate was that of a man tortured by his guilt in Christ's death. Several years after the Crucifixion, the governor says, philosophically, "I seem to remember everything about *that* day."

Flavius mentions that he recalls having seen a "great man" as a child and Pilate replies: "There was such a man. I crucified him."

Rathbone often said that he considered the performance to be one of the best of his entire career.

Unfortunately, the film was more successful in its straightforward melodrama than in the scenes dealing with religion. Foster, superb in the former sequences, was a bit awkward when he was called upon to be properly devout.

The special effects do not appear to be as carefully conceived as those producer Merian Cooper had employed in his successful *King Kong* two years earlier. The process work is obvious and crowd scenes seem limited by the budget. Today, the "spectacular" fall of Pompeii is a disappointment.

In spite of its drawbacks, the film does offer a certain amount of entertainment value and, if nothing else, Rathbone's performance is worth viewing.

CRITICAL COMMENT:

"But the hero of the occasion is Basil Rathbone, whose Pilate is a fascinating aristocrat, scornful in his hauteur and sly in his reasoning."

New York Times

"Basil Rathbone comes very close to stealing the picture with his playing of Pontius Pilate, the aristocrat not entirely without a conscience, who washes his hands of the blood of Jesus while tossing Him to the mob."

Variety

A FEATHER IN HER HAT

(1935)

A Columbia Production and Release. Directed by Alfred Santell. From a story by I. A. R. Wylie. Screenplay: Lawrence Hazard. Camera: Joseph Walker. Editor: Villa Lawrence. Released: October 1935. 72 minutes.

CAST: *Clarissa Phipps*: Pauline Lord; *Captain Courtney*: Basil Rathbone; *Richard Orland*: Louis Hayward; *Julia Anders*: Billie Burke; *Pauline Anders*: Wendy Barrie; *Paul Anders*: Victor Varconi; *Emily Judson*: Nydia Westman; *Sir Elroyd Joyce*: Thurston Hall; *Lady Drake*: Nana Bryant; *Pobjoy*: J. M. Kerrigan.

THE FILM: This tender little drama of mother love began production with Ruth Chatterton in the leading role. However, after one day of filming, the star quit the picture because of "artistic differences" and was replaced by Pauline Lord.

The plot revolves around Clarissa Phipps (Lord), the owner of

A Feather in Her Hat: **With Pauline Lord and Nydia Westman.**

A Feather in Her Hat: **With J. M. Kerrigan.**

a bookshop in the London slums, who wants her son to become a gentleman. The Cockney widow takes in Captain Courtney (Rathbone), an alcoholic aristocrat, so that her son, Richard (Louis Hayward), can assimilate his manner.

When the lad comes of age, Clarissa informs him that his "real" mother was a famous actress and had entrusted him to her care. She gives Richard her life savings of five thousand pounds on the pretext that it was left for him.

Believing his "real" mother to be Julia Anders (Billie Burke), a retired actress, Richard takes lodging with her family. Ultimately, he becomes a successful playwright.

Content with the knowledge that her son has matured into a real gentleman, Clarissa Phipps dies quietly on the evening of his initial success.

Both Rathbone and Miss Lord garnered good reviews from the picture, which, although moving at times, utilized worn-out clichés too often in order to make its dramatic points.

Louis Hayward remembers Rathbone as "a nice man, who portrayed the gentleman drunk beautifully."

CRITICAL COMMENT:
"Basil Rathbone's playing is flawless, although as a broken-down,

brandy guzzling ex-gentleman, he doesn't age sufficiently in appearance."

Variety

"Mr. Rathbone, sensitive to the spirit of the photoplay, is of admirable assistance as the bibulous aristocrat."

New York Times

A TALE OF TWO CITIES

(1935)

A Metro-Goldwyn-Mayer Picture. Directed by Jack Conway. Produced by David O. Selznick. From the novel by Charles Dickens. Screenplay: W. P. Lipscomb and S. N. Behrman. Music: Herbert Stothart. Photography: Oliver T. Marsh. Editor: Conrad A. Nervig. Released: November 1935. 121 minutes.

CAST: *Sydney Carton*: Ronald Colman; *Lucie Manette*: Elizabeth Allan; *Miss Pross*: Edna May Oliver; *Madame de Farge*: Blanche Yurka; *Stryver*: Reginald Owen; *Marquis St. Evremonde*: Basil Rathbone; *Dr. Manette*: Henry B. Walthall; *Charles Darnay*: Donald Woods; *Barsad*: Walter Catlett; *Gaspard*: Fritz Leiber; *Gabelle*: H.

A Tale of Two Cities: **With John Davidson.**

B. Warner; *Ernest de Farge*: Mitchell Lewis; *Jarvis Lorry*: Claude Gillingwater; *Jerry Cruncher*: Billy Bevan; *Seamstress*: Isabel Jewell; *LaVengeance*: Lucille LaVerne; *Woodcutter*: Tully Marshall; *Lucie, the Daughter*: Fay Chaldecott. *Also*: Elly Malyon, E. E. Clive, Lawrence Grant, Robert Warwick, Ralf Harolde, John Davidson, Tom Ricketts, Donald Haines, and Barlowe Borland.

THE FILM: David O. Selznick's lavish production of this Charles Dickens novel has become a screen classic. The attentive direction of Jack Conway, fine performances by an excellent cast, as well as the carefully conceived costumes and settings, helped to recreate the period of the French Revolution in vivid detail.

The screenplay by W. P. Lipscomb and S. N. Behrman remained faithful to the book, which was essentially a melodrama.

Sydney Carton (Ronald Colman), a lonely and dissipated London barrister, loves Lucie Manette (Elizabeth Allan). She, in turn, cares for him as a friend, but marries Charles Darnay (Donald Woods), nephew of the Marquis St. Evremonde (Rathbone), a cruel French aristocrat. Darnay had moved to England because he could not tolerate his uncle's inhumanity to the peasants. Shortly thereafter, the Marquis

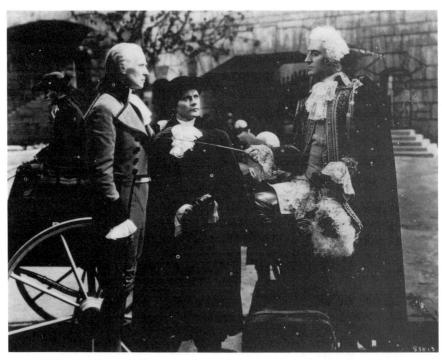

A Tale of Two Cities: **With H. B. Warner and Donald Woods.**

was murdered in his bed by the father of a boy who had been run down by the aristocrat's coach and horses.

When the Revolution comes, the most hated name among the populace is Evremonde. All members of the lineage, guilty or innocent, are sent to the guillotine. Through the efforts of the fanatical Madame de Farge (Blanche Yurka), Darnay is tricked into returning to Paris, where he is condemned.

Carton, not wanting his beloved Lucie or her daughter to suffer, redeems his purposeless life by exchanging places with Darnay. The next morning, as he goes to his death, he speaks those gallant words: "It is a far, far better thing that I do than I have ever done; it is a far, far better rest that I go to than I have ever known."

The Metro-Goldwyn-Mayer picture had many memorable moments: the sight of starving peasants drinking spilled wine from the muddy streets; the mock trial of Darnay before the blood-thirsty tribunal; the mob, cheering as the guillotine falls; and the spectacular re-enactment of the fall of the Bastille. Each sequence was extraordinary in its effectiveness.

Colman's sensitive portrayal of the tragic lawyer was one of the best of his career. Supporting performances were of the highest caliber also. Edna May Oliver as Miss Pross, Blanche Yurka's Madame de Farge, Henry B. Walthall as Dr. Manette, Claude Gillingwater as Jarvis Lorry, and Billy Bevan's Jerry Cruncher—each characterization managed to capture the Dickens flavor.

Rathbone, although having little to do, made a lasting impression. As the heartless Marquis, he managed to earn the loathing of the audience early in the film when he appeared to be more concerned with the condition of his horses rather than of the child they had just run down and killed. He later compounded the hatred when, after hearing the pleas of an aide to be more just with the populace, he replied: "Hunger is an indulgence with these peasants, as gout is with us."

Filmed at a budget of one million dollars, *A Tale of Two Cities* is a magnificent motion picture. It ranks as one of Selznick's finest contributions to the art form and is typical of the rich quality productions to come from Metro during the 1930s.

CRITICAL COMMENT:
"Basil Rathbone is a very model of cold hauteur as the cruel Evremonde."

New York Times

CAPTAIN BLOOD

(1935)

A Cosmopolitan Production; A First National Picture (Warner Brothers). Directed by Michael Curtiz. Executive Producer: Hal B. Wallis. Associate Producers: Harry Joe Brown and Gordon Hollingshead. From the novel by Rafael Sabatini. Screenplay: Casey Robinson. Photography: Hal Mohr. Music: Erich Wolfgang Korngold. Film Editor: George Amy. Art Director: Anton Grot. Sound: C. A. Riggs. Fencing Master: Fred Cavens. Released: December 1935. 119 minutes.

CAST: *Peter Blood*: Errol Flynn; *Arabella Bishop*: Olivia deHavilland; *Colonel Bishop*: Lionel Atwill; *Captain Levasseur*: Basil Rathbone; *Jeremy Pitt*: Ross Alexander; *Hagthorpe*: Guy Kibbee; *Lord Willoughby*: Henry Stephenson; *Wolverstone*: Robert Barrat; *Dr. Bronson*: Hobart Cavanaugh; *Dr. Whacker*: Donald Meek; *Mrs.*

Captain Blood: **With Errol Flynn.**

Captain Blood: **With Errol Flynn and Yola d'Avril.**

Captain Blood: **With Henry Stephenson, Olivia deHavilland, and J. Carrol Naish.**

Barlowe: Jessie Ralph; *Honesty Nuttall*: Forrester Harvey; *Reverend Ogle*: Frank McGlynn, Sr.; *Captain Gardner*: Holmes Herbert; *Andrew Baynes*: David Torrence; *Cahusac*: J. Carrol Naish; *Don Diego*: Pedro deCordoba; *Governor Steed*: George Hassell; *Kent*: Harry Cording. *Also*: Leonard Mudie, Ivan Simpson, Stuart Casey, Denis d'Auburn, Mary Forbes, E. E. Clive, Colin Kenny, and Vernon Steele.

THE FILM: The First National/Warner Brothers release was the second screen rendition of Rafael Sabatini's high-adventure novel. In 1924, J. Warren Kerrigan had starred in a silent adaptation for Vitagraph.

Robert Donat and Jean Muir were originally set for the leading roles in the new version. However, when contract negotiations with the British actor broke down, Olivia deHavilland and an unknown newcomer from Australia, Errol Flynn, were rushed into the parts in order to meet the film's production schedule.

Directed by Michael Curtiz, with a rousing score from Erich Wolfgang Korngold, *Captain Blood* was an excellent action-filled swashbuckling picture, which still holds much excitement when viewed today. Most important, it made major stars out of Flynn and Miss deHavilland.

Captain Blood: **With J. Carrol Naish and Errol Flynn.**

Captain Blood: **J. Carrol Naish, Basil Rathbone, Errol Flynn, Guy Kibbee, Ross Alexander, and Robert Barrat.**

The story, set during the reign of England's unpopular James II, tells of Dr. Peter Blood (Flynn), who is arrested while attending a wounded rebel. Convicted of treason, he is sent to Jamaica to be sold as a slave. While on the island, he falls in love with Arabella Bishop (deHavilland), niece of a plantation owner (Lionel Atwill). Blood's skill as a physician works in his favor and, after treating the governor's gout, he is made a trustee.

When Spanish pirates attack the British-held island, a group of slaves, led by Blood, defeat them. The slaves take the buccaneers' ship and become pirates themselves, joining forces with Captain Levasseur (Rathbone), a French corsair.

Levasseur captures a British ship, which carries as passengers Lord Willoughby (Henry Stephenson), an emissary from England's new king, William of Orange, and Arabella Bishop. To save Arabella from the Frenchman, Blood duels with his ally and kills him.

England is at war with France and Willoughby grants Blood a pardon, as well as a navy commission. The former buccaneer subsequently defeats two French ships, is appointed the new governor of Jamaica, and marries Arabella.

Rathbone's interpretation of the French pirate was a memorable one. As Levasseur, he was an able leader of men and smart enough to realize that an alliance with Blood would be to his benefit. *Pride* was his Achilles' heel. He could not allow *his* prize—the beautiful Arabella Bishop—to be taken from him. Saving face in front of his men became more important than maintaining a profitable relationship with Blood.

Their duel-to-the-death on the desolate rocky beach remains the high point of the picture. Although it never becomes as extravagant in its production values as the later Flynn/Rathbone duel in *The Adventures of Robin Hood,* the scene still contains excellent swordplay and is enthralling to watch. The shot of the waves washing over Rathbone's body is most effective.

CRITICAL COMMENT:

"Mr. Rathbone has a habit of dying violently in his pictures, but his demise in this one, when Blood punctures him at the conclusion of a desperately waged duel, seems more lamentable than usual. Perhaps it is because he lacks the proper seasoning of villainy this time."

New York Times

KIND LADY

(1935)

A Metro-Goldwyn-Mayer Release of a Lucien Hubbard Production. Directed by George B. Seitz. Adapted from the play by Edward Chodorov, which was taken from a story by Hugh Walpole. Screenplay: Bernard Schubert. Musical Score: Edward Ward. Camera: George Folsey. Released: December 1935. 76 minutes.

CAST: *Mary Herries*: Aline MacMahon; *Henry Abbott*: Basil Rathbone; *Phyllis*: Mary Carlisle; *Peter*: Frank Albertson; *Mr. Edwards*: Dudley Digges; *Lucy Weston*: Doris Lloyd; *Rose*: Nola Luxford; *Doctor*: Murray Kinnell; *Mrs. Edwards*: Eily Malyon; *Ada*: Justine Chase; *Aggie*: Barbara Shields; *Foster*: Donald Meek; *Roubet*: Frank Reicher.

Kind Lady: **With Aline MacMahon.**

Kind Lady: **With Frank Reicher and Dudley Digges.**

THE FILM: Rathbone starred with Aline MacMahon in this fairly well-done adaptation of Edward Chodorov's suspense play, which had featured Grace George and Henry Daniell in the Broadway production.

The story deals with Mary Herries (MacMahon), an English lady, who invites a strange man, Henry Abbott (Rathbone), his wife, and baby, to be guests in her palatial home. Once firmly implanted, Abbott's aides join him. Mary soon finds herself drugged daily and kept prisoner in her own house. She is eventually able to convey a message to the outside world and is rescued.

Rathbone received good notices for his performance; however, some critics felt that Miss MacMahon was miscast in her role.

Kind Lady was remade in 1951 with Ethel Barrymore and Maurice Evans.

CRITICAL COMMENT:
    "Rathbone makes a suave villain."

Variety

PRIVATE NUMBER

(1936)

A Twentieth Century-Fox Production. Directed by Roy Del Ruth. From the play, *Common Clay*, by Cleves Kinkead. Screenplay: Gene Markey and William Conselman. Camera: Peverell Marley. Editor, Allen McNeill. Released: June 1936. 75 minutes.

CAST: *Richard Winfield*: Robert Taylor; *Ellen Neal*: Loretta Young; *Wroxton*: Basil Rathbone; *Gracie*: Patsy Kelly; *Smiley Watson*: Joe Lewis; *Mrs. Winfield*: Marjorie Gateson; *Perry Winfield*: Paul Harvey; *Mrs. Frisbie*: Jane Darwell; *Rawlings*: Paul Stanton; *Stapp*: John Miljan; *Coakley*: Monroe Owsley; *Judge*: George Irving.

THE FILM: *Private Number* was an easily forgettable romantic melodrama, based on a play by Cleves Kinkead. First-rate performances by Rathbone, as well as stars Robert Taylor and Loretta Young, were the film's principal assets.

Richard Winfield (Taylor), scion of a wealthy family, falls in

Private Number: **With Robert Taylor.**

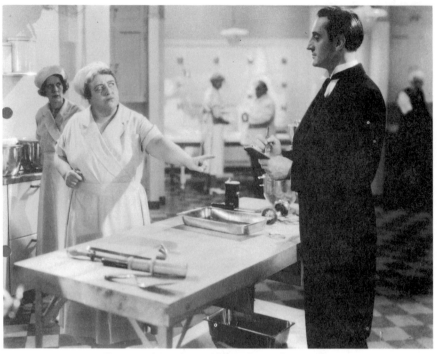

Private Number: **With Jane Darwell.**

love with the household maid, Ellen Neal (Young). Wroxton (Rathbone), the butler, has his own designs on the attractive servant.

Before he returns to college, Richard marries Ellen in a clandestine ceremony. Months pass and Ellen discovers she is pregnant. When Wroxton informs the family of this fact, they summon Richard back from college, but prior to his arrival, his wife flees the household.

An annulment suit is filed. However, in the courtroom, Richard proclaims his love for Ellen and they are reunited.

Most critics considered the basic premise of the picture, which was a remake of a 1930 film, *Common Clay,* with Lew Ayres and Constance Bennett, to be rather tiresome.

CRITICAL COMMENT:

"Mr. Rathbone is as hateful as Miss Young is charming, and Mr. Taylor is manly to a fault."

New York Times

ROMEO AND JULIET

(1936)

A Metro-Goldwyn-Mayer Picture. Directed by George Cukor. Produced by Irving Thalberg. From the play by William Shakespeare. Arranged for the screen by Talbot Jennings. Musical Score: Herbert Stothart. Art Director: Cedric Gibbons. Camera: William Daniels. Editor: Margaret Booth. Dance Director: Agnes De Mille. Costumes: Oliver Messel and Adrian. Released: July 1936. 127 minutes.

CAST: *Juliet*: Norma Shearer; *Romeo*: Leslie Howard; *Mercutio*: John Barrymore; *Nurse*: Edna May Oliver; *Tybalt*: Basil Rathbone; *Lord Capulet*: C. Aubrey Smith; *Peter*: Andy Devine; *Paris*: Ralph Forbes; *Benvolio*: Reginald Denny; *Balthasar*: Maurice Murphy; *Prince of Verona*: Conway Tearle; *Friar Laurence*: Henry Kolker; *Lord Montague*: Robert Warwick; *Lady Montague*: Virginia Hammond; *Lady Capulet*: Violet Kemble Cooper.

THE FILM: Irving Thalberg's production of *Romeo and Juliet* was a worthwhile adaptation of Shakespeare's classic romance. Its

Romeo and Juliet: **With Leslie Howard, Reginald Denny, and John Barrymore.**

Romeo and Juliet: **John Barrymore, Reginald Denny, Leslie Howard, and Basil Rathbone.**

assets included some good performances, skillful direction by George Cukor, beautiful photography, and an array of exquisitely designed sets and costumes.

Norma Shearer, as a youthful Juliet, and Rathbone, playing her cousin, Tybalt, contributed the film's strongest characterizations. Both were rewarded with Academy Award nominations.

Conversely, Leslie Howard was too old for Romeo and lacked the intensity particular scenes required. John Barrymore had some entertaining moments, but, on the whole, overdid the part of Mercutio. He was best in his death scene.

At times, the sumptuous production values seemed to work *against* the picture. Certain scenes, such as the Capulet's ball, employed costumes, settings, and pageantry, which appeared to be almost *too* extravagant for the simple, yet tragic, love story.

In old Verona, Romeo and Juliet meet, fall in love, and secretly marry, despite the enmity of their families, the Montagues and the Capulets.

The lovers' bliss is destroyed when Juliet's cousin, Tybalt, kills Romeo's friend, Mercutio, in a duel. Angered, Romeo slays Tybalt and is banished from Verona.

Unaware of their daughter's marriage, the Capulets insist that she wed Paris (Ralph Forbes). Juliet, at the suggestion of Friar Lawrence (Henry Kolker), takes a sleeping potion that will make her appear dead. His idea is to have the girl placed in the family vault. By the time she awakens, Romeo will have returned and they can flee together to Mantua.

The Friar's letter to Romeo informing him of the plan is delayed and, in the meantime, the young man learns that Juliet is "dead." He goes to the vault and, by her side, swallows poison. Juliet awakens. Upon seeing her husband's body, she plunges a dagger into her heart. The tragedy of the two lovers unites the warring Montagues and Capulets.

John Barrymore's love for "the bottle" caused production of *Romeo and Juliet* to be delayed on several occasions. At one point, William Powell was approached to replace the former matinee idol. However, Powell refused to take over for his old friend, who had helped him get started in films.

Rathbone's interpretation of the hot-tempered Tybalt was flawless, as it should have been. The actor was very familiar with the play. He'd essayed Romeo on the stage in over five hundred performances.

Although he isn't positive, director George Cukor believes that it was in connection with *Romeo and Juliet*, rather than *David Copperfield*, that Rathbone initially refused the role: "We received a letter from Basil in the morning mail, in which he explained why he couldn't accept our offer. Then, that same day, we got a telegram from him . . . saying 'yes.' I don't really recall the reason for either of his decisions."

Tybalt gave Rathbone the opportunity to utilize his fencing skills again—dueling with Reginald Denny, Barrymore, and Howard, the latter two being doubled in the long shots. Earlier in his career, Barrymore would have been an equal match for Rathbone, but, at fifty-three, he'd lost his skill.

Rathbone did *not* consider Tybalt to be a villain—and rightly so. As the actor put it in an interview: "Tybalt is a man who lives by his sword. He kills Mercutio in defense of the honor and dignity of his family."

Without questioning the quality of Rathbone's performance, one must express some misgivings about his Oscar nomination. The role of Tybalt is relatively short and, although important to the story, lacks any real "meat" that an actor can "sink his teeth into."

1936 was the first year that an award was given to supporting actors and the Shakespeare film was Rathbone's most impressive picture during that voting period. It's quite probable that the Academy was basing its decision on the performer's previous contributions, as he had given such memorable portrayals the prior year in *David Copperfield, Anna Karenina,* and *The Last Days of Pompeii*—all, of which, were ineligible for consideration. It is not unusual for an actor to be honored by the Academy for his cumulative work, rather than for a single performance.

CRITICAL COMMENT:

"And Basil Rathbone, a perfect devil of a Tybalt, fiery and quick to draw and an insolent flinger of challenges. No possible fault there."

New York Times

THE GARDEN OF ALLAH

(1936)

A Selznick-International Picture released through United Artists. Technicolor. Directed by Richard Boleslawski. Produced by David O. Selznick. From the novel by Robert Hichens. Screenplay: W. P. Lipscomb and Lynn Riggs. Photography: W. Howard Greene. Musical Score: Max Steiner. Art Directors: Sturges Carne, Lyle Wheeler, and Edward Boyle. Editors: Hal C. Kern and Anson Stevenson. Released: November 1936. 80 minutes.

CAST: *Domini Enfilden*: Marlene Dietrich; *Boris Androvsky*: Charles Boyer; *Count Anteoni*: Basil Rathbone; *Father Roubier*: C. Aubrey Smith; *Irena*: Tilly Losch; *Batouch*: Joseph Schildkraut; *Sand Diviner*: John Carradine; *DeTrevignac*: Alan Marshal; *Mother Superior*: Lucille Watson; *Hadj*: Henry Brandon. *Also*: Helen Jerome Eddy, Charles Waldron, John Bryan, Nigel DeBrulier, Robert Frazer, Bonita Granville, and David Scott.

THE FILM: The first dramatization of Robert Hichens's novel, dealing with a man's inner conflict with his God, was done on the

The Garden of Allah: **With Joseph Schildkraut.**

The Garden of Allah: **With Marlene Dietrich and John Carradine.**

Broadway stage in 1911 with Mary Mannering and Lewis Waller in the leading roles. There were two silent film versions: Helen Ware and Thomas Santschi for the Selig Company in 1917, followed by Alice Terry and Ivan Petrovich in a 1927 adaptation by Metro-Goldwyn-Mayer.

David O. Selznick's 1936 production was definitive. It offered a good screenplay and director Richard Boleslawski was able to elicit sensitive characterizations from his cast, headed by Marlene Dietrich, Charles Boyer, Rathbone, C. Aubrey Smith, Joseph Schildkraut, and John Carradine.

The Garden of Allah was the producer's first experience with the new three-color Technicolor process and he specified that costumes and settings be designed to take full advantage of the procedure. In order to enhance the color further, Selznick sent the cast and crew on location in the Mojave desert near Yuma, Arizona. Ultimately, the film won a special Academy Award for color cinematography.

Robert Hichens's story is well-known:

After the death of her father, Domini Enfilden (Dietrich) seeks a change of scene and moves to the Algerian desert. She meets and marries Boris Androvsky (Boyer), a Trappist monk, who has deserted his monastery in Tunis.

Through the efforts of a French officer (Alan Marshall) and a friend, Count Anteoni (Rathbone), Domini learns her husband's secret, which has tinged their relationship from the beginning.

Sadly, Domini and Boris realize that he must make amends for his sin. The former monk returns to the monastery—leaving Domini forever.

Rathbone accepted the role of Count Anteoni because he was anxious to play something other than a villain. It was the actor's fourth picture for Selznick—and his last.

Once filming had begun, the producer sent Rathbone new dialogue, which violated Anteoni's previously established character by placing him in an unsymypathetic light. Rathbone objected to shooting the scene and Selznick was called down to the set for a showdown. Angry words flew back and forth, with the producer eventually threatening to prefer charges against the actor with the Screen Actors Guild.

Realizing that such an action could result in his being informally "blacklisted" in Hollywood, Rathbone agreed to shoot the scene "under protest." But, Selznick never utilized his services again.

As the finished picture presents Anteoni from an entirely sympathetic point of view, it's probable that the scene in question was never used.

The Garden of Allah: **With Charles Boyer and Marlene Dietrich.**

Rathbone's role as the loyal friend to Domini was rather colorless, but the performer did what he could with it. He had one good scene toward the end, however, when he forces Boris to face up to his past deeds.

Although the plot has dated considerably, *The Garden of Allah* is still a memorable picture, due, for the most part, to the exquisite performances of Dietrich and Boyer.

CRITICAL COMMENT:

"Basil Rathbone and C. Aubrey Smith are excellent in fleeting supporting roles."

New York Times

CONFESSION

(1937)

A First National Production. Directed by Joe May. Associate Producer: Henry Blanke. From an original screenplay by Hans Rameau. Adaptation: Julius J. Epstein and Margaret LeVino. Photography: Sid Hickox. Art Director: Anton Grot. Musical Score and Songs: Peter Kreuder. Musical Director: Leo F. Forbstein. Editor: James Gibbon. Released: March 1937. 90 minutes.

CAST: *Vera*: Kay Francis; *Leonide Kirow*: Ian Hunter; *Michael Michailow*: Basil Rathbone; *Lisa*: Jane Bryan; *Presiding Judge*: Donald Crisp; *Nurse*: Dorothy Peterson; *Stella*: Laura Hope Crews; *Prosecuting Attorney*: Robert Barrat; *Defense Attorney*: Ben Welden; *Xenia*: Veda Ann Borg.

THE FILM: Filmed under the working title of *One Hour of Romance*, *Confession* was a remake of *Mazurka*, a successful 1936 German picture starring Pola Negri and directed by Willi Forst. Although the First National production had a few good performances and a promising storyline, it suffered from the unorthodox approach of a seemingly incompetent director.

Confession: **With Kay Francis.**

Confession: **With Mary Maguire and Jane Bryan.**

In brief, the screenplay, set in 1912, deals with Vera (Kay Francis), an opera singer working in Warsaw. She retires to marry Leonide Kirow (Ian Hunter), an officer. A few years pass and Vera gives birth to a daughter.

While her husband is off fighting, she attends a party hosted by an old friend, Michael Michailow (Rathbone), a famous composer/conductor. She has too much to drink and spends the night.

Leonide returns home, minus an arm, and, shortly thereafter, discovers Vera at Michael's apartment. He divorces his wife and moves with their child to another city.

Fifteen years pass. Vera, now a cabaret singer, has been unable to find her daughter. Arriving in a new city, she discovers her ex-husband's name in the phone directory. She visits the home, but learns from Leonide's second wife that he has been dead for three years and that the daughter, Lisa (Jane Bryan), believes that her step-mother is, in fact, her natural mother. Vera agrees not to reveal the truth to the girl.

Later that evening, as she sings in the cabaret, Vera spies Michael in the audience—kissing Lisa. In order to protect her daughter from this unscrupulous musician, she shoots him.

In a closed session at her trial, Vera tells her story and the court is lenient. Lisa wishes the singer luck, still unaware of her true identity.

Associate producer Henry Blanke recalls the problems with the project: "The original German version was excellent and quite innovative. My director, Joe May, who I had not wanted to hire in the first place, was so impressed with the earlier film that he decided that *his* production would be an exact duplicate.

"He spent weeks in an editing room . . . studying the Negri picture on a Movieola, frame-by-frame.

"When the production began filming, May sat on the set with a stop-watch to be sure that each scene ran the exact length as the original. . . . The whole thing was a total disaster."

Jane Bryan feels that she was never directed in a more "ridiculous" fashion in her life. "We were all marching through the film like sleepwalkers. There was absolutely no spontaneity."

In spite of this major handicap, both Rathbone and Miss Bryan managed to deliver interesting performances. Unfortunately, other cast members did not fare as well and, at times, the viewer senses that a performer is either rushing through his lines so that he can "catch a bus," or reading them off a cue card.

It was regrettable. In better hands, *Confession* could have been a good film.

CRITICAL COMMENT:
"Basil Rathbone, Donald Crisp, and Ian Hunter are fine in their roles."

Film Daily

LOVE FROM A STRANGER

(1937)

A United Artists Release of a Max Schach-Trafalgar Films Production. Directed by Rowland V. Lee. From the play by Frank Vosper, based on the short story by Agatha Christie. Screenplay: Frances Marion. Camera: Philip Tannura. Released: April 1937. 86 minutes.

CAST: *Carol Howard*: Ann Harding; *Gerald Lovell*: Basil Rathbone; *Kate Meadows*: Binnie Hale; *Ronald Bruce*: Bruce Seton; *Aunt Lou*: Jean Cadell; *Dr. Gribble*: Bryan Powley; *Emmy*: Joan Hickson; *Hobson*: Donald Calthrop; *Mr. Tuttle*: Eugene Leahy.

THE FILM: Produced in England, this first-rate thriller was based on a successful play that had been staged in New York the previous year, starring its author, Frank Vosper, and Jessie Royce Landis.

Simply, the story concerns Carol Howard (Ann Harding), a lottery winner, who, while on a European holiday, meets and marries

Love From a Stranger: **With Bruce Seton and Ann Harding.**

Love From a Stranger: **With Ann Harding.**

suave Gerald Lovell (Rathbone). Shortly after the wedding, Lovell
has his wife sign her fortune over to him, on the pretext that she is
merely affixing her signature to a mortgage transfer.

Carol learns that her husband is a psychopath who has already
murdered several women. The balance of the film involves her efforts
to avoid becoming his next victim.

Careful direction by Rowland V. Lee and superb performances
from Rathbone and Miss Harding were responsible for making *Love
from a Stranger* (working title: *A Night of Terror*) one of the best
suspense films of its day. Rathbone was particularly effective, creating
a villain that was both charming and frightening. Toward the end of
the picture, he plays a cat-and-mouse game of life and death with
Miss Harding in a lonely villa. The chilling sequence was unforgettable to theater audiences.

Vosper's play was filmed again in 1947 starring John Hodiak and
Sylvia Sidney.

CRITICAL COMMENT:

"Basil Rathbone makes an ideal neurotic, unbalanced scoundrel
who starts slowly and builds up to a tense finish. He skillfully avoids
the pitfalls of over-acting, which would normally come to a less talented player."

Variety

MAKE A WISH

(1937)

An RKO Radio Release of a Sol Lesser-Principal Production. Directed by Kurt Neumann. From an original story by Gertrude Berg. Screenplay: Mrs. Berg, Bernard Schubert, and Earle Snell. Additional Dialogue: William Hurlbut. Music: Oscar Straus. Other Songs by Straus, Louis Alter, and Paul Francis Webster. Musical Director: Dr. Hugo Riesenfeld. Camera: John Mescall. Editor: Arthur Hilton. Released: August 1937. 75 minutes.

CAST: *Chip*: Bobby Breen; *Selden*: Basil Rathbone; *Irene*: Marion Claire; *Moreta*: Henry Armetta; *Mays*: Ralph Forbes; *Brennan*: Leon Errol; *Pee Wee*: Billy Lee; *Joseph*: Donald Meek; *Dr. Stevens*: Herbert Rawlinson; *Moe*: Leonid Kinskey; *Minstrel*: Fred Scott.

THE FILM: This vehicle for child star Bobby Breen provided Rathbone with a change-of-pace. His undemanding role took him away from the heavier assignments he'd been used to and allowed the performer to relax in a part that required little more from him than to be pleasant.

Make a Wish: **With Bobby Breen and Marion Claire.**

Make a Wish was one of Master Breen's better pictures. It had a reasonably fresh story by Gertrude Berg, a nice score by Oscar Straus, with lyrics by Louis Alter and Paul Francis Webster, and marked the film debut of radio singer Marion Claire.

The plot was simple. Selden (Rathbone), a composer, befriends Chip (Breen), who is staying at a boys' camp in Maine. The musician has rented a cabin near the camp and is working on a new operetta. He meets Chip's widowed mother, Irene (Claire), and immediately falls in love with her, although she is engaged to the stuffy Mr. Mays (Ralph Forbes).

Irene, a retired singer, provides Selden with the inspiration he needs to write his musical. However, when mother and son leave for New York unexpectedly, he again loses interest in the project.

Depressed, Selden departs for Europe and entrusts Joseph (Donald Meek), his valet, with the completed third act of the operetta, which he is to deliver to the show's producer.

Joseph, a frustrated song writer, loses the manuscript, then attempts to reconstruct the material with the help of two other "tunesmiths" (Leon Errol and Henry Armetta). The result is disastrous.

Young Chip, having memorized the original score, saves the situation by singing Selden's melodies to the producer. Against Mays' wishes, Irene agrees to star in the production. It is, of course, a huge success.

The composer returns from Europe on opening night and is reunited with Irene.

The film gave Rathbone the opportunity to sing/speak the first few bars of the title song before Master Breen took over with his rich soprano voice. It was a nice moment and makes one wish that the actor had done other movie musical roles. He might have made an interesting Henry Higgins in *My Fair Lady*, had the play come on the scene earlier than it did.

There is a cute bit of dialogue in the picture, which is worth repeating:

Selden, realizing he is in love with Irene, happily races into his cabin, grabs Joseph, and sits him on top of the piano. He announces, "I feel marvelous!"

Joseph assesses his situation, then replies, "I feel like Helen Morgan."

CRITICAL COMMENT:

"Basil Rathbone is co-starred in a refreshing role as an operatic composer and demonstrates his ability to play a light romantic part as deftly as the heavy types which he usually handles."

Variety

TOVARICH

(1937)

A Warner Brothers Release of a Robert Lord Production. Directed by Anatole Litvak. From the play by Jacques Deval. Adaptation: Robert E. Sherwood. Screenplay: Casey Robinson. Camera: Charles Lang. Editor: Henri Rust. Dialogue Director: Rowland Leigh. Musical Score: Max Steiner. Musical Director: Leo F. Forbstein. Released: November 1937. 94 minutes.

CAST: *Tatiana*: Claudette Colbert; *Mikail*: Charles Boyer; *Gorotchenko*: Basil Rathbone; *Helene Dupont*: Anita Louise; *Charles Dupont*: Melville Cooper; *Fernande Dupont*: Isabel Jeans; *Chauffourier-Dubieff*: Morris Carnovsky; *Georges Dupont*: Maurice Murphy; *Count Brekenski*: Gregory Gaye; *M. Courtois*: Montagu Love; *Mme. Courtois*: Reine Riano; *Martelleau*: Fritz Feld; *Lady Kartegann*: Heather Thatcher. *Also*: Victor Killan, May Boley, Doris Lloyd, Curt Bois, and Grace Hayle.

THE FILM: Taken from Robert E. Sherwood's adaptation of Jacques

Tovarich: **With Claudette Colbert.**

Tovarich: **With Charles Boyer and Melville Cooper.**

Deval's stage play, *Tovarich* (meaning "comrade") was a highly
entertaining screen comedy.

The story deals with the Grand Duchess Tatiana Petrovana
(Claudette Colbert) and her consort, Prince Mikail Ouratieff (Charles
Boyer). They are White Russians, living in Paris to escape the after-
math of their country's revolution. Although Mikail controls a bank
account containing forty billion francs (a sum entrusted to him by
the late Czar), the couple live in poverty, rather than touch any of
the royal family's money.

Desperate, they accept jobs as butler and maid in the home of
Charles Dupont (Melville Cooper), a banker, and his family. Tatiana
and Mikail make excellent servants and the Duponts, not knowing
their true identity, are quite taken with them.

At a dinner party in honor of Soviet Commissar Gorotchenko
(Rathbone), the Duponts learn who their servants really are. The
employers are at a loss for the rest of the evening, as to whether they
should treat Tatiana and Mikail as royalty or household help.

The Ouratieffs hate Gorotchenko. Aside from being a high official
of the new Soviet Union, he was the interrogator who tortured
Mikail prior to the couple's escape. However, when the Commissar
asks the Prince for the forty billion francs he is holding, so the So-

viet Government will not have to sign away its rich oil fields to foreign nations, Mikail, at Tatiana's urging, agrees. The money will be used to help the people of Russia.

Tatiana and Mikail, feeling they were born for their roles, agree to stay on in the Dupont household for as long as they are welcome.

During production, the picture was called *Tonight's Our Night,* but, prior to release, Warner Brothers decided to go back to the original title.

Colbert and Boyer were perfectly cast as the royal fugitives, while Rathbone, appearing late in the film, presented an excellent portrait of the practical Soviet politician. Anatole Litvak's direction kept the story moving at exactly the right pace, resulting in an amiable and engaging motion picture.

CRITICAL COMMENT:
"Of the supporting cast, Melville Cooper, as the banker, and Rathbone contribute excellent characterizations."

Variety

THE ADVENTURES OF MARCO POLO

(1938)

A Samuel Goldwyn Production released through United Artists. Directed by Archie Mayo. Produced by Samuel Goldwyn. From a story by N. A. Pogson. Screenplay: Robert E. Sherwood. Photography: Rudolph Mate. Musical Score: Hugo Friedhofer; Musical Director: Alfred Newman; Art Director: Richard Day; Editor: Fred Allen. Released: February 1938. 100 minutes.

CAST: *Marco Polo*: Gary Cooper; *Princess Kukachin*: Sigrid Gurie; *Ahmed*: Basil Rathbone; *Binguccio*: Ernest Truex; *Kaidu*: Alan Hale; *Kublai Khan*: George Barbier; *Nazama*: Binnie Barnes; *Nazama's maid*: Lana Turner; *Bayan*: Stanley Fields; *Toctai*: Harold Huber; *Chen Tsu*: H. B. Warner. *Also*: Eugene Hoo, Helen Quan, Soo Yong, Henry Kolker, Hale Hamilton, Robert Greig, Ward Bond, and Jason Robards.

THE FILM: In *The Adventures of Marco Polo*, Rathbone played,

The Adventures of Marco Polo.

The Adventures of Marco Polo: **With Gary Cooper.**

for the first time, the type of role he was to repeat successfully in several future motion pictures—that of the sinister right hand to a chief of state.

Produced by Samuel Goldwyn, the slowly paced adventure film starred a miscast Gary Cooper as the Italian traveler to the court of Chinese emperor Kublai Khan (George Barbier). Polo had come to Peking to discover Oriental treasures and make trade agreements for his father, a leading Venice merchant.

At the court, Polo romances the Khan's daughter, Princess Kukachin (Sigrid Gurie), and makes an enemy of Ahmed (Rathbone), the evil foreign-born minister of state, who schemes to gain the throne for himself. Ahmed is the classic heavy—keeping vultures as pets and regularly feeding helpless victims to starving lions.

Polo is sent as a spy to the camp of rebel leader Kaidu (Alan Hale). He saves the rebel's life from an assassin sent by Ahmed and, as tribute, the warrior agrees to help Polo save the throne for Kublai Khan.

Kaidu's army attacks the palace, which has been taken over by Ahmed's men. Polo rescues the Princess from the minister and, after a fierce struggle between the two adversaries, the dastardly villain falls into the lion pit.

The Adventures of Marco Polo: **With Ernest Truex and Gary Cooper.**

John Carradine had originally been negotiated to play the role of Ahmed, however when Rathbone became available, having refused another assignment, producer Goldwyn decided to go with the more important name. The actor seemed to enjoy himself—doing the part tongue-in-cheek. His performance is one of the movie's few good points.

The project was five days into production when the director, John Cromwell, quit in a dispute over how the film ought to be approached. He had wanted to make it a serious drama. His replacement, Archie Mayo, seemed to have no concept whatsoever as to what the picture should be and the final result proved to be Cooper's only flop in seven films for the Goldwyn Company.

CRITICAL COMMENT:

"Basil Rathbone, minister of state and plotter against the throne, as well as the life of Polo, troupes his emphatic brand of sinister villainy."

Variety

THE ADVENTURES OF ROBIN HOOD

(1938)

A First National Picture (Warner Brothers). Technicolor. Directed by Michael Curtiz and William Keighley. Executive Producer: Hal B. Wallis. Associate Producer: Henry Blanke. Based upon ancient Robin Hood legends. Original Screenplay: Norman Reilly Raine and Seton I. Miller. Music: Erich Wolfgang Korngold. Photography: Sol Polito and Tony Gaudio. Dialogue Director: Irving Rapper. Film Editor: Ralph Dawson. Art Director: Carl Jules Weyl. Costumes: Milo Anderson. Archery Supervisor: Howard Hill. Fencing Master: Fred Cavens. Released: April 1938. 104 minutes.

CAST: Robin Hood: Errol Flynn; Maid Marian: Olivia deHavilland; Sir Guy of Gisbourne: Basil Rathbone; Prince John: Claude Rains; Will Scarlet: Patric Knowles; Friar Tuck: Eugene Pallette; Little John: Alan Hale; High Sheriff of Nottingham: Melville Cooper; King Richard: Ian Hunter; Bess: Una O'Connor; Much: Herbert Mundin; Bishop of the Black Canons: Montagu Love; Sir Essex: Leonard Willey. Also: Robert Noble, Kenneth Hunter, Robert War-

The Adventures of Robin Hood: **With Melville Cooper.**

The Adventures of Robin Hood: **With Claude Rains and Olivia deHavilland.**

wick, Colin Kenny, Lester Matthews, Harry Cording, and Howard Hill.

THE FILM: Many devotees of the genre consider *The Adventures of Robin Hood* to be the *ultimate* in swashbuckling films. Certainly, it gave Errol Flynn one of his greatest roles, and the climactic duel between the star and Basil Rathbone is one of the most exciting ever photographed.

The lavishly mounted picture seemed to have everything—elaborate sets, a stirring score, and was shot in the new three-color Technicolor process for the *then* record sum of two million dollars. Problems occurred early in the production, resulting in the original director, William Keighley, being replaced by Michael Curtiz after three weeks of filming. Associate producer Henry Blanke recalls the reason: "Keighley was a fine director, but he was the wrong man for this project. His footage had 'no guts' to it.

"Curtiz, on the other hand, would let no obstacle stand in his way. In the shooting script, there was a direction that read, 'Robin

Hood fights his way out of the castle.' It took Curtiz three weeks to film that action. Jack Warner would call down to the set every day and scream, 'Hasn't he gotten out yet?'"

The original screenplay by Norman Reilly Raine and Seton I. Miller was based on the various legends and ballads about the fabled outlaw. Their narrative told of how Sir Robin of Locksley (Flynn), a Saxon knight, rebels against the evil Prince John (Claude Rains) and the Norman barons, while King Richard the Lion-Hearted (Ian Hunter) is held for ransom in Austria, after taking part in the Third Crusade in Palestine.

Sir Guy of Gisbourne (Rathbone) is the chief conspirator in John's attempt to gain his brother's throne.

When Robin opposes the regent's oppressive treatment of the poor Saxon subjects in the realm, he is declared an outlaw and his lands are forfeit. He gathers a band of supporters, including Little John (Alan Hale), Friar Tuck (Eugene Pallette), and Will Scarlet (Patric Knowles) in Sherwood Forest and the group continually harasses and steals from the Normans. All spoils go to aid the needy and pay the English king's ransom.

During one of his raids, Robin meets Maid Marian (Olivia de-Havilland), a royal ward of Richard, and a romantic attachment develops between the two.

The Adventures of Robin Hood: **With Errol Flynn.**

The Adventures of Robin Hood: **With Harry Cording.**

Robin raids a large group of soldiers, led by Gisbourne and the High Sheriff of Nottingham (Melville Cooper). He steals their tax money and sends the two officials back to Prince John in rags.

This humiliation has incensed Gisbourne to the point that he agrees to hold an archery tournament as a method of capturing the outlaw. The prize is to be a gold arrow presented by Marian.

The trap works. Robin is captured and sentenced to hang. On the day of his execution, he is rescued by his men, who had been aided by Marian.

Richard, in disguise, returns to England. Learning of this, John makes plans to have himself crowned king and his brother assassinated. Marian attempts to inform Robin of the plan, but is caught by Gisbourne and imprisoned.

However, Robin and Richard join forces and, on John's coronation day, sneak into Nottingham Castle. A battle ensues, in which Gisbourne is killed by Robin. Richard banishes John and his followers, then restores Robin to his former rank, and gives him permission to marry Marian.

Rathbone was perfectly cast in his role. Constantly being frustrated by Robin Hood, the vicious knight would often let his anger obliterate his reason. Gisbourne may have been the man-of-action,

The Adventures of Robin Hood: **Errol Flynn, Olivia deHavilland, Harry Cording, Alan Hale, and Basil Rathbone.**

but the foppish Prince John was the more *cunning* villain of the story.

While filming Robin's escape from the castle, Rathbone was knocked to the floor and trampled by extras. A spear accidentally struck his right foot and the wound necessitated eight stitches.

The final duel with broadswords between Flynn and Rathbone is a masterpiece. Both actors had worked on their fencing skills since *Captain Blood* and the improvement showed. Director Curtiz utilized scenery, props, and lighting in the sequence for a maximum theatrical effect.

The Adventures of Robin Hood won Academy Awards for Original Music Score (Erich Wolfgang Korngold), Film Editing (Ralph Dawson), and Interior Decoration (Carl J. Weyl).

CRITICAL COMMENT:

"There are some convincing histrionics by Basil Rathbone, Claude Rains, Patric Knowles, Eugene Pallette, Alan Hale and Melville Cooper."

Variety

IF I WERE KING

(1938)

A Paramount Release of a Frank Lloyd Production. Directed by Frank Lloyd. From a play by Justin Huntly McCarthy. Screenplay: Preston Sturges. Camera: Theodor Sparkuhl. Special Effects: Gordon Jennings. Editor: Hugh Bennett. Released: September 1938. 100 minutes.

CAST: *François Villon*: Ronald Colman; *Louis XI*: Basil Rathbone; *Katherine de Vaucelles*: Frances Dee; *Huguette*: Ellen Drew; *Father Villon*: C. V. France; *Captain of the Watch*: Henry Wilcoxon; *The Queen*: Heather Thatcher; *Rene de Montigny*: Stanley Ridges; *Noel le Jolys*: Bruce Lester; *Tristan l'Hermite*: Walter Kingsford; *Colette*: Alma Lloyd; *Robin Turgis*: Sidney Toler; *Jehan le Loup*: Colin Tapley; *Oliver le Dain*: Ralph Forbes; *Thibaut d'Aussigny*: John Miljan; *General Dudon*: Montagu Love; *General Barbezier*: William Farnum. *Also*: Paul Harvey, Barry Macollum, Lester Matthews, and William Haade.

If I Were King: **With Ronald Colman.**

THE FILM: Justin McCarthy's historical play about Francois Villon was first filmed in 1920 starring William Farnum as the roguish poet. 1926 found John Barrymore essaying the part in *The Beloved Rogue*. Rudolph Friml's operetta, *The Vagabond King*, based on McCarthy's play, was made into a movie in 1930 with Dennis King and Jeanette MacDonald, then remade with Oreste Kirkop and Kathryn Grayson in 1955.

Frank Lloyd's nonmusical adaptation of *If I Were King* was made in 1938 starring Ronald Colman as Villon, with Basil Rathbone playing King Louis XI. William Farnum, incidentally, the star of the original version, had a minor role in this film also.

Although somewhat flawed by Colman's performance, it was an entertaining picture, which earned for Rathbone his second Academy Award nomination in the supporting actor category.

Simply, the story tells of the dashing knave, François Villon, who becomes Chief Constable of France through a whim of Louis XI. Villon adopts a benevolent policy in his dealings with the populace. This, in turn, makes the people feel more kindly toward the king.

Louis threatens to hang Villon when the generals refuse to support the Constable's plan to attack the Burgundian Army, which has sur-

If I Were King: **With Sidney Toler.**

If I Were King: **With Henry Wilcoxon, Ellen Drew, and Ronald Colman.**

rounded Paris. The poet appeals to the rabble and they take part in the fight against the would-be conquerers.

The Burgundians are defeated and François is a hero. However, Louis still has him banished from the city. The beautiful Katherine deVaucelles (Frances Dee), in love with Villon, decides to join him in his travels.

Colman was excellent as Villon when it came to reciting verse, but as a rogue, he left much to be desired. The actor, always the gentleman, was unable to convey anything less than that on the screen.

Rathbone, on the other hand, gave one of his finest screen performances. As the sly and cackling old king, he presented a character completely unlike anything he had ever done before. His scenes with Villon are the best in the film. The Oscar should have been Rathbone's that year, but was won by Walter Brennan for *Kentucky*.

CRITICAL COMMENT:

"Basil Rathbone brilliantly handles the difficult assignment of the eccentric, weazened Louis XI, a role that requires delicacy and shading of characterization in every scene."

Variety

THE DAWN PATROL

(1938)

A Warner Brothers Picture. Directed by Edmund Goulding. Executive Producer: Hal B. Wallis. Associate Producer: Robert Lord. From an original story, "Flight Commander," by John Monk Saunders and Howard Hawks. Screenplay: Seton I. Miller and Dan Totheroh. Music: Max Steiner. Photography: Tony Gaudio. Film Editor: Ralph Dawson. Art Director: John Hughes. Sound: C. A. Riggs. Released: December 1938. 103 minutes.

CAST: *Captain Courtney*: Errol Flynn; *Major Brand*: Basil Rathbone; *Lieutenant Scott*: David Niven; *Phipps*: Donald Crisp; *Sergeant Watkins*: Melville Cooper; *Bott*: Barry Fitzgerald; *Von Mueller*: Carl Esmond; *Hollister*: Peter Willes; *Ronnie*: Morton Lowry; *Squires*: Michael Brooke; *Flaherty*: James Burke. *Also*: Stuart Hall, Herbert Evans, and Sidney Bracy.

THE FILM: Rathbone gave one of the best performances of his

The Dawn Patrol.

The Dawn Patrol: **With Donald Crisp and Errol Flynn.**

motion picture career in this remake of Howard Hawks's World War I classic. He was Major Brand, commander of the 59th Squadron—British Royal Flying Corps. Neil Hamilton had played the role in the 1930 original.

Errol Flynn and David Niven, essaying the parts created by Richard Barthelmess and Douglas Fairbanks, Jr., were also starred.

For the most part, this new version followed the storyline of its predecessor very closely—revising only the dialogue. Edmund Goulding directed the screenplay by Seton I. Miller and Dan Totheroh.

The 59th Squadron, plagued with obsolete planes and equipment, is stationed in France during the First World War. Major Brand's thankless job is to utilize the little resources he has to work with in a valiant effort to stop the German onslaught. The mortality rate among his pilots is high.

His chief critic is Captain Courtney (Flynn). The air ace is unsympathetic to the problems of command and enraged that Brand is constantly sending inexperienced pilots out on dangerous missions.

The Major, in turn, is a man tortured with feelings of guilt. He blames himself for the loss of every man, yet realizes that these suicidal missions must continue if the Germans are to be defeated. As he blurts out to his aide, Phipps (Donald Crisp): "This is a slaughterhouse . . . and I'm the executioner!"

The Dawn Patrol: **With Donald Crisp.**

Eventually, Brand is promoted and, almost as a retaliation, he names Courtney his successor. The Captain soon comes to feel the agonies that go with such a responsibility and he turns to the bottle.

Lieutenant Scott (Niven) is Courtney's closest friend. When his younger brother, Ronnie (Morton Lowry), a freshman pilot, is killed on his first mission, he blames the Captain and their relationship is shattered.

Scott volunteers for a dangerous job—the bombing of a well-fortified ammunition dump. However, Courtney decides to undertake the mission, as he does not want to send his comrade to an almost certain death. After he destroys the target, Courtney shoots down von Richter, a German ace, then is himself killed by another pilot. The film concludes with Scott taking over as squadron commander.

Many critics felt that this 1938 version of *The Dawn Patrol* was better than the original. The performances were first-rate, with Rathbone walking away with the top acting honors.

Goulding's sensitive direction accented the air of doomed camaraderie that was inherent in the script and, thereby, made a grim statement on the futility of war. This impression prevails with the viewer, despite the excellent flying sequences, which stressed the heroic aspects of combat.

All of the aerial footage in the film, incidentally, was borrowed from the Hawks original.

CRITICAL COMMENT:

"Basil Rathbone is superb as the aviator who suffers inwardly the loss of every man while he is forced to remain in command on the ground."

Variety

SON OF FRANKENSTEIN

(1939)

A Universal Picture. Produced and Directed by Rowland V. Lee. Suggested by the novel by Mary Shelley. Screenplay: Willis Cooper. Photography: George Robinson. Special Effects: John P. Fulton. Editor: Ted Kent. Art Director: Jack Otterson. Music: Frank Skinner. Musical Director: Charles Previn. Costumes: Vera West. Makeup: Jack P. Pierce. Released: January 1939. 94 minutes.

CAST: *Baron Wolf von Frankenstein*: Basil Rathbone; *The Monster*: Boris Karloff; *Ygor*: Bela Lugosi; *Inspector Krogh*: Lionel Atwill; *Elsa von Frankenstein*: Josephine Hutchinson; *Peter*: Donnie Dunagan; *Amelia*: Emma Dunn; *Thomas Benson*: Edgar Norton; *Fritz*: Perry Ivins; *Burgomaster*: Lawrence Grant. *Also*: Lionel Belmore, Michael Mark, Caroline Cook, Gustav von Seyffertitz, and Edward Cassidy.

Son of Frankenstein: **With Boris Karloff.**

Son of Frankenstein: **With Lionel Atwill and Josephine Hutchinson.**

THE FILM: Few movie sequels match the quality of the original films upon which they are based—let alone surpass them. *Son of Frankenstein* was an exception. Whereas director James Whale's *Frankenstein* pictures may have been excellent mood pieces, the 1939 follow-up fares better with the test of time.

Inspired by the successful reissue of the original *Dracula* and *Frankenstein* on a double-bill, Rowland V. Lee's production was handsomely mounted and seemed to spare no expense. Acting and direction were excellent.

The story tells of Wolf von Frankenstein (Rathbone), son of the late Baron, who brings his wife (Josephine Hutchinson) and young boy, Peter (Donnie Dunagan), to his ancestral castle in the village Frankenstein. Inspector Krogh (Lionel Atwill), chief constable, warns Wolf that the villagers want him to leave, as they hate the family name and also suspect his complicity in six murders that have taken place since his father's Monster was "destroyed."

A shepherd, Ygor (Bela Lugosi), shows Wolf the hiding place of the Monster (Boris Karloff)—beneath the ruins of the old Frankenstein laboratory. The creature has been struck by lightning and is comatose.

Ygor asks Wolf to revive his "friend." The latter agrees, realizing that if he can humanize the Monster, his father's name will be vindicated.

The giant is restored and Ygor sends him out to kill. The victims are members of the jury who had, years before, condemned the shepherd to death. But Ygor cheated the noose, and has a broken neck to prove it.

When Wolf learns of the murders—and the Monster's visits to little Peter—he goes to the laboratory to confront Ygor. The shepherd attacks him and Wolf shoots the madman.

Discovering the body of his friend, the angry Monster destroys the rebuilt laboratory, then goes after Peter. Wolf and Krogh rush to the rescue. Frankenstein saves his son by knocking the creature into an underground pit of boiling sulpher.

Wolf and his family depart the village, bequeathing the castle to the populace.

One of the chief attributes of the film was its almost expressionistic sets. Art director Jack Otterson refered to them as "Psychological Sets." Departing entirely from any known style of architecture, his interiors, an arrangement of planes and masses, were designed

Son of Frankenstein: **With Bela Lugosi and Boris Karloff.**

Son of Frankenstein: **With Josephine Hutchinson, Donnie Dunagan, and Emma Dunn.**

to give the impression of an eerie locale—without intruding too strongly into the audience's consciousness.

Karloff played the Monster for the third and final time in this picture. He had created the role in 1931 for James Whale's original *Frankenstein,* then repeated the characterization in the 1935 sequel, *The Bride of Frankenstein.*

Rathbone was very convincing in a role that could easily have been overplayed, and Lugosi was properly sinister as Ygor.

Lee's tight direction, a well thought-out screenplay by Willis Cooper, and a splendid score from Frank Skinner, contributed to make *Son of Frankenstein* one of the finest films of the horror genre.

In 1946, Rathbone played the title role in a radio production of *Frankenstein,* which was heard on "Stars Over Hollywood," a CBS program.

CRITICAL COMMENT:

"For an offering of its type, the picture is well-mounted, nicely directed and includes a cast of capable artists. . . . Basil Rathbone carries the title spot. . . ."

Variety

THE HOUND OF THE BASKERVILLES

(1939)

A Twentieth Century-Fox Production. Directed by Sidney Lanfield. Associate Producer: Gene Markey. From the story by Sir Arthur Conan Doyle. Screenplay: Ernest Pascal. Photography: Peverell Marley. Art Directors: Richard Day and Hans Peters. Editor: Robert Simpson. Musical Direction: Cyril J. Mockridge. Released: March 1939. 78 minutes.

CAST: *Sir Henry Baskerville*: Richard Greene; *Sherlock Holmes*: Basil Rathbone; *Beryl Stapleton*: Wendy Barrie; *Dr. Watson*: Nigel Bruce; *Dr. James Mortimer*: Lionel Atwill; *Barryman*: John Carradine; *Frankland*: Barlowe Borland; *Mrs. Jennifer Mortimer*: Beryl Mercer; *John Stapleton*: Morton Lowry; *Sir Hugo Baskerville*: Ralph Forbes; *Cabby*: E. E. Clive; *Mrs. Barryman*: Elly Malyon; *Convict*: Nigel de Brulier; *Mrs. Hudson*: Mary Gordon.

THE FILM: Sherlock Holmes—master sleuth. Arthur Conan Doyle

The Hound of the Baskervilles: **With Lionel Atwill.**

The Hound of the Baskervilles: **Nigel Bruce, Rathbone, and Nigel de Bruller.**

described him as over six feet tall, excessively lean, penetrating eyes, and a hawklike nose.

The outline might fit Basil Rathbone. Evidently, Darryl Zanuck thought it did and, in 1939, he cast the British actor as the immortal detective of 221-B Baker Street. The mogul's decision assured Rathbone a definitive place in the history books of the American cinema.

There had been several previous versions of *The Hound of The Baskervilles* and more would follow. However, most fans of the Holmes stories consider this 1939 adaptation to be the best—thanks to the performances of Rathbone and Nigel Bruce, who played Watson.

The film stayed fairly close to the novel:

Since 1650 when Hugo Baskerville (Ralph Forbes) was killed by a giant hound, all male members of the Baskerville family have died violently. After the murder of Sir Charles Baskerville, Sir Henry (Richard Greene) inherits the family manor.

Dr. Mortimer (Lionel Atwill) enlists the aid of Sherlock Holmes and Dr. Watson to protect Sir Henry. While Holmes remains in London, Watson accompanies the handsome young man to Baskerville Hall, located on the desolate moors.

At the estate, Watson encounters Barryman (John Carradine), the butler, and his wife (Elly Malyon), as well as the Stapletons—John (Morton Lowry) and his sister, Beryl (Wendy Barrie). Sir Henry and Miss Stapleton are attracted to each other.

One night, Watson notices Barryman signaling from the window to somebody on the moor. When he and Henry investigate, the person, an escaped convict (Nigel de Brulier), unsuccessfully attempts to kill them. The convict is the brother of Mrs. Barryman. She and her husband had been sneaking him food and clothing.

Holmes appears on the scene. Actually, he'd been there all along, but had purposely kept out of sight, so he could observe the situation.

The convict, wearing Sir Henry's clothing, which was given him by the Barrymans, is attacked and killed by the hound. Holmes lets it be known that the dead man was the killer and states he will now be returning to London with Watson. It is, of course, a ruse to draw the real guilty party out into the open.

That evening, Sir Henry, after visiting with Beryl Stapleton, who has become his fiancée, decides to walk home—across the moor. He

The Hound of the Baskervilles: **Wendy Barrie, Richard Greene, and Rathbone.**

The Hound of the Baskervilles: **With Richard Greene and Lionel Atwill.**

is pursued by a giant starving hound, sent by the true murderer—John Stapleton.

Holmes and Watson have doubled back and rescue Sir Henry from the dog. Holmes goes after the wounded animal. He is, subsequently, locked in the beast's underground cage by Stapleton.

Left alone with Sir Henry, Stapleton attempts to poison him, but Holmes, having freed himself, enters in time to save his client. He announces that Stapleton is, in fact, a distant kin of the Baskervilles and, should Sir Henry die, would be next in line to inherit the estate. It was his plan to blame the murders on the Baskerville legend. Fortunately, Holmes had noted a resemblance to Stapleton in a portrait of Hugo Baskerville, thus enabling him to solve the case.

Stapleton attempts to escape, but is presumably captured by police that surround the manor.

His job completed, Holmes retires to bed. As he is about to exit, he turns and says, "Quick, Watson—the needle!" Considering Hollywood's strict Production Code at the time, this direct reference to the detective's narcotic habit was quite bold.

The Hound of the Baskervilles: **With Nigel Bruce.**

The Hound of the Baskervilles: **With Nigel Bruce and Morton Lowry.**

Critics felt that Rathbone was the perfect Sherlock Holmes and Bruce, although not quite fitting the Doyle conception of the character, made an excellent Watson. The pair worked well together in the film, as they would in thirteen more pictures dealing with the London sleuth.

The supporting performers also made effective contributions to the project, with John Carradine, Lionel Atwill, and Morton Lowry coming off the strongest. Because he was the studio's newest romantic lead, Richard Greene received top billing over Rathbone.

The production had drawbacks: a slow pace; a minimum of background music; exterior sets on a sound stage, which failed to convey the stark desolation of the moor. Each factor contributed in marring the necessary eerie mood, which was so important to the story. Nevertheless, Sidney Lanfield's picture did generate enough excitement to satisfy audiences and motivate Fox to film a sequel.

CRITICAL COMMENT:
"Rathbone gives a most effective characterization of Sherlock Holmes which will be relished by mystery lovers."
Variety

THE SUN NEVER SETS

(1939)

A Universal Picture. Produced and Directed by Rowland V. Lee. From a story by Jerry Horwin and Arthur Fitz-Richards. Screenplay: W. P. Lipscomb. Camera: George Robinson. Editor: Ted Kent. Art Director: Jack Otterson. Musical Director: Charles Previn. Musical Score: Frank Skinner. Released: June 1939. 98 minutes.

CAST: *John Randolph*: Douglas Fairbanks, Jr.; *Clive Randolph*: Basil Rathbone; *Phyllis Ransome*: Virginia Field; *Hugo Zurof*: Lionel Atwill; *Helen Randolph*: Barbara O'Neil; *Sir John Randolph*: C. Aubrey Smith; *Cosey*: Melville Cooper; *Mrs. Randolph*: Mary Forbes; *Gerald Randolph*: Arthur Mullinor; *Simon Randolph*: John Burton.

THE FILM: While watching *The Sun Never Sets,* one wonders if, at some point during pre-production, the writers toyed with the idea of making this story the basis for a Universal serial, instead of a feature motion picture. The film started out well enough as an engross-

The Sun Never Sets: **With Douglas Fairbanks, Jr.**

ing tale of two brothers in the British Colonial Service, but, shortly thereafter, adopted a totally unbelievable premise about a madman with plans for world domination—deteriorating into something right out of a Saturday matinee.

As producer/director Rowland V. Lee put it: "The project failed because it had a manufactured story that audiences wouldn't buy."

Clive Randolph (Rathbone) and his younger brother, John

The Sun Never Sets: **With Players.**

The Sun Never Sets: **With Lionel Atwill.**

The Sun Never Sets: **With Virginia Field and Barbara O'Neil.**

The Sun Never Sets: **With Harry Cording.**

(Douglas Fairbanks, Jr.), are stationed in the Gold Coast by the British Colonial Office. John had joined the service reluctantly—only after receiving a lecture about family tradition from his grandfather (C. Aubrey Smith).

The new recruit makes one very bad blunder, which almost ruins Clive's long career. He redeems himself by liquidating the evil munitions baron, Hugo Zurof (Lionel Atwill), whose propaganda broadcasts from a hidden radio station in the colony threatens to plunge the world into war.

The melodrama did give Rathbone a superb scene, however, in which two personal tragedies, as well as the strain of his job, cause him to suffer an emotional breakdown. Unfortunately, any positive effect scenes like this were to have on the production was diluted by the preposterous and heavy-handed situation of the would-be dictator hiding in his secret malalidium mine.

Barbara O'Neil played Rathbone's wife in the film: "This man was incarnate theatre. He commanded respect because he knew his craft well."

CRITICAL COMMENT:
". . . . Rathbone is excellent as the older brother."
Los Angeles Examiner

THE ADVENTURES OF SHERLOCK HOLMES

(1939)

A Twentieth Century-Fox Release of a Gene Markey Production. Directed by Alfred Werker. Based on the play, *Sherlock Holmes,* by William Gillette from the Sir Arthur Conan Doyle original. Screenplay: Edwin Blum and William Drake. Camera: Leon Shamroy. Editor: Robert Bischoff. Musical Director: Cyril J. Mockridge. Released: August 1939. 85 minutes.

CAST: *Sherlock Holmes*: Basil Rathbone; *Dr. Watson*: Nigel Bruce; *Ann Brandon*: Ida Lupino; *Jerrold Hunter*: Alan Marshal; *Billy*: Terry Kilburn; *Professor Moriarty*: George Zucco; *Sir Ronald Ramsgate*: Henry Stephenson; *Inspector Bristol*: E. E. Clive; *Bassick*: Arthur Hohl; *Mrs. Jameson*: May Beatty; *Lloyd Brandon*: Peter Willes; *Mrs. Hudson*: Mary Gordon; *Justice*: Holmes Herbert. *Also*: George Regas, Mary Forbes, Frank Dawson, William Austin, and Anthony Kemble Cooper.

THE FILM: Twentieth Century-Fox claimed that their follow-up

The Adventures of Sherlock Holmes: **With Nigel Bruce and Player.**

The Adventures of Sherlock Holmes: **With Ida Lupino.**

to *The Hound of the Baskervilles* was taken from William Gillette's play, *Sherlock Holmes,* which had been the basis of two earlier Holmes films starring John Barrymore and Clive Brook, respectively. To be exact, the new production, with the exception of the Holmes/Moriarty conflict, bore little relationship to any earlier dramatization.

The Adventures of Sherlock Holmes was a better picture than *Hound* in every respect. Director Alfred Werker kept Edwin Blum

The Adventures of Sherlock Holmes: **With Nigel Bruce, Ida Lupino, and Alan Marshal.**

The Adventures of Sherlock Holmes: **With Ida Lupino and Nigel Bruce.**

The Adventures of Sherlock Holmes: **With Ida Lupino and Nigel Bruce.**

and William Drake's exciting screenplay moving at a keen pace and was able to create an atmosphere of mystery, which was sadly lacking at times in Lanfield's film. Settings and costumes were first rate.

Once again, Rathbone and Bruce were fine as the Baker Street residents. George Zucco was excellent in the role of Moriarty, as was Ida Lupino playing the picture's heroine.

Holmes's arch-enemy, Professor Moriarty, advises the detective that he plans to commit the most incredible crime of his career, then sends an anonymous letter to Sir Ronald Ramsgate (James Stephenson), custodian of the crown jewels, warning that the price-less Star of India emerald will be stolen.

Ramsgate comes to Holmes for help. However, the sleuth is more interested in the problems of Ann Brandon (Lupino). She has re-ceived a mysterious sketch of a man with an albatross around his neck —similar to the one her father had received ten years previously, prior to his murder in South America. When Ann's brother (Peter Willes) is killed, the police suspect her fiancé, Jerrold Hunter (Alan Marshal). Watson has reported to Holmes that he had seen Moriarty leaving Hunter's law office, but the detective does not believe Jerrold to be guilty. Yet, he is curious about the attorney's relationship with the master criminal.

Holmes sends Watson to assist Ramsgate in guarding the valuable emerald, while he, in disguise, goes with Ann to a garden party. A club-footed South American gaucho tries to kill the girl with a bolas, but Holmes shoots the attacker.

Watson informs Holmes that he and Ramsgate had foiled an attempt to steal the Star of India from the Tower of London. The

The Adventures of Sherlock Holmes: **With Nigel Bruce.**

detective realizes that Moriarty was behind the plan and had used Ann Brandon to decoy him away from his main objective—the crown jewels. Holmes rushes to the Tower and catches the Professor, disguised as a police officer, in the process of stealing the stones. A fight ensues—with the sleuth knocking Moriarty off of the Tower to his death.

After it is explained to Miss Brandon that Moriarty had visited Jerrold only to throw Holmes off the track, she is reunited with her fiancé.

Rathbone had a delightful moment in the production when, in the guise of a London music hall entertainer, he performs a lively song and dance at the garden party. There were other memorable scenes: the "civilized" conversation between Holmes and Moriarty in the cab; the sinister gaucho stalking Ann Brandon; the final confrontation in the Tower of London. All were splendid touches.

During the filming of the picture, Ida Lupino became the "victim" of Rathbone and Bruce's marvelous sense of humor. She recalls the incident: "I'd come down with a cold and was feeling pretty tired. Basil suggested I get away from things on the coming weekend and spend the two days as guests of the Bruces. Willy thought that it was a great idea and told me for the rest of the week how quiet and peaceful his place was. When I finally agreed to go, they gave me the address. . . . Nigel Bruce lived in Beverly Hills . . . one block from my own house. But, I went anyway and had a wonderful time."

Following *The Adventures of Sherlock Holmes,* Fox decided to discontinue the series.

CRITICAL COMMENT:

"The Holmes character seems tailored for Rathbone, who fits the conception of the famed book sleuth."

Variety

RIO

(1939)

A Universal Production and Release. Directed by John Braum. From an original story by Jean Negulesco. Screenplay: Stephen Morehouse Avery, Frank Partos, Edwin Justus Mayer, and Aben Kandel. Camera: Hal Mohr. Editor: Phil Cahn. Musical Director: Charles Previn. Songs: Jimmy McHugh, Frank Skinner, and Ralph Freed. Released: September 1939. 78 minutes.

CAST: *Paul Reynard*: Basil Rathbone; *Dirk*: Victor McLaglen; *Irene Reynard*: Sigrid Gurie; *Bill Gregory*: Robert Cummings; *Roberto*: Leo Carrillo; *Manuelo*: Billy Gilbert; *"Mushy"*: Irving Bacon; *Old Convict*: Maurice Moscovich; *Lamartine*: Samuel S. Hinds; *Rocco*: Irving Pichel; *Maria*: Ferike Boros.

THE FILM: *Rio* was a low-budget programmer from Universal. However, unlike most pictures of that class, it garnered above-average reviews from the nation's critics. The melodrama was carefully di-

Rio: **With Sigrid Gurie.**

Rio: **With Irving Pichel and Irving Bacon.**

Rio: **With Sigrid Gurie and Robert Cummings.**

rected by John Braham and offered interesting performances from Rathbone, Victor McLaglen, Sigrid Gurie, and Robert Cummings.

The plot concerns Paul Reynard (Rathbone), a crooked financier sent to a French penal colony for dealing in forged bonds. His wife, Irene (Gurie), and aide, Dirk (McLaglen), move from France to Rio, so they can be closer to Paul and, if necessary, help him escape. Irene meets and falls in love with Bill Gregory (Cummings), an American engineer.

Reynard escapes, murdering another convict in the process. When he arrives in Rio, he learns of his wife's involvement with Gregory, then attempts to shoot the engineer. Dirk interferes and kills Reynard to preserve Irene's happiness.

Robert Cummings reflects on the production: "Basil was very popular on the set and quite considerate of his fellow performers.

"He was a little distant with me, however, because, I think, he believed I was 'crazy.' I'd been talking to him about my interest in health foods and he must have thought the theory was complete idiocy. He never invited me to his house . . . probably because he wouldn't have known what to serve me."

CRITICAL COMMENT:

"Yarn is of a made-to-order variety for Rathbone, giving him excellent opportunity to exhibit his unique ability of playing at the same time sympathetic and unsympathetic parts."

Variety

TOWER OF LONDON

(1939)

A Universal Picture. Produced and Directed by Rowland V. Lee. Story and Screenplay: Robert N. Lee. Photography: George Robinson. Editor: Edward Curtiss. Art Director: Jack Otterson. Musical Director: Charles Previn. Makeup: Jack P. Pierce. Costumes: Vera West. Released: November 1939. 92 minutes.

CAST: *Richard III*: Basil Rathbone; *Mord*: Boris Karloff; *Queen Elizabeth*: Barbara O'Neil; *Edward IV*: Ian Hunter; *Duke of Clarence*: Vincent Price; *Lady Alice Barton*: Nan Grey; *John Wyatt*: John Sutton; *Lord Hastings*: Leo G. Carroll; *Henry VI*: Miles Mander; *Beacon*: Lionel Belmore; *Anne Neville*: Rose Hobart; *Henry Tudor*: Ralph Forbes; *Isobel*: Frances Robinson; *Tom Clink*: Ernest Cossart. *Also*: G. P. Huntley, John Rodion, Ronald Sinclair, and Donnie Dunagan.

THE FILM: With the exception of a brief speech by John Barrymore in the 1929 revue *Show of Shows*, Basil Rathbone was the first actor to play Richard III in a *talking* motion picture. Unlike Laurence

Tower of London: **With Boris Karloff.**

Tower of London: **With John Sutton.**

Tower of London: **With Miles Mander and Player.**

Tower of London: **With Vincent Price.**

Olivier and Vincent Price, who both essayed the role later, Rathbone did not portray the evil Duke of Gloucester as a grotesque hunchback, but presented the audience with a rather handsome character, stricken with only a slight deformity.

According to Vincent Price: "Basil gave an excellent performance and, in the light of modern research on the subject, was probably more correct in his interpretation of Richard than either Olivier or myself."

The Rowland V. Lee production begins in 1471, after Edward IV (Ian Hunter) has deposed his uncle, Henry VI (Miles Mander), and proclaimed himself king. Richard, Edward's brother, plots to gain the throne for himself and, when Henry's son, the Prince of Wales (G. P. Huntley), lands in England with an army, he tricks the old king into leading an attack against his offspring. The Prince is killed, but Henry survives the battle. Richard orders Mord (Boris Karloff), the executioner of the Tower of London, to assassinate Henry. Then, Richard marries Anne Neville (Rose Hobart), widow of the Prince of Wales.

The Duke of Clarence (Price) is arrested for plotting against Edward and is sent to the Tower. Richard gets the Duke drunk, after which, with the aid of Mord, he drowns him in a vat of wine.

Tower of London: **With Rose Hobart.**

Edward dies in 1483. Richard is named Protector until Prince Edward (Ronald Sinclair) is crowned. Fearing her brother-in-law, the Queen (Barbara O'Neil) takes Prince Richard (Donnie Dunagan) and seeks sanctuary in Westminster Abbey. Nevertheless, at his uncle's suggestion, the young king sends for his brother to re-join him in the Tower.

John Wyatt (John Sutton), with the help of his cousin, the Queen, steals the royal treasure on behalf of Henry Tudor (Ralph Forbes). He is captured, but his fiancée, Lady Alice Barton (Nan Gray) assists in his escape.

Richard has Mord kill the young princes—an act that makes him King of England. Two years later, Richard and Mord are slain in battle by Henry Tudor's forces and the latter takes the throne.

Although it was handicapped with a poorly constructed and episodic screenplay, *Tower of London* offered audiences an engrossing look at one of the bloodiest periods in English history. Rathbone resisted an actor's *natural* tendency to "chew up the scenery" in such a flamboyant role and, instead, portrayed Richard in a very quiet manner—thereby making him even more sinister than if he had gone

Tower of London: **With Ian Hunter.**

in the opposite direction with his delineation of the character. The film also gave the public an opportunity to again view his superb ability as a swordsman.

Strangely enough, the production's weakest performance came from Boris Karloff. Universal wanted to enhance the actor's horror image. Accordingly, the character of Mord was written as a murderous fiend and a bizarre makeup, complete with bald pate and club-foot, was designed for him. It was an interpretation that seemed out of place in the picture and was difficult to take seriously.

Vincent Price, a relative newcomer in the movie industry when he did the film, recalls a practical joke played on him by Rathbone and Karloff: "It was the scene where Basil and Boris drown me in the vat of wine. Being young and foolish, I insisted on going into the vat myself. The stunt co-ordinator instructed me to grab onto a bar at the bottom of the vat, count ten, then come up for air. The ten count would allow Basil to finish the take and, also, give the crew enough time to reopen the lid of the vat.

"Anyway, while I was down at the bottom of that tank . . . holding onto the bar and counting . . . I heard the crew breaking into the vat with axes. It seems that my friends, Boris and Basil, had sat on top of the lid and the thing was stuck. Luckily for me, they got it open before I was in any serious danger."

Price continues: "The crew on that picture loved Basil. There was one grip, who would always be making good-natured insults about England. Basil would feign anger and chase the man up into the catwalks."

Sir Laurence Olivier starred in a 1956 film version of Shakespeare's *Richard III* and, in 1962, Price played the Duke of Gloucester in a remake of *Tower of London*.

CRITICAL COMMENT:

"Rathbone provides a most vivid portrayal of the ambitious Duke who schemes and murders to achieve his ends."

Variety

RHYTHM ON THE RIVER

(1940)

A Paramount Release of a William LeBaron Production. Directed by Victor Schertzinger. From a story by Billy Wilder and Jacques Thery. Screenplay: Dwight Taylor. Camera: Ted Tetzlaff. Editor: Hugh Bennett. Songs: Johnny Burke and James V. Monaco. "I Don't Want to Cry Anymore" by Victor Schertzinger. Released: August 1940. 92 minutes.

CAST: *Bob Summers*: Bing Crosby; *Cherry Lane*: Mary Martin; *Oliver Courtney*: Basil Rathbone; *Starbuck*: Oscar Levant; *Charlie Goodrich*: Oscar Shaw; *Uncle Caleb*: Charlie Grapewin; *Millie*: Lillian Cornell; *Westlake*: William Frawley; *Patsy Flick*: Phyllis Kennedy. *Also*: John Scott Trotter, Jean Cagney, Wingy Mannone, Brandon Hurst, Charles Lane, and Pierre Watkin.

THE FILM: *Rhythm on the River* was, simply, an excellent vehicle for the musical talents of Bing Crosby and Mary Martin. It was well received as such.

Unknown to each other, Bob Summers (Crosby) and Cherry

Rhythm on the River: **With Mary Martin and Oscar Levant.**

Rhythm on the River: **With Bing Crosby and Mary Martin.**

Lane (Martin) work independently as music and lyric ghost-writers for a popular composer, Oliver Courtney (Rathbone). The couple eventually meet, fall in love, and write a song together, "Only Forever," which they plan to keep as their own. When they discover that they both have the same employer, Bob and Cherry decide to try to crash the music business themselves. They have their problems until "Only Forever" becomes a hit—and the new songwriting team is on its way.

Rathbone's part, although important, did little to further his career. It allowed him, in any case, a brief pause from the more serious roles he had been used to.

Bing Crosby recalls working with the performer: "All of us in the cast were very much impressed at being in the company of such a distinguished actor. A legitimate actor . . . particularly an English actor . . . had tremendous stature with people like us—crooners, etc. His crisp diction, and the way he handled himself, certainly affected us all.

"He was, however, a man of tremendous good humor and we soon lost our awe of him . . . and had a lot of fun on the film."

CRITICAL COMMENT:
"Rathbone's prominent role is handled in the player's usually competent style."

Variety

THE MARK OF ZORRO

(1940)

A Twentieth Century-Fox Production. Directed by Rouben Ma-
moulian. From the story, "The Curse of Capistrano," by Johnston
McCulley. Screenplay: John Taintor Foote. Adaptation: Garrett
Fort and Bess Meredith. Camera: Arthur Miller. Editor: Robert
Bischoff. Released: November 1940. 93 minutes.

CAST: *Diego*: Tyrone Power; *Lolita Quintero*: Linda Darnell; *Capt.
Esteban Pasquale*: Basil Rathbone; *Inez Quintero*: Gale Sonder-
gaard; *Fray Felipe*: Eugene Pallette; *Don Luis Quintero*: J. Edward
Bromberg; *Rodrigo*: Robert Lowery; *Turnkey*: Chris-Pin Martin;
Don Alejandro Vega: Montagu Love; *Senora Isabella Vega*: Janet
Beecher; *Maria*: Belle Mitchell. *Also*: George Regas, John Belifer,
Frank Puglia, Eugene Borden, and Guy D'Ennery.

THE FILM: *The Mark of Zorro* was Twentieth Century-Fox's answer to Warner's *The Adventures of Robin Hood*. As if to empha-
size the similarities between the two swashbuckling epics, the studio

The Mark of Zorro: **With J. Edward Bromberg.**

The Mark of Zorro: **With Tyrone Power.**

cast three actors from the earlier film in their picture—Basil Rathbone, Eugene Pallette, and Montagu Love—and ordered Alfred Newman to deliver a score reminiscent of the action themes composed
by Erich Wolfgang Korngold.

The story, based on Johnston McCulley's "The Curse of Capistrano," had previously been filmed in 1920 with Douglas Fairbanks,
Sr. Tyrone Power, star of the new version, lacked Fairbanks's strong
personality, but was equal to the limited demands of the role. Rouben Mamoulian directed the adventure yarn to play at a lively clip
and, on the whole, the final result was a pleasing one.

The narrative tells of Diego Vega (Power), the son of the benevolent Alcade (Love) of early Los Angeles, who resigns his commission in the Spanish army and returns home to California when he receives an urgent summons from his father.

Upon his arrival, he learns that his father no longer holds office and Don Luis Quintero (J. Edward Bromberg) is the new Alcalde. Quintero, aided by Captain Esteban Pasquale (Rathbone), rules by fear—over-taxing the peons and either torturing or killing those that resist. Because the dictator controls the military power in the area, Diego's father and the other caballeros are unable to oust him.

Diego plays the fop for both Quintero and Pasquale, as well as the caballeros, and is, therefore, dismissed as being harmless by all parties.

A masked avenger, Zorro (the fox), appears on the scene. He vows that the Alcalde will either resign or suffer his wrath. The posted notice bears the writer's signature—a Z cut with a sword.

Zorro begins his reign of terror: attacking soldiers; stealing tax revenues; and even visiting Quintero in his office to issue an in-person demand for his resignation. The Alcalde is frightened, and it is

The Mark of Zorro: **With Gale Sondergaard.**

The Mark of Zorro: **With Tyrone Power and George Regas.**

only Pasquale who prevents him from obeying Zorro's orders. They are making too much money in their high offices to give them up in order to satisfy a lone highwayman.

Zorro (the audience knows he's really Diego) meets Lolita (Linda Darnell), the Alcalde's niece. The senorita, disapproving of her uncle's activities, is smitten with the mysterious adventurer.

Meanwhile, the Alcalde's wife, Inez (Gale Sondergaard), although in the midst of an affair with Pasquale, is taken with Diego and his knowledge of the upper social classes of old Spain. The pair go riding almost daily.

Pasquale, in turn, suggests to Quintero that a marriage be arranged between Lolita and Diego, as this union would form an alliance between the government and the caballeros. Diego, in love with the girl, agrees. However, Lolita is unhappy at the prospect of marrying a fop—until her future husband reveals to her his alternate identity.

Zorro's war against Quintero continues. He hides his stolen money with Padre Felipe (Pallette). The priest, in turn, distributes the spoils to the peons. After Pasquale accidentally discovers Felipe's secret, he imprisons him and confiscates the money.

Angered, Zorro concentrates on getting Quintero to quit. He makes it known to the Alcalde that he can penetrate his well-guarded mansion. Frightened, and urged on by a "concerned" Diego, Quintero is about to sign his resignation when Pasquale enters and, after a few angry words, challenges Diego to a duel. Vega kills the dastardly soldier-of-fortune.

When a secret passage, leading from the cellar to Quintero's office, is discovered, the Alcalde has Diego arrested for being Zorro. He reasons since the bandit had been in the cellar earlier that evening and, as the mansion once belonged to Diego's family, the young Vega *must* be the masked outlaw.

Diego and the Padre break out of jail and, with the help of both the caballeros and the peons, overthrow Quintero, who resigns. The elder Vega is reinstated as Alcalde and Diego marries Lolita.

Captain Esteban Pasquale must be counted as Rathbone's finest screen villain. The role was the ultimate progression from the black knight of *Robin Hood*. Both cunning *and* a man-of-action, Pasquale was a more dangerous adversary than Gisbourne could ever hope to be.

The Mark of Zorro: **With Tyrone Power and J. Edward Bromberg.**

The Mark of Zorro: **With Tyrone Power.**

The soldier-of-fortune was seldom without his sword—always carrying it in his hand to accent his gestures. He explains early in the film to Diego: "Most men have objects that they play with. . . . Churchmen have their beads. . . . I toy with a sword."

At a dinner party, Diego notes that Pasquale is jabbing his knife into an orange and he remarks: "Captain . . . you seem to find that poor fruit an enemy."

Eyeing him coldly, Pasquale retorts, "A rival!"

The duel between the two men, although lacking the elaborate staging of Warner Brothers' *Robin Hood,* is an example of fine swordsmanship. Rathbone sustained two cuts on the forehead during the filming of this sequence.

The production's major flaw can be found in the story construction. The error is so obvious that one wonders how Mamoulian overlooked it.

Pasquale, the only *real* danger to Diego, is killed approximately twenty minutes before the end of the film .This leaves only Quintero standing in the way of Diego's ultimate victory and the audience is already aware that the character is little more than a buffoon. No matter what Quintero or his men do to Diego, we know they are not a serious threat and that the hero will easily triumph. Although

the only sizable battle scene takes place close to the picture's conclusion, it somehow seems like an anti-climax.

The movie is *still* a good entertainment. However, because of
the aforementioned problem, it misses being one of the great adventure classics.

CRITICAL COMMENT:

"Supporting Power in the starring spot is a competent cast, with
Rathbone and Bromberg particularly effective as the villainous officials."

Variety

THE MAD DOCTOR

(1941)

A Paramount Release of a George Arthur Production. Directed by
Tim Whelan. Story and Screenplay: Howard J. Green. Camera: Ted
Tetzlaff. Editor: Archie Marshek. Released: February 1941. 90 min-
utes.

CAST: *Dr. George Sebastian*: Basil Rathbone; *Linda Boothe*: Ellen
Drew; *Gil Sawyer*: John Howard: *Louise Watkins*: Barbara
Allen; *Dr. Charles Downer*: Ralph Morgan; *Maurice Gretz*: Martin
Kosleck; *Winnie*: Kitty Kelly; *Lawrence Watkin*: Hugh O'Connell;
Hatch: Hugh Sothern.

THE FILM: *The Monster, Destiny,* and *A Date with Destiny* were
the titles this Paramount programmer went through before a final
one, *The Mad Doctor,* was settled upon.

Rathbone had originally rejected the script, but finally agreed

The Mad Doctor: **With Martin Kosleck.**

to play the title role after certain rewrites were completed.

The actor was Dr. George Sebastian, who makes a habit of marrying wealthy women, then murdering them. His first two victims supposedly died from pneumonia and his third wife, Linda Boothe (Ellen Drew), appears to be very accommodating to his purposes, as she has a suicide complex.

Gil Sawyer (John Howard), a newspaper reporter in love with

The Mad Doctor: **With Ellen Drew.**

Linda, is suspicious of Sebastian, who seems to have a Svengali-like effect on the girl. As is the case with most melodramas of this sort, Sawyer, the hero, thwarts the plans of Sebastian, the heavy, to do away with the heroine—and the evil doctor kills himself.

Rathbone turned in his usual competent job in the picture, which made virtually no impression on either critics or audiences.

Martin Kosleck, playing Rathbone's "hatchet man" in the film, recalls the star: "I enjoyed working on *Mad Doctor* more than anything else in my career *because* of Basil Rathbone. He was a wonderful man . . . very precise . . . he rehearsed everything until it was perfect. Between scenes, we would walk around the Paramount lot and go over our lines. . . . I loved that man."

CRITICAL COMMENT:
". . . . Rathbone creates a character of staggering stature, dominating the film with the finesse and skill of his portrayal."
Hollywood Reporter

THE BLACK CAT

(1941)

A Universal Production. Directed by Albert S. Rogell. Associate Producer: Burt Kelly. Suggested by the Edgar Allan Poe story. Screenplay: Robert Lees and Fred Rinaldo, Eric Taylor and Robert Neville. Photography: Stanley Cortez. Art Director: Jack Otterson. Editor: Ted Kent. Musical Director: H. J. Salter. Special Photographic Effects: John Fulton. Released: April 1941. 69 minutes.

CAST: *Hartley*: Basil Rathbone; *Mr. Penny*: Hugh Herbert; *Hubert Smith*: Broderick Crawford; *Eduardo*: Bela Lugosi; *Abigail Doone*: Gale Sondergaard; *Elaine Winslow*: Anne Gwynne; *Myrna Hartley*: Gladys Cooper; *Henrietta Winslow*: Cecilia Loftus; *Margaret Gordon*: Claire Dodd; *Stanley Borden*: John Eldredge; *Richard Hartley*: Alan Ladd.

THE FILM: Borrowing only the title from Edgar Allan Poe, this insignificant mystery/comedy was a project to which most of the cast wished they had never been assigned. According to Gale Sondergaard: "I hated doing that thing. It was beneath me."

The Black Cat: **With Anne Gwynne.**

The Black Cat: **With Broderick Crawford, Alan Ladd, and John Eldredge.**

The plot had to do with a murderer prowling around the Winslow family mansion, killing off the greedy heirs. Hartley (Rathbone) is the leader of the relatives and Hubert Smith (Broderick Crawford) is the amateur sleuth, out to solve the four deaths—the murderer eventually being revealed as Hartley's wife, Myrna (Gladys Cooper).

Although top-billed, Rathbone's role was secondary and the actor made the most of the little he had to work with. Hugh Herbert, Bela Lugosi, and newcomer Alan Ladd were also in the film.

The major problem with the picture was a silly and uninteresting screenplay, which did not warrant the talented performers who comprised its cast.

CRITICAL COMMENT:
"The proper eerie touch is given to the character portrayed by Rathbone, a sinister relative. . . ."

Variety

INTERNATIONAL LADY

(1941)

A United Artists Release of an Edward Small Production. Directed by Tim Whelan. Produced by Edward Small. Associate Producer: Stanley Logan. From an original story by E. Lloyd Sheldon and Jack DeWitt. Screenplay: Howard Estabrook. Photography: Hal Mohr. Art Director: John DuCasse Schulze. Editor: William Claxton. Musical Director: Lud Gluskin. Musical Score: Lucien Moraweck. Sound: Earl Sitar. Released: October 1941. 101 minutes.

CAST: *Tim Hanley*: George Brent; *Carla Nillson*: Ilona Massey; *Reggie Oliver*: Basil Rathbone; *Sidney Grenner*: Gene Lockhart; *Webster*: George Zucco; *Dr. Rowan*: Francis Pierlot; *Bruner*: Martin Kosleck; *Tetlow*: Charles D. Brown; *Mrs. Grenner*: Marjorie Gateson. *Also*: Leland Hodgson, Clayton Moore, Gordon DeMain, and Frederic Worlock.

THE FILM: This superficial Edward Small production was loaded with clichés, but audiences still found it fun to watch. The film also afforded Rathbone another opportunity to play comedy.

Carla Nillson (Ilona Massey), a radio singer in London during

International Lady: **With George Brent.**

International Lady: **With George Brent.**

1941, transmits coded messages through her music to a group of spies. Utilizing the secret information, the Nazis are able to destroy Allied defense materials. F.B.I. agent Tim Hanley (George Brent) and Reggie Oliver (Rathbone) of Scotland Yard are investigating the espionage ring. Hanley falls in love with Carla, who, eventually, reforms and assists the two representatives of the Allied cause in capturing the other conspirators.

Rathbone and Brent developed a good rapport during production and their scenes together are the strongest in the film. Brent reflects: "It was really an unimportant picture, but I looked forward to going to the set every day because Basil made it a joy to be there."

CRITICAL COMMENT:

"Basil Rathbone, in a sympathetic comedy role, gives a charming and amusing performance."

Hollywood Reporter

PARIS CALLING

(1941)

A Universal Release of a Charles K. Feldman Group Production. Directed by Edwin L. Marin. Produced by Benjamin Glazer. Original Screenplay: Benjamin Glazer and Charles Kaufman. Original Story Collaboration: John S. Toldy. Photography: Milton Krasner. Art Director: Jack Otterson. Editor: Edward Curtiss. Musical Director: H. J. Salter. Musical Score: Richard Hageman. Road sequences by Jean Negulesco. Released: December 1941. 95 minutes.

CAST: *Marianne*: Elisabeth Bergner; *Nick*: Randolph Scott; *Benoit*: Basil Rathbone; *Colette*: Gale Sondergaard; *Schwabe*: Lee J. Cobb; *Lantz*: Charles Arnt; *Mouche*: Edward Ciannelli; *McAvoy*: Patric O'Malley. *Also*: Elisabeth Risdon, George Ranavent, William Edmunds, George Metaxa, Paul Leysaac, Gene Garrick, Paul Bryar, Otto Reichow, and Grace Lenard.

THE FILM: Rathbone had another villainous role in this enter-

Paris Calling: **With Elisabeth Bergner.**

Paris Calling: **With Randolph Scott and Elisabeth Bergner.**

taining, but unexceptional, espionage picture, which marked the American film debut of Elisabeth Bergner, the famous European actress.

Released at the start of the United States' involvement in World War II, the story tells of Marianne (Bergner), a well-to-do Parisian girl, engaged to a high government official, André Benoit (Rathbone). When the Germans arrive, she flees Paris with her mother, but after the parent is killed by Nazi bombs, returns to the city and joins the underground movement. While she is involved in her espionage activities, the girl meets and falls in love with Nick (Randolph Scott), a stranded RAF pilot.

Marianne discovers that Benoit is a traitor and she, subsequently, shoots him for some vital papers he possesses. As the Nazis close in on the underground group, a British plane lands and a detachment of sailors rescue Nick and Marianne.

Critics were impressed with Miss Bergner, as well as the performances of Rathbone, Lee J. Cobb, playing a Gestapo chief, and Gale Sondergaard. Unfortunately, their feelings about the remaining aspects of the picture, such as script, direction, and other performances, were rather negative.

CRITICAL COMMENT:

"Basil Rathbone, the traitor who sells out to the Nazis, is his suave, villainous self."

Variety

FINGERS AT THE WINDOW

(1942)

A Metro-Goldwyn-Mayer Production. Directed by Charles Lederer. Produced by Irving Starr. From an original story by Rose Caylor. Screenplay: Rose Caylor and Lawrence P. Bachmann. Photography: Harry Stradling and Charles Lawton. Editor: George Boemler. Released: March 1942. 90 minutes.

CAST: *Oliver Duffy*: Lew Ayres; *Edwina Brown*: Laraine Day; *Dr. Santelle*: Basil Rathbone; *Dr. Cromwell*: Walter Kingsford; *Dr. Kurt Immelman*: Miles Mander; *Inspector Gallagher*: Charles D. Brown; *Ogilvie*: Russell Gleason; *Devlan*: William Tannen; *Hagney*: Mark Daniels; *Krum*: Bert Roach; *Dr. Chandley*: Russell Hicks.

THE FILM: Lew Ayres recalls this low-budget Metro programmer as being "the kind of film that actors do when they need work." Many of the nation's critics felt the same way.

Ayres was cast as Oliver Duffy, an actor turned detective. With the help of dancer Edwina Brown (Laraine Day), he attempts to

Fingers at the Window: **With Laraine Day and Lew Ayres.**

find the "master-mind" behind a series of axe murders in Chicago.

The villain of the piece is a stage magician (Rathbone). He has assumed the identity of Dr. Santelle, a deceased Paris psychiatrist, and come to Chicago to collect an inheritance due the dead man. The bogus doctor had hypnotized several lunatics and sent them to kill persons that knew him as a stage performer.

Edwina, who had seen the magician work in Paris, is to be his final victim. Naturally, Oliver and the police arrive in time to rescue her.

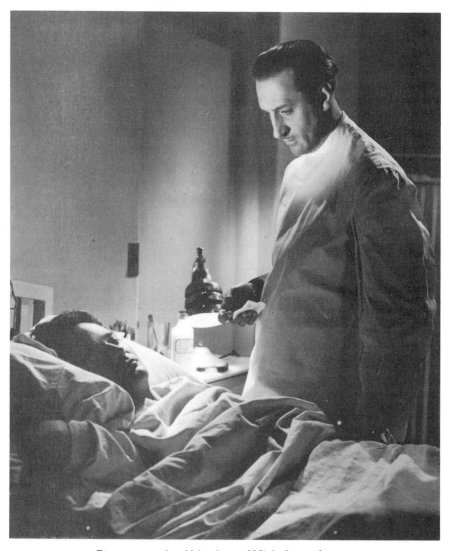

Fingers at the Window: **With Lew Ayres.**

Rathbone turned in his usual competent performance in the picture, which marked the directing debut of writer Charles Lederer.

Rathbone's co-star, Laraine Day, remembers that she was impressed with the way the actor handled himself on the project: "Other actors . . . if they had to do things they felt did not measure up to their abilities . . . would be miserable to work with. They'd take their frustration out on the cast and crew. But, Mr. Rathbone was different. He never seemed to resent doing the film and was very nice to everybody involved."

CRITICAL COMMENT:

"Rathbone makes an elegant menace, cold, bitter, determined to kill all who might cause him to lose his stolen riches."

Variety

CROSSROADS

(1942)

A Metro-Goldwyn-Mayer Production. Directed by Jack Conway. Produced by Edwin B. Knoph. From an original story by John Kafka and Howard Emmett Rogers. Screenplay: Guy Trosper. Photography: Joseph Ruttenberg. Musical Score: Bronislau Kaper. Art Director: Cedric Gibbons. Editor: George Boemler. Released: June 1942. 83 minutes.

CAST: *David Talbot*: William Powell; *Lucienne*: Hedy Lamarr; *Henri Sarrou*: Basil Rathbone; *Michele Allaine*: Claire Trevor; *Dr. Andre Tessier*: Felix Bressart; *President of the Court*: Guy Bates Post; *Prosecuting Attorney*: H. B. Warner; *Mrs. Pelletier*: Margaret Wycherly; *Le Duc*: Vladimir Sokoloff; *Dr. Alex Dubroc*: Sig Rumann; *Deval*: Fritz Leiber; *Defense Attorney*: Frank Conroy.

THE FILM: On the plus side, *Crossroads* had a good director, a stellar cast, and first-class production values. Its negative aspect was

Crossroads: **With William Powell.**

Crossroads: **With Margaret Wycherly and Claire Trevor.**

a clumsily developed and antiquated screenplay. The result—a well-mounted film that belonged in the "B" picture market.

David Talbot (William Powell) is a French diplomat, whose memory stops at a railway accident ten years previous. Shortly after his marriage to Lucienne (Hedy Lamarr), three blackmailers (Rathbone, Claire Trevor, and Margaret Wycherly) appear on the scene. They convince the amnesiac that he is really a former thief and murderer.

Talbot is about to acquiesce to the demands of the trio, when he discovers they have made a mistake. He realizes that their claims about his past are false. The diplomat sets a trap, which ultimately snares the crooks.

Rathbone, who appeared to have put on some weight, was fine in another of his suave villain roles. The sinister Henri Sarrou seemed very cool in his confrontations with Talbot, but became highly agitated while awaiting the results of his devious plans. To regain his composure, the blackmailer would pick out a few notes on the piano. It was an interesting touch to the characterization.

The film's other performances, especially those of Powell and Miss Trevor, were also of high quality. Had the script been better, *Crossroads* could have been an intriguing picture.

Claire Trevor remembers lunching with Rathbone and composer Bronislau Kaper almost every day the production was filming: "Basil had a great sense of humor and kept us laughing with his 'suave' English stories. Those lunches were the best thing about doing the picture."

CRITICAL COMMENT:

"Top performances are also turned in by Basil Rathbone as the extortionist and by his aide, Claire Trevor. . . ."

Variety

SHERLOCK HOLMES AND THE VOICE OF TERROR

(1942)

A Universal Production. Directed by John Rawlins. Associate Producer: Howard Benedict. From the story, "His Last Bow," by Sir Arthur Conan Doyle. Screenplay: Lynn Riggs. Adaptation: Robert D. Andrews. Photography: Woody Bredell. Art Director: Jack Otterson. Musical Director: Charles Previn. Musical Score: Frank Skinner. Editor: Russell Schoengarth. Released: September 1942. 65 minutes.

CAST: *Sherlock Holmes*: Basil Rathbone; *Dr. Watson*: Nigel Bruce; *Kitty*: Evelyn Ankers; *Sir Evan Barham*: Reginald Denny; *Sir Alfred Lloyd*: Henry Daniell; *General Jerome Lawford*: Montagu Love; *Meade*: Thomas Gomez; *Jill*: Hillary Brooke; *Mrs. Hudson*: Mary Gordon; *Crosbie*: Arthur Blake; *Captain Roland Shore*: Leyland Hodgson; *Admiral Fabian Prentice*: Olaf Hytten.

Sherlock Holmes and the Voice of Terror: **Olaf Hytten, Leyland Hodgson, Henry Daniell, Basil Rathbone, Reginald Denny, Nigel Bruce, and Montagu Love.**

Sherlock Holmes and the Voice of Terror: **With Thomas Gomez and Evelyn Ankers.**

THE FILM: Universal's initial entry in their updated Sherlock Holmes series was inspired by Conan Doyle's story, "His Last Bow," and filmed with the working title of *Sherlock Holmes Saves London.*

Set in war-torn England, Holmes is summoned by a member of the British Inner Council, Sir Evan Barham (Reginald Denny), to help apprehend the Nazi agents behind a series of terrifying radio broadcasts, which have foretold acts of sabotage against Allied planes and war materials. The detective suspects that "the voice" belongs to a member of the Council.

Holmes enlists the aid of Kitty (Evelyn Ankers), a Limehouse bar girl. She becomes "friendly" with a known Nazi agent, Meade (Thomas Gomez), and keeps Holmes apprised of his activities.

When "the voice" predicts a German attack on the Northern English Coast one week hence, Holmes suspects a trick, as the radio broadcasts had previously only foretold events that were to take place immediately. He surmises that the announcement is a decoy to draw British military strength away from the real landing point —the South Coast.

Holmes and Watson, accompanied by the Council and British troops, rush to the South Coast and, in a bombed-out church, capture the enemy spies. The detective unmasks Barham as "the voice."

Upon learning that Kitty has been working with Holmes, Meade kills her. Then, he is shot down himself by the troops. The Nazi attack is repulsed and Holmes ends the film with a most stirring speech—right out of "His Last Bow": "There's an East wind, Watson . . . . Such a wind as never blew in England yet. It will be cold and bitter, Watson . . . and a good many of us may wither before its blast. But it's God's own wind, nonetheless. And a greener, better, stronger land will be in the sunshine when the storm has cleared."

Sherlock Holmes and the Voice of Terror was the only episode of the Universal series that was *not* directed by Roy William Neill. John Rawlins handled those duties on this film and, although *his* work was adequate, the project suffered from a dull screenplay. It was one of the series' weakest segments.

Rathbone, abandoning the deerstalker hat he had worn in the two entries at Fox, and Bruce were at their best in the roles, which

Sherlock Holmes and the Voice of Terror: **With Hillary Brooke and Nigel Bruce.**

Sherlock Holmes and the Voice of Terror: **With Evelyn Ankers and Nigel Bruce.**

they were, by now, quite familiar with. Mary Gordon, who had played Mrs. Hudson, the landlady of 221 Baker Street, in the earlier films, repeated the part in this picture.

CRITICAL COMMENT:

"Rathbone carries the Sherlock Holmes role in great style, getting able assistance from the flustery Bruce as Dr. Watson."

Variety

SHERLOCK HOLMES AND THE SECRET WEAPON

(1942)

A Universal Production. Directed by Roy William Neill. Associate Producer: Howard Benedict. From the story, "The Dancing Men," by Sir Arthur Conan Doyle. Screenplay: Edward T. Lowe, W. Scott Darling, and Edmund L. Hartmann. Adaptation: W. Scott Darling and Edmund L. Hartmann. Photography: Les White. Art Director: Jack Otterson. Editor: Otto Ludwig. Musical Director: Charles Previn. Music Score: Frank Skinner. Released: December 1942. 68 minutes.

CAST: *Sherlock Holmes*: Basil Rathbone; *Dr. Watson*: Nigel Bruce; *Charlotte*: Kaaren Verne; *Moriarty*: Lionel Atwill; *Lestrade*: Dennis Hoey; *Peg Leg*: Harold DeBecker; *Dr. Tobel*: William Post, Jr.; *Mrs. Hudson*: Mary Gordon; *Mueller*: Paul Fix; *Braun*: Robert O. Davis; *Sir Reginald*: Holmes Herbert; *Brady*: Harry Cording; *Kurt*: Phillip Van Zandt.

Sherlock Holmes and the Secret Weapon: **With William Post, Jr.**

THE FILM: Director Roy William Neill's first assignment on the Holmes series had a screenplay based on Doyle's "The Dancing Men." The film was a vast improvement over the series' initial entry—in all areas of production.

Joining Rathbone and Bruce in this episode were Lionel Atwill, as an excellent Moriarty, and Kaaren Verne. Dennis Hoey made his initial appearance in the role of Inspector Lestrade of Scotland Yard and Mary Gordon was back as Mrs. Hudson.

Sherlock Holmes and the Secret Weapon: **With Kaaren Verne.**

Sherlock Holmes and the Secret Weapon: **With Lionel Atwill and Nigel Bruce.**

With the aid of Sherlock Holmes, Dr. Franz Tobel (William Post, Jr.), inventor of a secret bombsight, escapes from Nazi agents in Switzerland. Arriving in London, Tobel refuses to turn his invention over to the British War Ministry. Instead, he divides the bombsight into four units—each useless without the others—and gives them to four scientists for safekeeping. None of the four men know the identity of their counterparts.

Tobel is kidnapped by Professor Moriarty, who is being paid by the Nazis to get the bombsight.

The doctor's fiancée, Charlotte Eberle (Verne) gives Holmes an envelope, which she believes contains a coded message from Tobel that identifies the four scientists. But, in place of the message, there is a note: "We meet again, Holmes."

The detective realizes that Moriarty has beaten him to the original letter. However, he is able to get a copy by photographing, under ultra-violet light, the top page of the pad upon which the message was written. The alphabet substitution code is made up of a series of stick figures drawn in different positions—dancing men.

Holmes deciphers the complicated message, learning the names of the four scientists. Unfortunately, Moriarty beats him to three of the men and kills them for their bombsight parts. The disguised

Sherlock Holmes and the Secret Weapon: **With Players.**

sleuth changes places with the last man, Frederick Hofner (Henry Victor), and is abducted by the Professor's accomplices. Upon opening the box, which supposedly contains the final section of the bombsight, Moriarty finds a note—"We meet again, Professor."

Holmes informs Moriarty that the real Hofner and the remainder of the invention is in the hands of Scotland Yard. Moriarty vows that, since he cannot send Germany the bombsight, he will send them Tobel, the inventor.

Stalling for time, Holmes suggests that the Professor do away with him in an "imaginative" way, rather than just using a gun. He recommends that Moriarty drain his blood—drop by drop. Intrigued by the idea, the master criminal cannot help but make reference to the detective's drug habit, "The needle to the last, eh Holmes?"

Utilizing a device they'd attached to Moriarty's car while he was at Hofner's house, Watson and Lestrade arrive at the criminal's hideout in time to save Holmes and rescue Tobel. Moriarty is killed when he drops sixty feet through a trap-door to the sewers below.

Tobel gives his invention to the British and Holmes concludes the picture with another patriotic speech about England—this one

adapted from Shakespeare: "This fortress built by nature for herself.
This blessed plot. This earth. This realm. This England."

The working title for the picture was *Sherlock Holmes Fights
Back*.

CRITICAL COMMENT:

"Basil Rathbone assumes the part of Sherlock Holmes with the
suavity that is his stock in trade."

Hollywood Reporter

Sherlock Holmes and the Secret Weapon: **With Nigel Bruce and Holmes
Herbert.**

SHERLOCK HOLMES IN WASHINGTON

(1943)

A Universal Release. Directed by Roy William Neill. Associate Producer: Howard Benedict. Based on the characters created by Sir Arthur Conan Doyle. Original Story: Bertram Millhauser. Screenplay: Bertram Millhauser and Lynn Riggs. Photography: Lester White. Editor: Otto Ludwig. Art Director: Jack Otterson. Musical Director: Charles Previn. Music Score: Frank Skinner. Released: March 1943. 70 minutes.

CAST: *Sherlock Holmes*: Basil Rathbone; *Dr. Watson*: Nigel Bruce; *Nancy Partridge*: Marjorie Lord; *William Easter*: Henry Daniell; *Stanley*: George Zucco; *Lt. Peter Merriam*: John Archer; *Bart Lang*: Gavin Muir; *Detective Lt. Grogan*: Edmund MacDonald; *Howe*: Don Terry; *Cady*: Bradley Page; *Mr. Ahrens*: Holmes Herbert; *Senator Henry Babcock*: Thurston Hall; *Marchmont*: Gilbert Emery; *Clerk*: Ian Wolfe.

THE FILM: The first segment of the Holmes series, which did not

Sherlock Holmes in Washington: **With George Zucco and Marjorie Lord.**

Sherlock Holmes in Washington: **With Gavin Muir, Nigel Bruce, and Clarence Muse.**

use a Doyle story as its basis, had the detective crossing the Atlantic to recover an important document that has been microfilmed and concealed in a match-folder. Also after the folder are a group of Nazi agents, headed by William Easter (Henry Daniell) and Richard Stanley (George Zucco).

Before he'd been abducted by the spies from a Washington-bound train, the British agent transporting the document had passed the match-folder to Nancy Partridge (Marjorie Lord), a fellow passenger, who is completely unaware of what she now carries.

The courier's body is delivered in a trunk to Holmes at his Washington hotel and the sleuth surmises that the spies do not have the document either. By questioning the porter from the train, Holmes learns of the matches being passed to Miss Partridge. He rushes to her home, however the spies have been there first and kidnaped the young lady.

The trunk the courier's body arrived in is examined by Holmes in the police lab, and he discovers that it probably came from an antique shop. Holmes, with Watson in tow, finds the shop and, while the Doctor goes for the police, investigates the premises.

Sherlock Holmes in Washington: **With Ian Wolfe.**

Sherlock Holmes in Washington: **With Nigel Bruce and Irving Mitchell.**

Holmes is captured by Stanley, a Moriarty-like villain. The detective notices the match-folder on the enemy agent's desk, but it is obvious that Stanley does not know he has the elusive document in his possession.

Watson arrives with the police. The spies, with the exception of Stanley, are apprehended and Miss Partridge rescued. The ringleader, thinking that another train passenger, Senator Babcock (Thurston Hall), has the document, escapes with the match-folder in his pocket. Holmes captures Stanley at the Senator's office and retrieves the document.

Rathbone and Bruce received excellent support in this episode from both a former (Zucco) and a future (Daniell) Moriarty. The screenplay had interesting moments, but its story was somewhat similar to *Sherlock Holmes and the Secret Weapon*. Unfortunately, the script was not as well written as the previous film and the picture must, therefore, be classified as only an average series entry.

CRITICAL COMMENT:

"Basil Rathbone is just what he should be in the title role, and Nigel Bruce as Doctor Watson is supplied with much bright comedy of which he is quick to make the most."

Hollywood Reporter

ABOVE SUSPICION

(1943)

A Metro-Goldwyn-Mayer Production. Directed by Richard Thorpe. Produced by Victor Saville. From the novel by Helen MacInnes. Screenplay: Keith Winter, Melville Baker, and Patricia Coleman. Camera: Robert Planck. Art Director: Randall Duell. Music Score: Bronislau Kaper. Released: April 1943. 89 minutes.

CAST: *Frances Myles*: Joan Crawford; *Richard Myles*: Fred Mac-Murray; *Hassert Seidel*: Conrad Veidt; *Sig von Aschenhausen*: Basil Rathbone; *Dr. Mespelbrunn*: Reginald Owen; *Peter Galt*: Richard Ainley; *Aunt Ellen*: Ann Shoemaker; *Aunt Hattie*: Sara Haden; *Mr. A. Werner*: Felix Bressart; *Thornley*: Bruce Lester; *Frau Kleist*: Johanna Hofer; *Ottilie*: Lotta Palfi.

THE FILM: *Above Suspicion* was a delightful melodrama that didn't take itself too seriously. Richard Thorpe directed the picture at a smart pace, making the most of the suspense that was inherent in the neatly constructed screenplay, while, at the same time, play-

Above Suspicion: **With Joan Crawford and Fred MacMurray.**

Above Suspicion: **With Philip Van Zandt and Joan Crawford.**

ing up its comedic aspects. Cast and production values were outstanding.

Set just prior to the outbreak of World War II, the Metro-Goldwyn-Mayer production follows the adventures of newlyweds Frances and Professor Richard Myles (Joan Crawford and Fred MacMurray) as they travel across the European Continent to Germany on assignment for the British Secret Service. Their job is to obtain, through a series of secret agents, the confidential plans for a new weapon.

Gestapo chief Sig von Aschenhausen (Rathbone), an old school chum of Richard's, suspects the married couple of being espionage agents and attempts to thwart their mission. On the other hand, Hassert Seidel (Conrad Veidt), a most unconventional tourist guide, assists them in their efforts.

The Myleses get what they are after, but Frances is captured by von Aschenhausen and interrogated in a remote castle. She is rescued by Seidel and her husband, who shoots the Nazi official. The trio escapes across the border into Italy.

Although Rathbone played the cruel, but sophisticated, villain with competence, the high points of this chase picture were the scenes

between Crawford and MacMurray. Their banter was quite entertaining.

One bit has MacMurray returning a Gestapo agent's "Heil Hitler!" greeting with "Good morning, dope."

The Nazi, unable to understand much English, is more confused
than angered, as he asks a comrade, "Vhat is dis dope?"

Conrad Veidt, getting away from his "bad guy" roles in what

Above Suspicion: **With Fred MacMurray.**

was to be his last film, was also amusing as the Myleses' roguish benefactor.

CRITICAL COMMENT:
   "Basil Rathbone is a rather heavy heavy, but he motivates the
action in latter sequences."

Variety

SHERLOCK HOLMES FACES DEATH

(1943)

A Universal Production. Produced and Directed by Roy William Neill. From the story, "The Musgrave Ritual," by Sir Arthur Conan Doyle. Screenplay: Bertram Millhauser. Photography: Charles Van Enger. Art Directors: John B. Goodman and Harold MacArthur. Musical Director: H. J. Salter. Editor: Fred Feitchans. Released: September 1943. 68 minutes.

CAST: *Sherlock Holmes*: Basil Rathbone; *Dr. Watson*: Nigel Bruce; *Sally Musgrave*: Hillary Brooke; *Captain Vickery*: Milburn Stone; *Dr. Sexton*: Arthur Margetson; *Brunton*: Halliwell Hobbes; *Lestrade*: Dennis Hoey; *Philip Musgrave*: Gavin Muir; *Geoffrey Musgrave*: Frederic Worlock; *Captain MacIntosh*: Olaf Hytten; *Major Langford*: Gerald Hamer; *Lieutenant Clavering*: Vernon Downing; *Mrs. Howells*: Minna Phillips; *Mrs. Hudson*: Mary Gordon.

THE FILM: Conan Doyle's "The Musgrave Ritual" inspired the fourth entry in this Universal series. Although the identity of the

Sherlock Holmes Faces Death: **With Mary Gordon.**

Sherlock Holmes Faces Death: **With Hillary Brooke.**

killer was obvious to most mystery fans about halfway through the picture, the film had several intriguing moments—thanks to a good script by Bertram Millhauser and Neill's direction.

Joining Rathbone and Bruce for this outing were Milburn Stone (of "Gunsmoke" fame), Hillary Brooke, and, in a bit, Peter Lawford. Dennis Hoey repeated as Lestrade, as did Mary Gordon in the part of Mrs. Hudson.

Dr. Watson is in charge of a convalescent hospital for army officers, which is located in Musgrave Manor. Following an attack by an unknown assailant on his assistant, Dr. Sexton (Arthur Margetson), Watson calls in Holmes. The sleuth arrives at the estate to find a host of potential suspects among the resident patients.

The tower clock in the manor strikes *thirteen*—twice—and the brothers Philip (Gavin Muir) and Geoffrey (Frederic Worlock) Musgrave are both murdered. Holmes believes that the key to the crimes will be found in the weird Musgrave Ritual—a chant traditionally read after the death of a family member. Sally Musgrave (Brooke), the last of the clan, gives Holmes a copy of the Ritual and he deduces that the floor of the manor's main hall is, in fact, a giant chess board. Utilizing the services of the patients and staff as chessmen, the detective directs an elaborate game—moving each person to a different square until he discovers the mansion's secret.

Holmes finds a subterranean crypt beneath the house, dating back to the fourteenth century. In the burial chamber is the body of the butler (Halliwell Hobbes). The investigator announces that the dead man has written something on the floor in blood—probably the name of his murderer. Holmes departs the manor to get some special chemicals, so he can apply them to the markings and, thereby, be able to read them better.

Actually, there are no markings. This is a device on the part of the detective to unmask the killer, who turns out to be Sexton. Holmes confronts the murderer in the crypt and, during a struggle, allows him to gain possession of his pistol. Confident that he will soon do away with the sleuth, Sexton confesses his crimes to him: The doctor wants to marry Sally Musgrave, as he has discovered an extremely valuable land grant in the crypt, which she would inherit. He was never attacked, but to divert suspicion, had wounded himself.

Sexton shoots the detective and is, almost immediately, arrested by Lestrade, who, with Watson, had witnessed the previous scene. Naturally, Holmes is not dead. He had loaded the gun with blanks, intending for Sexton to get a hold of it.

Sherlock Holmes Faces Death: **With Arthur Margetson.**

Milburn Stone's role in the film was that of Sally Musgrave's romantic interest. The performer is a short man—a fact, evidently, that the producers did not consider when they cast him. Recalls Stone: "Everybody in the picture was taller than me. There was this shot where Basil and I had to walk across the room together. He walked on the floor, but they built a special platform for me, so I'd look taller.

"I had a love scene with Hillary Brooke, which was even worse. We were sitting on the sofa and I looked almost like a midget next to her. The property man supplied me with some pillows to prop me up."

Sherlock Holmes Faces Death employed a good many stock mystery story devices: howling winds, a mysterious old mansion, secret passages. The clichés worked, however, and helped create a suspenseful atmosphere for Holmes to operate in. It was one of the better segments of the series.

CRITICAL COMMENT:

"As drawing cards, there are Basil Rathbone and Nigel Bruce giving expertly smooth accounts of Holmes and the blundering Watson."

Hollywood Reporter

CRAZY HOUSE

(1943)

A Universal Picture. Directed by Edward F. Cline. Associate Producer: Erle C. Kenton. Screenplay: Robert Lees and Frederic I. Rinaldo. Camera: Charles Van Enger. Art Directors: John B. Goodman and Harold H. MacArthur. Editor: Arthur Hilton. Musical Director: Charles Previn. Released: October 1943. 80 minutes.

CAST: *Olsen and Johnson*: Themselves; *Sadie*: Cass Daley; *Mac*: Patric Knowles; *Margie*: Martha O'Driscoll; *Johnny*: Leighton Noble; *Wagstaff*: Thomas Gomez; *Col. Merriweather*: Percy Kilbride; *Roco*: Hans Conried; *Hanley*: Richard Lane; *Gregory*: Andrew Tombes; *Stone*: Billy Gilbert; *Fud*: Chester Clute; *Judge*: Edgar Kennedy; *Hotel Clerk*: Franklin Pangborn; *Mumbo*: Shemp Howard; *Jumbo*: Fred Sanborn. *Also*: Tony and Sally DeMarco, Count Basie and His Orchestra, Marion Hutton and The Glenn Miller Singers, Chandra

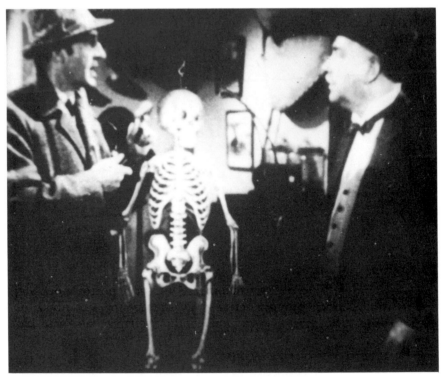

Crazy House: **With Nigel Bruce.**

Kaly and His Dancers, The Delta Rhythm Boys, and Leighton Noble and His Orchestra. *Guest Stars*: Allan Jones, Leo Carrillo, Andy Devine, Robert Paige, and Alan Curtis. *Unbilled Guest Appearance*: Basil Rathbone and Nigel Bruce.

THE FILM: The picture was nothing more than a vehicle for the madcap antics of comics Ole Olsen and Chic Johnson. Numerous Hollywood celebrities, such as Rathbone and Nigel Bruce (playing Sherlock Holmes and Dr. Watson), made brief appearances in the film.

THE SPIDER WOMAN

(1944)

A Universal Release of a Roy William Neill Production. Directed by Neill. From a story by Sir Arthur Conan Doyle. Screenplay: Bertram Millhauser. Camera: Charles Van Enger. Editor: James Gibbon. Released: January 1944. 62 minutes.

CAST: *Sherlock Holmes*: Basil Rathbone; *Dr. Watson*: Nigel Bruce; *Adrea Spedding*: Gale Sondergaard; *Lestrade*: Dennis Hoey; *Norman Locke*: Vernon Downing; *Radlik*: Alec Craig; *Mrs. Hudson*: Mary Gordon; *Gilflower*: Arthur Hohl; *Larry*: Teddy Infuhr.

THE FILM: Super Sleuth went up against a female Moriarty in this well-done episode of the Universal series. Academy Award winner Gale Sondergaard was cast as the sinister Adrea Spedding, and her scenes with Rathbone, in which the two talented performers play a "cat-and-mouse" game of innuendoes, were the high points of the film.

The Spider Woman: **With Gale Sondergaard.**

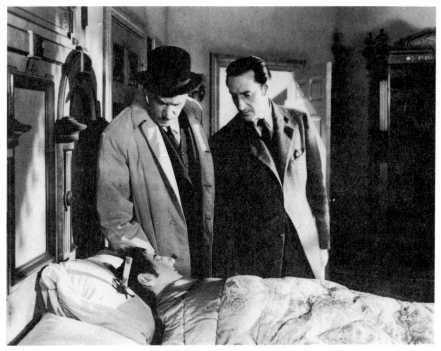

The Spider Woman: **With Dennis Hoey.**

The story deals with Holmes's investigation of what the newspapers term "Pajama Suicides," a series of violent deaths that have been taking place in London hotel rooms. After faking his own demise, so he can work undetected, Holmes adopts the guise of a Hindu. He meets Miss Spedding and, eventually, learns that she is responsible for the crimes. The victims have all been bitten by a deadly African spider, the bite being so painful that the sufferer goes mad and destroys himself. The arachnid, which had been transported by a pygmy, entered the hotel rooms through an air shaft.

The motive: Miss Spedding and her associates have loaned the dead men money in exchange for the victims making them the beneficiaries on their insurance policies. The murderers simply want to collect the death benefits.

An attempt to kill Holmes with the spider fails, as does an effort to poison the detective and Watson with lethal gas.

Holmes is captured by Adrea and her men in an amusement park. The sleuth is tied behind a metal caricature of Hitler, while customers of a shooting gallery, including Dr. Watson, fire live ammunition at the target, which has an exposed heart. Needless to say, Holmes frees himself in time to capture the criminals.

The Spider Woman: **With Alec Craig and Gale Sondergaard.**

Hoping to appeal to larger audiences, the producers dropped the detective's name from this and all subsequent entries in the series.

The film served as a spin-off for a later picture starring Gale Sondergaard, *The Spider Woman Strikes Back* (1946).

CRITICAL COMMENT:

"Basil Rathbone plays the versatile detective with his usual serene elegance."

New York Times

THE SCARLET CLAW

(1944)

A Universal Production. Produced and Directed by Roy William Neill. Based on the characters created by Sir Arthur Conan Doyle. Screenplay: Edmund L. Hartmann and Roy William Neill. Original Story: Paul Gangelin and Brenda Weisberg. Camera: George Robinson. Musical Director: Paul Sawtell. Art Directors: John B. Goodman and Ralph M. DeLacy. Editor: Paul Landres. Special Photography: John P. Fulton. Released: April 1944. 74 minutes.

CAST: *Sherlock Holmes*: Basil Rathbone; *Dr. Watson*: Nigel Bruce; *Alistair Ramson*: Gerald Hamer; *Lord Penrose*: Paul Cavanagh; *Emil Journet*: Arthur Hohl; *Judge Brisson*: Miles Mander; *Marie Journet*: Kay Harding; *Sergeant Thompson*: David Clyde; *Nora*: Victoria Horne; *Drake*: Ian Wolfe.

THE FILM: *The Scarlet Claw* was, unquestionably, the best picture in the Sherlock Holmes series. The suspenseful screenplay by Roy Neill and Edward L. Hartmann was almost a horror story and

The Scarlet Claw: **With Gerald Hamer.**

The Scarlet Claw: **With Nigel Bruce and Victoria Horne.**

The Scarlet Claw: **With David Clyde and Nigel Bruce.**

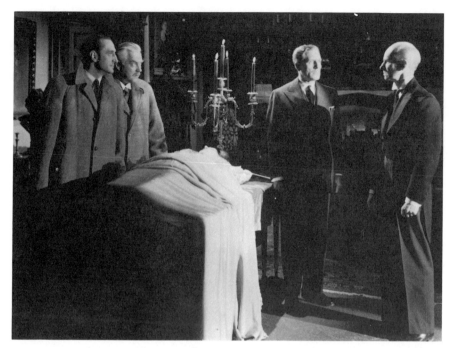

The Scarlet Claw: **With Nigel Bruce, Paul Cavanagh, and Ian Wolfe.**

Neill's imaginative direction, aided by the superb special effects of John P. Fulton, turned the film into a minor masterpiece of that genre.

The production had many unforgettable moments: a dead woman's hand clutching a bellrope; the luminous "monster" stalking Holmes in the marsh; the murder of the judge, with the killer being disguised as a woman. Each scene helped to create a film that kept audiences guessing until the conclusion, as to the identity of the "monster."

Briefly, the story takes Holmes and Watson to a small village in Canada to investigate a series of ghastly murders, supposedly committed by a legendary phantom. The sleuth surmises that there is no monster at all, but only a murderer dressed in luminous clothing and using a garden weeder to tear out the throats of his victims.

Holmes discovers that the killer is Alistair Ramson (Gerald Hamer), an insane actor, who has vowed to destroy the residents in the village responsible for his being sent to prison. The performer is a master at makeup and has established several different personalities for himself over the past two years. Therefore, ferreting him out will not be an easy task.

However, Holmes is able to accomplish the job by assuming the guise of one of Ramson's intended victims. The killer attacks Holmes in the marsh, but flees when he is surrounded by the townspeople. Emil Journet (Arthur Hohl), the father of a recent victim, ends the murderer's life.

Rathbone and Bruce were at their best in this, their eighth fling at the Holmes and Watson roles, and they received fine support from Gerald Hamer and Miles Mander, who played the ill-fated judge.

Paul Landres, editor of the picture, recalls that "everybody involved was very excited about this film because we all knew that it was far superior to anything else in the series."

CRITICAL COMMENT:
   "Mr. Rathbone does his usual stiff-backed job."

New York Times

BATHING BEAUTY

(1944)

A Metro-Goldwyn-Mayer Picture. Technicolor. Directed by George Sidney. Produced by Jack Cummings. From an original story by Kenneth Earl, M. M. Musselman, and Curtis Kenyon. Screenplay: Dorothy Kingsley, Allen Boretz, and Frank Waldman. Adaptation: Joseph Schrank. Camera: Harry Stradling. Art Directors: Cedric Gibbons, Stephen Goosson, and Merril Pye. Musical Direction: Johnny Green. Dance Direction: Jack Donohue and Robert Alton. Water Ballet: John Murray Anderson. Released: May 1944. 104 minutes.

CAST: *Steve Elliott*: Red Skelton; *Caroline Brooks*: Esther Williams; *George Adams*: Basil Rathbone; *Willis Evans*: Bill Goodwin; *Organist*: Ethel Smith; *Jean Allenwood*: Jean Porter; *Carlos*: Carlos Ramirez; *Chester*: Donald Meek; *Marie*: Jacqueline Dalya. *Also*: Harry James and His Orchestra with Helen Forrest, and Xavier Cugat and His Orchestra with Lina Romay.

Bathing Beauty: **With Jean Porter and Red Skelton.**

Bathing Beauty: **With Red Skelton, Esther Williams, and Jacqueline Dalya.**

THE FILM: This Metro-Goldwyn-Mayer musical extravaganza, filmed under the working title of *Mr. Co-Ed*, presented Esther Williams with her first starring role in motion pictures. Designed as a showcase for her swimming abilities, as well as the comedy antics of Red Skelton, the production, as such, was quite successful.

The story concerns Steve Elliott (Skelton), a songwriter, who becomes a student at a young ladies' seminary in order to be near his wife, Caroline (Williams).

Rathbone was totally wasted in the picture, playing the role of Skelton's manager.

For audiences that enjoyed this type of entertainment, complete with lavish water ballets, big band numbers, and the like, *Bathing Beauty* was certainly no disappointment.

CRITICAL COMMENT:
    "Rathbone is efficient in a new environment."

Los Angeles Times

THE PEARL OF DEATH

(1944)

A Universal Release. Produced and Directed by Roy William Neill. From "The Six Napoleons" by Sir Arthur Conan Doyle. Screenplay: Bertram Millhauser. Photography: Virgil Miller. Editor: Ray Snyder. Art Directors: John B. Goodman and Martin Obzina. Musical Director: Paul Sawtell. Released: August 1944. 67 minutes.

CAST: *Sherlock Holmes*: Basil Rathbone; *Dr. Watson*: Nigel Bruce; *Naomi Drake*: Evelyn Ankers; *Giles Conover*: Miles Mander; *Lestrade*: Dennis Hoey; *The Creeper*: Rondo Hatton; *Bates*: Richard Nugent.

THE FILM: Howard S. Benedict, executive producer of Universal's Sherlock Holmes films, lists *Pearl of Death* as his personal favorite in the series. Certainly, as a mystery-thriller, it can be considered second only to *The Scarlet Claw,* which immediately preceded it.

Bertram Millhauser delivered an excellent script, based on Doyle's "The Adventure of the Six Napoleons," and Roy Neill's di-

The Pearl of Death: **With Miles Mander.**

rection was up to its usual standard, building the suspense at a steady pace.

Again, Rathbone and Bruce received able support from Dennis Hoey as Lestrade, as well as Miles Mander in the role of the master jewel thief, Giles Conover. However, the most interesting character in the picture was The Creeper, played by Rondo Hatton. This homicidal brute killed his victims by breaking their backs.

The plot deals with Holmes's search for the valuable Borgia Pearl, which has been stolen by Conover from the Royal Regent Museum and hidden in a wet plaster bust of Napoleon. Six identical busts have been distributed around London. The purchasers, one by one, are being murdered by Conover's henchman, The Creeper.

Conover's attempts to murder Holmes fail and the detective ultimately beats the criminal to the owner of the last bust, which, in fact, contains the pearl.

Thinking he has been double-crossed by Conover, The Creeper kills his boss, then is himself shot by Holmes. Watson arrives with Lestrade and the case is closed.

Rondo Hatton, a victim of acromegaly, reprised his role of The Creeper in a minor 1946 horror epic for Universal, *House of Horrors*.

The Pearl of Death: **With Nigel Bruce, Karl Bassick, and Dennis Hoey.**

The Pearl of Death: **With Rondo Hatton and Miles Mander.**

CRITICAL COMMENT:

"The Rathbone-Bruce team turns in a good, solid performance, as does Miles Mander, who plays the role of a nefarious and clever jewel thief."

New York Times

FRENCHMAN'S CREEK

(1944)

A Paramount Picture. Technicolor. Directed by Mitchell Leisen. Produced by B. G. DeSylva. From the novel by Daphne duMaurier. Screenplay: Talbot Jennings. Camera: George Barnes. Editor: Alma Macrorie. Art Directors: Hans Dreier and Ernst Fegté. Costumes: Raoul Pene Du Bois. Music Score: Victor Young. Released: September 1944. 110 minutes.

CAST: *Dona St. Columb*: Joan Fontaine; *The Frenchman*: Arturo deCordova; *Lord Rockingham*: Basil Rathbone; *Lord Godolphin*: Nigel Bruce; *William*: Cecil Kellaway; *Harry St. Columb*: Ralph Forbes; *Edmond*: Harald Ramond; *Pierre Blanc*: Billy Daniels; *Lady Godolphin*: Moyna MacGill; *Henrietta*: Patricia Barker. *Also*: David James, Mary Field, David Clyde, Charles Coleman, Paul Oman, Denis Green, and Bob Stevenson.

THE FILM: Taking Nigel Bruce along with him, Rathbone moved

Frenchman's Creek: **With Joan Fontaine.**

Frenchman's Creek: **With Joan Fontaine.**

over to the Paramount lot to play a supporting role in his first swashbuckler since *The Mark of Zorro*. The stars of the screen version
of Daphne du Maurier's bestselling novel were Joan Fontaine and
the totally miscast Arturo deCordova.

Director Mitchell Leisen was unable to instill much life into
Talbot Jennings's slow-moving and poorly constructed screenplay,
although his manipulation and control of color in the film was so
outstanding that many critics consider *Frenchman's Creek* to be one
of the most beautiful Technicolor pictures of the decade.

The story, set in seventeenth-century England, tells of unhappily
married Lady Dona St. Columb (Fontaine) and her romance with
a French pirate (deCordova). The adventurer's ship is anchored in
a creek near Dona's country estate, where she has come to get away
from her weakling husband (Ralph Forbes) and his lecherous friend,
Lord Rockingham (Rathbone).

Dona meets the Frenchman, who has been terrorizing the coun-
tryside, and is charmed by him. They spend several blissful days
together and she takes part in a raid on the estate of Lord Godolphin
(Bruce), a country squire.

When her husband, Harry, and Rockingham come down from
London to help capture the pirates, Dona sends a household servant, William (Cecil Kellaway), to warn the Frenchman to set sail

Frenchman's Creek: **With Joan Fontaine.**

for the open sea. That night, to divert their attention, she invites
the squires to a dinner party.

Dona, as well as her company, are surprised when the pirates
capture the house. With the squires locked up, the Frenchman pleads
with the lady to sail away with him, then, after she refuses, departs.
Rockingham gets Dona alone and reveals that he had overheard
her conversation with the pirate. Failing to blackmail her into bed,
he attempts to rape her. Dona kills her attacker by pushing a suit
of armor down on him as he chases her upstairs.

The Frenchman is captured by the squires and imprisoned. Dona
helps him to escape and he sails away without her—she having realized that she cannot desert her children.

Rathbone, repeating the type of role he'd played so many times
during the 1930s, was excellent as Lord Rockingham. The scene in
which he confronts Dona is definitely the most effective moment in
the picture. Unfortunately, audiences were denied the opportunity
to see a display of the actor's excellent swordsmanship in the film.

Victor Young gave the production a magnificent score, centering
around the main theme of "Clair de Lune." The sets by art direc-

tors Hans Dreier and Ernst Fegté and set decorator Sam Comer
earned the picture an Academy Award in the category of Interior
Decoration.

The popularity of the original novel and the name of Joan Fontaine on the marquee, helped to make the picture a commercial
success, in spite of its artistic drawbacks.

CRITICAL COMMENT:
  "Basil Rathbone manages some capital moments."
  Hollywood Reporter

THE HOUSE OF FEAR

(1945)

A Universal Release of a Roy William Neill Production. Directed by Neill. From a story, "The Adventure of the Five Orange Pips," by Sir Arthur Conan Doyle. Screenplay: Roy Chanslor. Camera: Virgil Miller. Editor: Saul Goodkind. Released: March 1945. 68 minutes.

CAST: *Sherlock Holmes*: Basil Rathbone; *Dr. Watson*: Nigel Bruce; *Alastair*: Aubrey Mather; *Lestrade*: Dennis Hoey; *Simon Merrivale*: Paul Cavanagh; *Alan Cosgrave*: Holmes Herbert; *John Simpson*: Harry Cording; *Mrs. Monteith*: Sally Shepherd; *Chalmers*: Gavin Muir; *Alison MacGregor*: Florette Hillier; *Alex MacGregor*: David Clyde.

THE FILM: This entry in the Holmes series was unique in that Dr. Watson was the first to discover the answer to the mystery. Other-

The House of Fear: **With Nigel Bruce, Dennis Hoey, and Harry Cording.**

The House of Fear: **Harry Cording, Paul Cavanagh, Holmes Herbert, Dick Alexander, Cyril Delevanti, Basil Rathbone, and Dennis Hoey.**

wise, Roy Chanslor's muddled screenplay, based on Conan Doyle's "The Adventure of the Five Orange Pips," was rather a bore and Roy William Neill's efforts to instill some life into it were unsuccessful.

In brief, the story deals with The Good Comrades, a unique club of group-insured men, who reside in a dreary Scottish mansion. One-by-one, the club members receive envelopes containing orange pips in decreasing numbers. The recipient of each is later found murdered—his body mutilated beyond recognition.

Sherlock Holmes, aided by Watson and Inspector Lestrade (Dennis Hoey), enters the case. Eventually, all of the members disappear, with the exception of Alastair (Aubrey Mather). Watson notes that the favorite pipe tobacco of one of the "deceased" is missing and, immediately thereafter, the good doctor vanishes.

In a cave beneath the mansion, Holmes and Lestrade discover a bound-and-gagged Watson and the answer to the riddle: The Good Comrades are not dead, but had faked their own murders in order to collect the insurance money. Their "bodies" were recently buried corpses—borrowed from the local cemetery.

Rathbone seemed to be a bit weary of the detective role by this time. His press notices, as well as those for the film itself, were generally disappointing.

CRITICAL COMMENT:

"But neither the mystery nor the solution are anything to get nervous about, and Mr. Rathbone's performance of the detective is as pedestrian as a cop's on patrol."

New York Times

THE WOMAN IN GREEN

(1945)

A Universal Release. Produced and Directed by Roy William Neill. Based on the characters created by Sir Arthur Conan Doyle. Screenplay: Bertram Millhauser. Photography: Virgil Miller. Musical Director: Mark Levant. Art Directors: John B. Goodman and Martin Obzina. Editor: Edward Curtiss. Released: June 1945. 63 minutes.

CAST: *Sherlock Holmes*: Basil Rathbone; *Dr. Watson*: Nigel Bruce; *Lydia*: Hillary Brooke; *Professor Moriarty*: Henry Daniell; *Fenwick*: Paul Cavanagh; *Inspector Gregson*: Matthew Boulton; *Maude*: Eve Amber; *Onslow*: Frederic Worlock; *Williams*: Tom Bryson; *Crandon*: Sally Shepherd; *Mrs. Hudson*: Mary Gordon.

THE FILM: *The Woman in Green* had the potential of being a first-class thriller. Certainly, it offered a fascinating story, which "reincarnated" Professor Moriarty in the person of Henry Daniell. In fact, both Rathbone and executive producer Howard S. Benedict thought Daniell to be "the best Moriarty of all."

The Woman in Green: **With Sally Shepherd and Nigel Bruce.**

The Woman in Green: **With Nigel Bruce.**

However, the film's problems far outweighed its assets: Bertram Millhauser wrote a screenplay, suggested by Doyle's "The Adventure of the Empty House," that was inferior to his earlier work; Roy Neill's direction seemed lackluster; production values were shoddy; and, once again, Rathbone appeared bored with his role. In sum, the picture was a big disappointment.

Scotland Yard asks Sherlock Holmes to assist them in the investigation of a series of murders, in which the victims, all beautiful women, have had their right forefinger amputated after death.

The detective suspects that the crimes are the work of his old nemesis, Professor Moriarty, and he sets out to trap the fiend.

The killings are part of an elaborate plan to blackmail Sir George Fenwick (Paul Cavanagh), who is murdered by Moriarty after Holmes is retained by the gentleman's daughter (Sally Shepherd) to check into his strange behavior. The sleuth surmises that Fenwick was hypnotized into believing he was responsible for the "Finger Murders."

Lydia (Hillary Brooke), an attractive and cunning hypnotist, has been working with Moriarty on his scheme. Holmes allows her to entice him to her apartment, where she "puts him under." Moriarty enters and is about to arrange for the detective to fall off a balcony when Watson arrives with the police. In attempting to escape, the evil professor falls from a rooftop. Holmes, of course, was never actually hypnotized, but stalling for time until help arrived.

Dennis Hoey wasn't available to reprise his role of Inspector Lestrade for this episode of the series, so a new character was created to represent Scotland Yard—Inspector Gregson, competently portrayed by Matthew Boulton.

Hillary Brooke, making her third appearance in the Holmes films, recalls that the projects were always enjoyable to work in: "Basil was constantly fooling around on the set. We had a scene in the picture where the two of us were in a cocktail lounge. For some reason, the sequence was taking a long time to shoot, so, to break the monotony, we pretended we were getting drunk . . . slurring our speech and the like . . . with the scene ending by both of us sliding under the table and 'passing out.'

"Willy Bruce was also a lot of fun . . . always 'ho-ho-ho-ing' and blustering about. The only complainer on the set was Henry Daniell . . . invariably getting upset when things were delayed. He was a great Moriarty though."

CRITICAL COMMENT:

"Basil Rathbone and Nigel Bruce as Holmes and Watson . . . play their respective roles in a manner now best described as 'familiar.' "

New York Times

The Woman in Green: **With Henry Daniell, Hillary Brooke, and Percival Vivian.**

PURSUIT TO ALGIERS

(1945)

A Universal Picture. Produced and Directed by Roy William Neill. Based on the characters created by Sir Arthur Conan Doyle. Screenplay: Leonard Lee. Camera: Paul Ivano. Musical Director: Edgar Fairchild. Art Directors: John B. Goodman and Martin Obzina. Editor: Saul A. Goodkind. Released: October 1945. 65 minutes.

CAST: *Sherlock Holmes*: Basil Rathbone; *Dr. Watson*: Nigel Bruce; *Sheila*: Marjorie Riordan; *Agatha Dunham*: Rosalind Ivan; *Mirko*: Martin Kosleck; *Jodri*: John Abbott; *Prime Minister*: Fredric Worlock; *Sanford*: Morton Lowry; *Nikolas*: Leslie Vincent.

THE FILM: "Routine" is the most generous description that can be applied to this shabby entry in the Sherlock Holmes series. *Pursuit to Algiers* was inferior to the preceding episodes in every respect: story, direction, acting (with the possible exception of Nigel Bruce's comedy antics), and production values.

Pursuit to Algiers: **With Leslie Vincent and Nigel Bruce.**

Pursuit to Algiers: **Sven Hugo Borg, Leslie Vincent, Basil Rathbone, Nigel Bruce, and Martin Kosleck.**

The story took place on board an ocean liner and had Holmes and Watson escorting Nikolas (Leslie Vincent), the king of Ruritania, to Algiers, where he is to be met by representatives of his government. The ship's passengers include several assassins, who attempt to do in the detective, as well as the young monarch.

The villains make their final move when the ship anchors off Algiers. They subdue Holmes and kidnap Nikolas. Watson arrives with the Ruritanian agents and informs Holmes that the spies have been captured and the king freed. The sleuth reveals that the young man Watson believed to be Nikolas was, in fact, a decoy and the real monarch has been on board all along—masquerading as a steward.

Holmes's closing line is amusing, considering the mediocre quality of the production: "Watson, let me advise you. If you ever consider taking up another profession, never even *think* of becoming an actor."

The fact that the villains are captured *off-screen* is typical of the second-rate treatment this project received. The audience is only told of this event, presumably because the producers did not wish to spend the time and money required to film it.

Martin Kosleck, appearing for the third time with Rathbone,

Pursuit to Algiers: **With Marjorie Riordan and Leslie Vincent.**

played one of the spies. He reflects that he recommended an associate for a role in the picture: "The actor gave a terrible performance. One day, near the end of filming, Basil came up to me and kidded, 'Martin, you are such a good actor. How can you have a friend so untalented?' "

CRITICAL COMMENT:

"Neill's direction keeps the matters on the move, and he obtains expected performances from Basil Rathbone as Holmes and Nigel Bruce as Watson."

Hollywood Reporter

TERROR BY NIGHT

(1946)

A Universal Release. Directed by Roy William Neill. Executive Producer: Howard Benedict. Based on the characters created by Sir Arthur Conan Doyle. Screenplay: Frank Gruber. Camera: Maury Gertsman. Released: February 1946. 60 minutes.

CAST: *Sherlock Holmes*: Basil Rathbone; *Dr. Watson*: Nigel Bruce; *Maj. Duncan Bleek*: Alan Mowbray; *Lestrade*: Dennis Hoey; *Vivian Vedder*: Renee Godfrey; *Lady Margaret*: Mary Forbes; *Train Attendant*: Billy Bevan; *Prof. Kilbane*: Frederic Worlock; *Conductor*: Leyland Hodgson; *Ronald Carstairs*: Geoffrey Steele; *McDonald*: Boyd Davis; *Mrs. Shallcross*: Janet Murdoch; *Sands*: Skelton Knaggs.

THE FILM: Frank Gruber's tightly-plotted screenplay was responsible for this episode being one of the best in the Universal series. Perhaps the quality of the script inspired both Rathbone and direc-

Terror By Night: **Renee Godfrey, Billy Bevan, Basil Rathbone, Dennis Hoey, and Nigel Bruce.**

Terror By Night: **With Dennis Hoey, Billy Bevan, Alan Mowbray, and Nigel Bruce.**

tor Roy Neill to take a renewed interest in their jobs, as their respective performances in this picture were vastly improved over the dull work they had contributed to the previous three installments.

Virtually the entire action of the film, which ran a scant but fast-moving sixty minutes, takes place on a train bound from London to Edinburgh. Holmes and Watson are aboard to guard a priceless diamond, "The Star of Rhodesia." Inspector Lestrade (Dennis Hoey), embarking on a fishing trip, is also along for the ride.

Following the theft of the stone and the murder of its owner, the private detective interrogates the train's colorful group of passengers and discovers that the killer, Sands (Skelton Knaggs), was brought aboard in the false bottom of a coffin.

Holmes suspects Colonel Sebastian Moran, an associate of the late Professor Moriarty, as being the mastermind behind the crime. Sands murders two more people with small poison darts shot from an air gun and is then done in himself by Moran, who has boarded the train under the guise of Major Duncan Bleek (Alan Mowbray), an old friend of Watson's.

Ultimately, Holmes exposes Bleek's true identity. With the help of Lestrade, he recovers the gem and prevents the criminal's henchmen from aiding his escape.

Terror by Night marked Dennis Hoey's final appearance in the series. Other interesting portrayals were provided by Alan Mowbray, as a superb heavy, and silent movie comedian Billy Bevan in the role of a train attendant.

CRITICAL COMMENT:
"Mr. Rathbone is silky smooth as usual."

New York Times

HEARTBEAT

(1946)

An RKO Release of a Robert and Raymond Hakim Production. Directed by Sam Wood. From an original screenplay by Hans Wilhelm, Max Kolpe, and Michael Duran. Adaptation: Morrie Ryskind. Additional Dialogue: Rowland Leigh. Photography: Joseph Valentine. Musical Score: Paul Misraki. Musical Director: C. Bakaleinikoff. Song, "Can You Guess," by Paul Misraki and Ervin Drake. Released: April 1946. 101 minutes.

CAST: *Arlette*: Ginger Rogers; *Pierre*: Jean Pierre Aumont; *Ambassador*: Adolphe Menjou; *Prof. Aristide*: Basil Rathbone; *Baron Dvorak*: Eduardo Ciannelli; *Yves Cadubert*: Mikhail Rasumny; *Roland Medeville*: Melville Cooper; *Ambassador's Wife*: Mona Maris; *Minister*: Henry Stephenson.

THE FILM: The producers of *Heartbeat* intended for their picture to be a French-style romantic comedy. Unfortunately, due to a

Heartbeat: **With Ginger Rogers.**

Heartbeat: **With Players.**

weak screenplay and the humorless direction of Sam Wood, the final result wasn't very funny.

The plot concerns Arlette (Ginger Rogers), who has recently graduated from a school for pickpockets run by Professor Aristide (Rathbone). She attends an embassy party, where she meets Pierre (Jean Pierre Aumont), a diplomat. A romance develops between the couple and he subsequently reforms her.

Rathbone's scenes, although limited to the early part of the film, were the production's most amusing. The British actor contributed his usual interesting performance to the project.

Conversely, Ginger Rogers, a talented actress/comedienne, was hampered by her poorly developed role. The star remembers Rathbone as "a marvelous actor, congenial and amusing. He did his job well."

CRITICAL COMMENT:

"Most memorable performances are delivered by Rathbone, as the professor, and Mikhail Rasumny, an inept pupil who befriends Miss Rogers."

Variety

DRESSED TO KILL

(1946)

A Universal Release. Produced and Directed by Roy William Neill. Executive Producer: Howard Benedict. From a story by Sir Arthur Conan Doyle. Adaptation: Frank Gruber. Screenplay: Leonard Lee. Camera: Maury Gertsman. Editor: Saul Goodkind. Musical Director: Milton Rosen. Art Directors: Jack Otterson and Martin Obzina. Released: May 1946. 72 minutes.

CAST: *Sherlock Holmes*: Basil Rathbone; *Dr. Watson*: Nigel Bruce; *Hilda Courtney*: Patricia Morison; *Gilbert Emery*: Edmond Breon; *Colonel Cavanaugh*: Frederic Worlock; *Inspector Hopkins*: Carl Harbord; *Hamid*: Harry Cording.

THE FILM: Even very successful movie series must sometime end and most do so on a sour note. Universal's Sherlock Holmes films were no exception. *Dressed to Kill* was, without doubt, a "lemon."

Rathbone and Bruce seemed to be totally uninterested in Leonard Lee's inauspicious screenplay and Roy Neill's direction lacked any

Dressed to Kill: **With Patricia Morison.**

Dressed to Kill: **With Nigel Bruce.**

Dressed to Kill: **With Player.**

inspiration whatsoever. Supporting performances were inferior to those in earlier episodes of the series, as were the production values, which appeared paltry.

In this adventure, Sherlock Holmes is on the trail of stolen Bank of England engraving plates. The key to finding their hiding place can be found in the coded tunes from three music boxes, manufactured in Dartmoor Prison. The detective's antagonists in this instance are Hilda Courtney (Patricia Morison) and her henchmen.

As he did in such previous installments as *Pearl of Death* and *Sherlock Holmes and the Secret Weapon,* the sleuth races his opponents in an attempt to gain possession of the music boxes first.

Ultimately, the musical messages are decoded, revealing that the plates are hidden at the museum home of Dr. Samuel Johnson. Accompanied by a representative of Scotland Yard, Holmes thwarts the criminals when they attempt to retrieve the stolen engravings.

Dressed to Kill was a dismal conclusion to an often exceptional motion picture series.

CRITICAL COMMENT:

"Basil Rathbone and Nigel Bruce are up to usual form, as Holmes and Dr. Watson, respectively. . . ."

Variety

ICHABOD AND MR. TOAD

(1949)

A Walt Disney Production. Released by RKO Radio Pictures. Technicolor. Directed by Jack Kinney, Clyde Geronimi, and James Algar. Production Supervisor: Ben Sharpsteen. Based on *The Legend of Sleepy Hollow* by Washington Irving and *The Wind in the Willows* by Kenneth Grahame. Story: Erdman Penner, Winston Hibler, Joe Rinaldi, Ted Sears, Homer Brightman, and Harry Reeves. Directing Animators: Franklin Thomas, Oliver Johnston, Jr., Wolfgang Reitherman, Milt Kahl, John Lounsbery, and Ward Kimball. Musical Director: Oliver Wallace. Vocal Arrangements: Ken Darby. Songs: "Ichabod," "Katrina," "The Headless Horseman" by Don Raye, Gene DePaul. "Merrily on Our Way," music by Frank Churchill and Charles Wolcott, lyrics by Larry Morey and Ray Gilbert. Film Editor: John O. Young. Released: October 1949. 68 minutes.

CAST: *Ichabod* narrated by Bing Crosby. *Mr. Toad* narrated by Basil Rathbone. *Voices*: *Mr. Toad*: Eric Blore; *Cyril*: Pat O'Malley; *Water Rat*: Claud Allister; *Prosecutor*: John Ployardt; *Mole*: Collin Campbell; *Angus MacBadger*: Campbell Grant; *Winky*: Ollie Wallace.

THE FILM: Originally titled *Two Fabulous Characters*, the picture was hailed by most critics as being Disney's best animated feature in some time. Rathbone was an effective narrator for Kenneth Grahame's *The Wind in the Willows*, which comprised the first and better half of the film. Bing Crosby took over the narration chores in the second part, *The Legend of Sleepy Hollow* by Washington Irving.

CRITICAL COMMENT:
"Basil Rathbone's clipped narration is entirely in keeping with the tone of this fairy tale of rural England."

New York Times

Publicity shot from Ichabod and Mr. Toad.

CASANOVA'S BIG NIGHT

(1954)

A Paramount Production and Release. Technicolor. Directed by Norman Z. McLeod. Produced by Paul Jones. From a story by Aubrey Wisberg. Screenplay: Hal Kanter and Edmund Hartmann. Camera: Lionel Lindon. Art Directors: Hal Pereira and Albert Nozaki. Editor: Ellsworth Hoagland. Score: Lyn Murray. Song: Jay Livingston and Ray Evans. Released: March 1954. 85 minutes.

CAST: *Pippo Popolino*: Bob Hope; *Francesca Bruni*: Joan Fontaine; *Lucio*: Basil Rathbone; *Elena DiGambetta*: Audrey Dalton; *Stefano DiGambetta*: Hugh Marlowe; *The Doge of Venice*: Arnold Moss; *Foressi*: John Carradine; *Maggiorin*: John Hoyt; *Duchess of Genoa*: Hope Emerson; *Raphaele*: Robert Hutton; *Emo*: Lon Chaney; *Bragadin*: Raymond Burr; *Corfa*: Primo Carnera. *Also*: Frieda Inescort, Frank Puglia, and Paul Cavanagh. *Unbilled Guest Appearance*: Vincent Price as *Casanova*.

THE FILM: After an eight-year absence, Rathbone returned to the screen to play straight man for the antics of Bob Hope. *Casanova's*

Casanova's Big Night: **With Bob Hope.**

Big Night (working title: *Mr. Casanova*) was a predictable farce—typical of most of the comedian's films for Paramount.

Hope was Pippo Popolino, a tailor's apprentice, called upon to pose as the great lover, Casanova (Vincent Price), who has skipped town to avoid paying his creditors. With the help of Francesca Bruni (Joan Fontaine) and Casanova's valet, Lucio (Rathbone), Pippo takes on an assignment to retrieve the crested petticoat of a Venetian noblewoman. Unknown to Pippo, his success in the venture could be the cause of a war. As with all Hope pictures, the comedian performs the noble act, which brings about a happy ending.

Rathbone played well with Hope and the comic considered the actor a definite asset to the film: "It was a privilege to work with Basil. Character actors like him made entertainers like myself look good on the screen. He was terribly charming and funny. A great guy."

CRITICAL COMMENT:

"Basil Rathbone gives a slick performance as the valet of the real Casanova."

Los Angeles Examiner

WE'RE NO ANGELS

(1955)

A Paramount Picture. In VistaVision. Technicolor. Directed by Michael Curtiz. Produced by Pat Duggan. From the play, *La Cuisine des Anges*, by Albert Husson. Screenplay: Ranald MacDougall. Photography: Loyal Griggs. Editor: Arthur Schmidt. Art Directors: Hal Pereira and Roland Anderson. Costumes: Mary Grant. Music: Frederick Hollander. Songs: "Sentimental Moments" by Frederick Hollander and Ralph Freed; "Ma France Bien-Aimee" by G. Martini and Roger Wagner. Released: June 1955. 103 minutes.

CAST: *Joseph*: Humphrey Bogart; *Albert*: Aldo Ray; *Jules*: Peter Ustinov; *Amelie Ducotel*: Joan Bennett; *Andre Trochard*: Basil Rathbone; *Felix Ducotel*: Leo G. Carroll; *Paul Trochard*: John Baer; *Isabelle Ducotel*: Gloria Talbott; *Madame Parole*: Lea Penman; *Arnaud*: John Smith.

THE FILM: *Angels Cooking* was the working title of this pleasant comedy, an independent adaptation of Albert Husson's play, *La Cuisine des Anges*. The screenplay was written by Ranald MacDougall and was *not* based on the 1953 Broadway success, *My Three Angels*

We're No Angels: **With Humphrey Bogart.**

We're No Angels: **Peter Ustinov, Rathbone, Humphrey Bogart, and Aldo Ray.**

by Sam and Bella Spewack, which also credited the Husson play as its original source.

Although Michael Curtiz's direction was rather slowly paced, the film still provided enough laughs to make audiences happy—and, with Humphrey Bogart as its star, the picture was a commercial success.

The story tells of three escaped convicts from Devil's Island, Joseph (Bogart), Albert (Aldo Ray), and Jules (Peter Ustinov), who befriend a kind shopkeeper (Leo G. Carroll) and his family (Joan Bennett and Gloria Talbott) on Christmas Eve.

When a tyrannical relative, Andre Trochard (Rathbone), and his nephew (John Baer) pay the family a visit in order to inspect the firm's books, the convicts attempt to help their friends. It seems that the shopkeeper, Felix Ducotel, only *manages* the store for Trochard. Felix, unfortunately, has never kept proper books and his employer, after scanning the ledgers, suspects him of embezzlement.

Trochard insists on examining a basket containing Albert's pet snake and the reptile's poisonous bite soon sends him to his just reward. His nephew meets a similar end when he encounters the pet while picking his dead uncle's pocket.

The final order of business for the convicts is to find a future husband for Miss Ducotel. A young naval officer is "drafted" for the job.

Having solved the Ducotels' problems, the three "angels" discover they are homesick for their prison and decide to return. After all, if they escaped once, they can do it again.

Irene Dunne, Gig Young, and John Derek were originally negotiated to play the roles that were subsequently essayed by Miss Bennett, Ustinov, and Baer.

Rathbone's assignment was a relatively short one, but he managed to inject the proper comedic touch into his portrayal of the nasty uncle.

Aldo Ray remembers the actor as being quite gregarious: "Basil was a hell of a nice guy and a constant talker. Between scenes, he kept the cast entertained with his show business anecdotes."

CRITICAL COMMENT:

"Rathbone plays the Mr. Witch uncle in just the right blend of villainy and exaggeration."

Los Angeles Examiner

THE COURT JESTER

(1956)

A Paramount Release of a Dena Production. In VistaVision. Technicolor. Written, Produced, and Directed by Norman Panama and Melvin Frank. Camera: Ray June. Art Directors: Hal Pereira and Roland Anderson. Editor: Tom McAdoo. Songs: Sylvia Fine and Sammy Cahn. Music Scored and Conducted by Victor Schoen. Choreography: James Starbuck. Released: January 1956. 101 minutes.

CAST: *Hawkins*: Danny Kaye; *Maid Jean*: Glynis Johns; *Sir Ravenhurst*: Basil Rathbone; *Princess Gwendolyn*: Angela Lansbury; *King Roderick*: Cecil Parker; *Griselda*: Mildred Natwick; *Sir Griswold*: Robert Middleton; *Sir Locksley*: Michael Pate; *Captain of the Guard*: Herbert Rudley; *Fergus*: Noel Drayton; *The Fox*: Edward Ashley; *Giacomo*: John Carradine; *Sir Brockhurst*: Alan Napier. *Also*: Lewis Martin, Patrick Aherne, Richard Kean, and Hermine's Midgets.

The Court Jester: **With Hermine's Midgets, Danny Kaye, and Glynis Johns.**

The Court Jester: **With Alan Napier.**

THE FILM: Rathbone had a grand time spoofing himself in this delightful Danny Kaye vehicle for Paramount. According to the comedian: "Basil's roles in movies like *Robin Hood* and *Zorro* made him the obvious choice to play our dastardly Sir Ravenhurst."

The story concerns a band of rebels, led by The Fox (Edward Ashley), who attempt to regain the English throne for its rightful heir—an infant. The unscrupulous King Roderick (Cecil Parker) had usurped the crown years before.

In order to gain entrance to the castle, one of the outlaws, Hubert Hawkins (Kaye), knocks out a court jester (John Carradine) and switches places with him. Once inside, he discovers that Maid Jean (Glynis Johns), while secretly transporting the young monarch, had been abducted by the royal guards and brought to the fortress also. Fortunately, the captors are unaware that the child is hidden in Jean's cart.

The remainder of the film concerns the efforts of Hubert and Jean to keep the tot out of the clutches of Roderick's chief henchman, Sir Ravenhurst (Rathbone), and to aid The Fox in capturing the palace. Naturally, Hubert's methods of accomplishing these feats places him in one absurd predicament after another—all of which makes for a very funny motion picture.

Sylvia Fine (Mrs. Kaye) and Sammy Cahn delivered a charming score for the production, which included several memorable tunes, including "The Maladjusted Jester" and "Life Could Not Better Be."

Basil Rathbone, Hollywood's expert swordsman, found his match in Danny Kaye. Although the comedian had virtually no experience with rapiers prior to doing the film, after two weeks of instruction from both a fencing master and the British actor, he was able to out-fight Rathbone to the point that the latter had to be doubled in some of the long shots. Sylvia Fine explains: "Danny's mind works like a camera and he picks things up very quickly. Basil was well into his sixties when we did this film and Danny's movements were just too quick for him.

"Basil was marvelous to work with. He really added stature to the picture."

CRITICAL COMMENT:

". . . and Basil Rathbone is all that could be desired as a villainous straight man."

Hollywood Reporter

THE BLACK SLEEP

(1956)

A United Artists Release of an Aubrey Schenck, Howard W. Koch (Bel-Air) Production. Directed by Reginald LeBorg. From a story by Gerald Drayson Adams. Screenplay: John C. Higgins. Camera: Gordon Avil. Editor: John F. Schreyer. Music: Les Baxter. Released: June 1956. 82 minutes.

CAST: *Sir Joel Cadman*: Basil Rathbone; *Odo*: Akim Tamiroff; *Mungo*: Lon Chaney; *Borg*: John Carradine; *Casimir*: Bela Lugosi; *Dr. Gordon Ramsey*: Herbert Rudley; *Laurie*: Patricia Blake; *Daphne*: Phyllis Stanley; *Curry*: Tor Johnson; *Nancy*: Sally Yarnell; *K-6*: George Sawaya; *Miss Daly*: Claire Carleton.

THE FILM: The title of this mild horror film refers to a fictional East Indian drug, which, when administered to an individual, puts him into a cataleptic state.

Rathbone was Sir Joel Cadman, a prominent British surgeon. The year—1872.

Cadman gives the drug to his former student, Dr. Gordon Ramsey (Herbert Rudley). Ramsey is in prison, awaiting execution for a

The Black Sleep: **With Akim Tamiroff.**

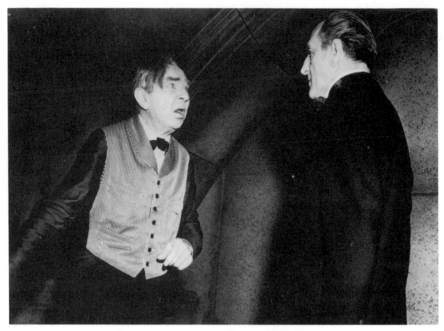

The Black Sleep: **With Bela Lugosi.**

murder he did not commit. When the authorities find him under the influence of the potion, they believe him to be dead and turn his "body" over to Cadman. The doctor revives the "dead man" and Ramsey agrees to assist his benefactor with his research on the human brain.

The pair travel to Cadman's estate outside of London. Shortly after his arrival, Ramsey learns that Sir Joel is experimenting on the brains of living people, in order that he may learn enough to operate on his wife, who has been in a coma for a year due to a tumor. Cadman's victims are left with mutilated brains, reducing them to nothing more than freaks.

A romance develops between Ramsey and a resident nurse, Laurie (Patricia Blake). Her father was one of Cadman's early guinea pigs. He is now the psychopathic Mungo (Lon Chaney), roaming through the house—attacking the staff.

The freaks, led by Borg (John Carradine), break out of their chains. They kill Cadman, his wife, and Mungo; however Ramsey and Laurie are able to escape their wrath.

Budgeted at approximately two hundred-fifty thousand dollars, the production's strongest asset was its cast, which included three performers (Chaney, Carradine, and Bela Lugosi) closely associated with the horror genre. Their talents were sadly wasted, as no overall mood of terror or suspense was created in the film.

Lugosi, in one of his last screen performances, found his role to be frustrating. The actor played a mute, yet, in order to call attention to himself, kept begging director Reginald LeBorg for some dialogue. To placate the former Count Dracula, LeBorg shot a few close-ups of him, which were not utilized in the final cut.

The director recalls that, whenever Rathbone blew a line, he would scold himself. On the final day of filming, the actor was having problems with a particularly long sequence and, between takes, the cast and crew could hear his angry voice, "Damn it, Basil! Get it right next time."

CRITICAL COMMENT:

"Rathbone is quite credible as the surgeon, enough so that the brain operations he performs will horrify many viewers."

Variety

THE LAST HURRAH

(1958)

A Columbia Picture. Produced and Directed by John Ford. From the novel by Edwin O'Connor. Screenplay: Frank Nugent. Photography: Charles Lawton, Jr. Editor: Jack Murray. Art Director: Robert Peterson. Released: November 1958. 121 minutes.

CAST: *Skeffington*: Spencer Tracy; *Adam Caulfield*: Jeffrey Hunter; *Maeve Caulfield*: Dianne Foster; *John Gorman*: Pat O'Brien; *Norman Cass, Sr.*: Basil Rathbone; *The Cardinal*: Donald Crisp; *Cuke Gillen*: James Gleason; *Ditto Boland*: Edward Brophy; *Amos Force*: John Carradine; *Roger Sugrue*: Willis Bouchey; *Bishop Gardner*: Basil Ruysdael; *Sam Weinberg*: Ricardo Cortez; *Hennessey*: Wallace Ford; *Festus Garvey*: Frank McHugh; *Gert*: Anna Lee; *Delia*: Jane Darwell; *Msgr. Killian*: Ken Curtis. Also: Carleton Young, Frank Albertson, Bob Sweeney, William Leslie, O. Z. Whitehead, Arthur Walsh, Ruth Warren, Charles Fitzsimmons, Helen Westcott, James Flavin, and Frank Sully.

The Last Hurrah: **Edward Brophy, James Gleason, Basil Rathbone, Ricardo Cortez, Carleton Young, and Pat O'Brien.**

THE FILM: Based on Edwin O'Connor's best-selling novel, *The Last Hurrah* proved to be an excellent vehicle for the talents of Spencer Tracy, as well as several top character stars of the 1930s and 40s. John Ford directed this fine sentimental film, a fictionalized account of the career of Boston's former mayor, James M. Curley.

Briefly, the screenplay tells of Irish Mayor Frank Skeffington's (Tracy) final campaign for re-election. He wants one more term in office—a "last hurrah." The mayor invites his nephew, Adam Caulfield (Jeffrey Hunter), a syndicated writer for the opposition newspaper owned by Amos Force (John Carradine), to observe the campaign.

In a surprise upset, Skeffington loses the election and, shortly thereafter, suffers a heart attack, which proves to be fatal.

Rathbone, working for the first time with both Tracy and director Ford, was Norman Cass, an influential Boston banker and political enemy of Skeffington. When Cass's bank refuses to grant a loan for a new city housing project, the mayor appoints Norman Jr. (O. Z. Whitehead) fire commissioner and threatens to let the seemingly retarded young man disgrace the family name—unless his father backs down. Skeffington gets what he wants, except that in retaliation, Cass now throws his full financial support behind the opposition candidate.

Rathbone was excellent in the short, but impressive, role. Ford had the actor play *under* Carradine, who was always screaming about Tracy's activties. The actor's part called for him to lose his temper only once—when his family name was placed in jeopardy.

Pat O'Brien recalls that both the director and Tracy had a great admiration for Rathbone. John Carradine, a member of Ford's "stock company," agrees and adds: "John Ford didn't usually like actors trained in the theatre and would often ridicule them. He *didn't* ridicule Basil Rathbone."

CRITICAL COMMENT:

". . . and Basil Rathbone is malevolently authoritative as Tracy's arch-enemy."

Variety

THE MAGIC SWORD

(1962)

A United Artists Release of a Bert I. Gordon Production. Eastman Color. Produced and Directed by Bert I. Gordon. From a story by Mr. Gordon. Screenplay: Bernard Schoenfeld. Photography: Paul Vogel. Editor: Harry Gerstad. Art Director: Franz Bachelin. Special Effects: Milt Rice. Music: Richard Markowitz. Released: April 1962. 80 minutes.

CAST: *Lodac*: Basil Rathbone; *Sybil*: Estelle Winwood; *Princess Helene*: Anne Helm; *St. George*: Gary Lockwood; *Sir Branton*: Liam Sullivan; *Sir Patrick*: John Mauldin; *Sir Dennis*: Jacques Gallo; *Sir Ulrich*: Leroy Johnson; *Sir Pedro*: David Cross; *Sir James*: Angus Duncan. *Also*: Taldo Kenyon, Maila Nurmi, Jack Kosslyn, Lorrie Richards, Ann Graves, Marlene Callahan, Merritt Stone, Danielle de Metz, and Dick Kiel.

THE FILM: Designed to attract a juvenile audience, *The Magic Sword* (working title: *St. George and the Seven Curses*) was an inexpensively produced "epic," dealing with knighthood in fourth-century England.

The Magic Sword.

The Magic Sword: **With Liam Sullivan.**

The picture told of George (Gary Lockwood), the adopted son of Sybil (Estelle Winwood), a well-meaning sorceress. With the help of his magic sword and armor, as well as six brave knights, George sets out to rescue the Princess Helene (Anne Helm) from the evil sorcerer, Lodac (Rathbone). Lodac hampers the young man's attempts to save his lady fair by laying down seven horrible curses (such as a twenty-five foot tall Ogre, a boiling crater, a fire ball, and so forth), which, ultimately, claim the lives of all George's companions. However, our hero reaches Lodac's castle, slays a two-headed dragon, and rescues Helene. Sybil, in the form of a black panther, kills the wicked sorcerer.

As would be expected, the veterans in the cast delivered the best performances. Rathbone was an effective heavy and Estelle Winwood was fun as the flighty sorceress. Gary Lockwood came through with a properly heroic characterization, but the rest of the players were less than adequate.

Director Bert I. Gordon's approach to the project was somewhat confusing. It was never quite clear if the picture was intended to be a spoof of knighthood or a straight adventure story. The production also suffered from cheaply built sets and drab-looking costumes. The special effects were acceptable.

According to Lockwood: "It was an insignificant film. We all did it for the money and nothing else."

CRITICAL COMMENT:

"Basil Rathbone is well-cast as an awesome and menacing sorcerer."

Hollywood Reporter

TALES OF TERROR

(1962)

An American-International Release of a Roger Corman Production. Color. Directed by Roger Corman. Based on stories by Edgar Allan Poe. Screenplay: Richard Matheson. Camera: Floyd Crosby. Editor: Anthony Carras. Art Director: Daniel Haller. Released: May 1962. 90 minutes.

CAST: "Morella"—*Locke*: Vincent Price; *Leonora*: Maggie Pierce; *Morella*: Leona Gage; *Driver*: Ed Cobb. "The Black Cat"—*Fortunato*: Vincent Price; *Montresor*: Peter Lorre; *Annabel*: Joyce Jameson; *Policeman*: Lennie Weinrib; *Bartender*: Wally Campo. "The Case of M. Valdemar"—*Valdemar*: Vincent Price; *Carmichael*: Basil Rathbone; *Helene*: Debra Paget; *Dr. James*: David Frankham.

THE FILM: During the 1960s, American-International produced a generally excellent series of color horror pictures, which were loosely based on the short stories of Edgar Allan Poe. Vincent Price was the star of virtually all of the films.

Tales of Terror, produced and directed by Roger Corman, was a

Tales of Terror: **With Debra Paget and Vincent Price.**

Tales of Terror: **With Debra Paget and David Frankham.**

trilogy of Poe stories—"Morella," "The Black Cat," and "The Case of M. Valdemar." Price appeared in all three segments, however Rathbone was only in the final one.

Price was Valdemar, an elderly gentleman, dying from an incurable disease. He has come under the influence of an unscrupulous hypnotist, Carmichael (Rathbone), who mesmerizes his patient, so he will feel no pain.

Ultimately, Carmichael hypnotizes the old man on his deathbed. Although his body dies, Valdemar's spirit remains aware and is able to communicate. Helene (Debra Paget), Valdemar's wife, and Dr. James (David Frankham) beg the hypnotist to release her husband in order that he may find peace. He refuses and keeps Valdemar in this suspended state for months.

Finally, even Valdemar begs for release. Carmichael agrees, but *only* if Helene will marry him.

Valdemar rises from his bed to protect his wife, who is being assaulted by the hypnotist. The doctor rushes into the room to discover his patient's body lying on top of Carmichael's.

Rathbone gave an effective performance in this above-average horror picture, as did the rest of the cast.

Roger Corman recalls his experience directing the actor: "I found him to be an intelligent and disciplined performer.

"Most actors find it difficult to maintain the same level of performance from one camera set-up to another. This was not the case with Basil Rathbone. He was able to recreate his performance *exactly* . . . no matter how many times we repeated a scene."

CRITICAL COMMENT:

"Basil Rathbone has an icy authority as a Machiavellian hypnotist."

Hollywood Reporter

TWO BEFORE ZERO

(1962)

An Ellis Films Release of a Motion Picture Corporation of America Production. Directed by William D. Faralla. Produced by Fred A. Niles. Narration written by Bruce Henry. Camera: Jack Whitehead. Editor: Robert L. Sinise. Music: Sid Siegel. Released: October 1962. 78 minutes.

CAST: Basil Rathbone and Mary Murphy appearing as the narrators.

THE FILM: Rathbone and Mary Murphy served as on-screen narrators in this poorly conceived documentary that detailed the rise of communism, while tracing the lives of the men behind the movement. Newsreel footage was utilized to illustrate the points made by the two performers.

The film employed an unusual technique, whereby Rathbone, dressed in judicial robes, and Miss Murphy, attired in a flowing white gown, dramatized the communist double-talk and the naiveté of its victims.

Two Before Zero.

Two Before Zero: **With Mary Murphy.**

Most critics were unimpressed with the project and it did not receive a wide release.

CRITICAL COMMENT:
"The actors do the best they can with their lines, but the fault is not to be found in the stars."

Variety

THE COMEDY OF TERRORS

(1963)

An American-International Release. Color. Directed by Jacques Tourneur. Executive Producers: James H. Nicholson and Samuel Z. Arkoff. Producers: Anthony Carras and Richard Matheson. Screenplay: Richard Matheson. Camera: Floyd Crosby. Editor: Anthony Carras. Art Director: Daniel Haller. Special Effects: Pat Dinga. Music: Les Baxter. Costumes: Marjorie Corso. Released: December 1963. 88 minutes.

CAST: *Waldo Trumbull*: Vincent Price; *Amos Hinchley*: Boris Karloff; *Felix Gillie*: Peter Lorre; *John F. Black*: Basil Rathbone; *Caretaker*: Joe E. Brown; *Amaryllis Trumbull*: Joyce Jameson; *Mrs. Phipps*: Beverly Hills. *Also*: Paul Barsolow, Linda Rogers, Luree Nicholson, Buddy Mason, and Rhubarb.

THE FILM: As a change-of-pace from their Edgar Allan Poe series of chillers, American-International decided to produce a black comedy starring the members of their horror repertory company—Vincent Price, Peter Lorre, Boris Karloff, and Basil Rathbone. Although the

The Comedy of Terrors: **With Joe E. Brown.**

The Comedy of Terrors.

final picture was not entirely successful, it *was* a very funny movie, which has grown more popular through the years.

The story takes place in a small New England town during the 1890s. Amos Hinchley (Karloff), a senile, deaf old man of ninety-two, and his drunken son-in-law, Waldo Trumbull (Price), run the local funeral parlor. Trumbull works only when a financial crisis presents itself and, then, he usually goes out and "creates" a customer with the help of his assistant, Felix Gillie (Lorre).

The rent is past due and landlord John F. Black (Rathbone)

threatens eviction. To solve the problem, Trumbull decides to "do in" Mr. Black and make him the firm's next client. Black, a frustrated actor, obliges by *apparently* dropping dead from a stroke. In reality, he has only gone into a temporary cataleptic state.

The undertakers' efforts to deliver the "departed" to his final resting place are constantly being thwarted by the "departed" himself. Black awakens, discovers he is in a coffin, and asks: "What place is this?" Unfortunately, before he can escape, Trumbull and Gillie hit him on the head and return his "remains" to the casket.

After Black is placed in his family mausoleum, a caretaker (Joe E. Brown) hears a pounding noise from the coffin. He releases the enraged Black, who has regained consciousness. The landlord rampages through the Trumbull home, swinging an axe, until he is shot down by the inebriated undertaker.

Gillie and Trumbull's wife, Amaryllis (Joyce Jameson), are in love and decide to run off together. Hinchley, thinking his son-in-law is ill, gives him poison, which he believes to be medicine. The picture fades out and we hear Black's voice, "What place is this?"

Rathbone enjoyed doing *The Comedy of Terrors*, since it gave him the opportunity to work again with his old friends, Price, Karloff, and Lorre. He also considered the script the best he'd had in several years.

Price recalls the project: "I hadn't seen Basil for some time and was shocked at how much he had aged. But he was still marvelous in the picture and we had a lot of fun.

"I remember that he hated lying in that coffin. He was almost violent about getting out of it after every set-up . . . and he fought like hell to avoid retakes. I guess the thing made him nervous."

Rathbone contributed some of the picture's funniest moments. The sequence in which he "hams" a scene from *Macbeth* is classic. It was the last film of any real merit that the actor was associated with.

CRITICAL COMMENT:

"There is not much about timing and attack to be learned by such as Price, Lorre, Boris Karloff and Basil Rathbone. They play together smooth as silk, extracting the last ounce of fun from the mock-macabre events."

Hollywood Reporter

"Rathbone is excruciatingly funny in satirizing the Shakespearean actor, who, though ostensibly mortally wounded, keeps rising from the floor to give one more line."

Los Angeles Herald Examiner

PONTIUS PILATE

(1964)

An Italian/French Coproduction: Glomer Film, Rome - Lux C. C. F., Paris. A U. S. Films Release. In Cinemascope. Technicolor. Directed by Irving Rapper. Executive Producer: Enzo Merolle. Screenplay: Gino DeSanctis. Photography: Massimo Dallamano. Music: A. F. Lavagnino. Music Director: Pierluigi Urbini. Released: 1964. 100 minutes.

CAST: *Pontius Pilate*: Jean Marais; *Claudia Procula*: Jeanne Crain; *Caiaphas*: Basil Rathbone; *Sarah*: Leticia Roman; *Nicodemus*: Massimo Serato; *Galba*: Riccardo Garrone; *Barabbas*: Livio Lorenzon; *Jonathan*: Gianni Garko; *Jesus and Judas*: John Drew Barrymore. *Also*: Roger Treville, Carlo Giustini, Dante Di Paolo, Paul Muller, Alfredo Varelli, Manoela Ballard, Emma Baron, and Raffaella Carra.

THE FILM: This expensively mounted Italian/French co-production was filmed in Rome during the Summer of 1961—at the same time 20*th* Century-Fox was there shooting their disastrous *Cleopatra*, starring Elizabeth Taylor and Richard Burton. Unlike the more pres-

Pontius Pilate: **With Players.**

tigious picture, *Pontius Pilate* was not plagued with bad luck during
production, but, unfortunately, the final result wasn't much better
either. A rambling screenplay, Irving Rapper's lethargic direction,
poor dubbing, and, for the most part, uninteresting performances, de-
tracted from what could have been a fascinating character study of
the man who sent Christ to the Cross.

Produced under the title of *Ponzio Pilato,* the picture depicts the
political struggles of the Roman governor (Jean Marais) from the
time of his arrival in Palestine, until he is recalled to Rome after
Christ's death.

Rathbone's role was that of Caiaphas, chief rabbi of the Temple
in Caesarea. Although it was a relatively minor part, the actor under-
played his few good scenes to perfection. It was the most effective
performance in the picture. His confrontation scene with Christ, in
which he attempts to induce the Messiah to admit his heresy, is exceptional.

After Pilate has condemned Jesus, Caiaphas, who feared the
Prophet was a threat to his position of leadership over the Jews, is
taken aback when the governor writes the plaque to be nailed on
the Cross—"Jesus of Nazareth, King of the Jews."

Pontius Pilate: **With John Drew Barrymore, Jean Marais, and Players.**

Pontius Pilate: **With Jean Marais and Players.**

The elderly religious leader stammers: "Do not write 'King of the Jews,' but that he *said* he was King of the Jews!"

Pilate retorts: "It will say what I have written!"

Caiaphas realizes his efforts to rid himself of this Messiah have failed. Instead of a man, now he will have to contend with a martyr. It was a powerful moment in the drama.

Jean Marais's interpretation of Pilate was inferior to that of Rathbone's in *The Last Days of Pompeii*. The French actor seemed unable to convey the sensitivity that his colleague had brought to the role many years before. On the other hand, Jeanne Crain acquitted herself well in the part of the governor's wife, but John Drew Barrymore was a bit hammy as the guilt-ridden Judas. Barrymore, incidentally, also played Christ.

The epic was not released until 1964 and had little success in theaters.

QUEEN OF BLOOD

(1966)

An American-International Release of a George Edwards Production. Color. Written and Directed by Curtis Harrington. Camera: Vilis Lapenieks. Editor: Leo Shreve. Sound: Harold Garver. Art Director: Albert Locatelli. Music: Leonard Morand. Released: March 1966. 81 minutes.

CAST: *Allan*: John Saxon; *Dr. Farraday*: Basil Rathbone; *Laura*: Judi Meredith; *Paul*: Dennis Hopper; *Velana*: Florence Marly. *Also*: Robert Boon, Don Eitner, Virgil Frye, Robert Porter, Terry Lee, and Forrest Ackerman.

THE FILM: Roger Corman had purchased a Russian-made science-fiction movie about space travel, with the idea of spending an additional fifty thousand dollars to give it the appearance of being an American project.

He hired Rathbone (at three thousand dollars per day) and John Saxon for name value, as well as several other familiar faces. George Edwards was set to produce. Curtis Harrington wrote and directed

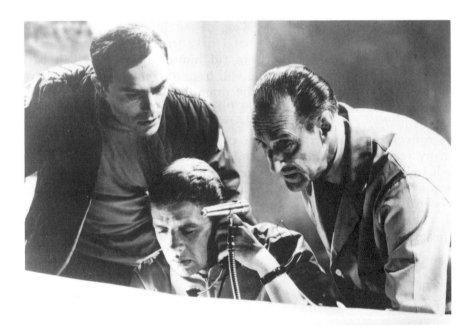

Queen of Blood: **With John Saxon and Player.**

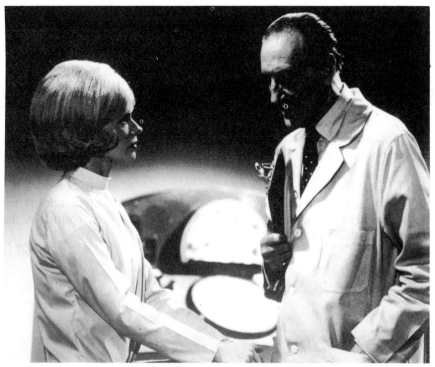

Queen of Blood: **With Judi Meredith.**

additional scenes, which were filmed during a one-week period on some cheaply constructed sets. All that remained of the original picture after this new material was cut into it were the special effects sequences and various long shots.

Queen of Blood was set in the year 1990. Dr. Farraday (Rathbone) dispatches astronauts Allan (Saxon), Laura (Judi Meredith), and Paul (Dennis Hopper), among others, to rescue a group of superior beings from another planet, who have crashed their space vehicle on Mars. Velana (Florence Marley) is the only survivor of the crash and she is taken aboard the spaceship from Earth.

Velana is a vampire. Unfortunately, before this is discovered, she kills two of the crew members, including Paul. Laura saves Allan from a similar fate. In doing so, she wounds Velana, a hemophiliac, causing her to bleed to death. However, the vampire has produced a considerable number of eggs, which Farraday, despite warnings from the surviving astronauts, plans to study.

The finished picture looked exactly like what it was—a patchwork. Nevertheless, the special-effects footage from the original Russian film was very good and the scenes on the spacecraft *after* the vampire is brought aboard had an eerie quality.

Rathbone, contracted for two days work on the film, was held over for a third. The actor had arrived at the studio to begin his role, only to discover that the set had not been completed. He amused himself for the better part of that first day by drinking coffee, munching doughnuts, and watching the producer, director, and art director working feverishly to get things ready, so filming could commence.

The British actor's part in the picture had him doing little more than radioing orders to the astronauts. The assignment required no special talent—just a well-known name for the marquee.

Reviews were generally poor.

CRITICAL COMMENT:

"Acting values are strong, Rathbone taking individual honors for credibility. He makes every moment he's on the screen count, in the accepted tradition of leading man performance."

Boxoffice

GHOST IN THE INVISIBLE BIKINI

(1966)

An American-International Release. Color. Directed by Don Weis. Executive Producers: James H. Nicholson and Samuel Z. Arkoff. Producer: Anthony Carras. From a story by Louis M. Heyward. Screenplay: Louis M. Heyward and Elwood Ullman. Camera: Stanley Cortez. Editor: Fred Feitshans. Released: April 1966. 82 minutes.

CAST: *Chuck Phillips*: Tommy Kirk; *Lilli Morton*: Deborah Walley; *Bobby*: Aron Kincaid; *Reginald Ripper*: Basil Rathbone; *Sinistra Ripper*: Quinn O'Hara; *Hiram Stokeley*: Boris Karloff; *The Ghost*: Susan Hart; *J. Sinister Hulk*: Jesse White; *Eric Von Zipper*: Harvey Lembeck; *Vicki*: Nancy Sinatra; *Lulu*: Claudia Martin; *Malcolm*: Francis X. Bushman; *Chicken Feather*: Benny Rubin; *Princess Yolanda*: Bobbi Shaw; *Myrtle Forbush*: Patsy Kelly. *Also*: George Barrows, Luree Holmes, Alberta Nelson, and Andy Romano.

THE FILM: This "epic" went through several titles before a final one was decided upon. Among the earlier labels were: *Bikini Party in a Haunted House*, *Slumber Party in a Horror House*, *Pajama Party in a Haunted House*, and *Ghost in a Glass Bikini*. The film was

Ghost in the Invisible Bikini.

nothing more than another entry in American-International's *Beach Party* series that was popular during the 1960s.

Rathbone had a fairly lengthy role as Reginald Ripper, a villainous attorney trying to cheat three heirs (Tommy Kirk, Deborah Walley, and Patsy Kelly) out of the estate left them by Hiram Stokeley (Boris Karloff). Stokeley dispatches The Ghost (Susan Hart) to thwart Ripper's plans, which, of course, she does.

Rathbone was totally wasted in the picture, although he seemed to be enjoying himself in the part, which he accepted only for the monetary rewards.

CRITICAL COMMENT:

"Boris Karloff and Basil Rathbone and Patsy Kelly add class to the picture with their comedy skills. They are provided many sharp lines of dialogue."

Los Angeles Herald Examiner

VOYAGE TO A PREHISTORIC PLANET

(1967)

An American-International Release. Color. Written and Directed by
John Sebastian. Producer: George Edwards. Released: 1967. 80
minutes.

CAST: *Prof. Hartman*: Basil Rathbone; *Marcia*: Faith Domergue.

THE FILM: While *Queen of Blood* was filming, Roger Corman delivered to producer George Edwards two pages of additional dialogue
for Rathbone and requested that the new material be photographed
before the actor was dismissed. This was done.

Prior to the picture itself being wrapped, actress Faith Domergue
was brought in for a day to film several more pages on a space capsule
set.

This footage involving the two performers was later cut into an-

Voyage to a Prehistoric Planet.

other Russian science-fiction movie owned by Corman, *Storm Planet.* Thus was created *Voyage to a Prehistoric Planet* (original title: *Gill Women*), which has been seen in the United States on syndicated television, but never in theaters.

The story deals with the first spaceship landing on Venus in the year 2000. The passengers include two astronauts and a robot. Another space vehicle stays in orbit around the planet. Radio contact is lost and the astronauts confront many dangers, such as dinosaurs and quicksand, before they are rescued.

Rathbone wore the same costume, worked on the same set, and had the same function as in *Queen of Blood.* He gave orders to Miss Domergue in the orbiting space vehicle. She, in turn, relayed the messages to the astronauts on Venus. Except for the stars' individual scenes, all the footage in the picture was from the Russian film.

John Sebastian, credited as being writer/director, is actually a pseudonym for Curtis Harrington.

AUTOPSY OF A GHOST

(1967)

An Azteca Films Release. Color. Written, Produced, and Directed by Ismael Rodriguez. Spanish Title: *Autopsia de un Fantasma*. Released: 1967. 100 minutes.

CAST: *Canuto Perez*: Basil Rathbone; *Satan*: John Carradine; *Moleculo*: Cameron Mitchell. *Also*: Amedee Chabot, Carlos Pinar, Vitola, Susana Cabrera, Pancho Cordova, and Pompin Iglesias.

THE FILM: This little-known film seldom shows up on Rathbone's list of screen credits. Produced in Mexico City a few months before the actor's death, *Autopsy of a Ghost* has only been released in Spanish and, as far as can be determined, there is no English-language version in existence.

The picture was the creation of Mexico's "mad genius" director, Ismael Rodriguez, who imported Rathbone, John Carradine, and Cameron Mitchell to head an otherwise all-Mexican cast. Mitchell spoke Spanish fluently and it was his voice that audiences heard from

Autopsy of a Ghost: **With John Carradine and Player.**

the screen. However, Rathbone and Carradine said their lines in English, their voices being dubbed later by Mexican actors.

Reminiscent of Rostand's *The Last Night of Don Juan*, this black comedy tells of Canuto Perez (Rathbone), a 1567 suicide victim. As punishment, he is denied eternal peace until he finds a woman willing to sacrifice her life for him.

Four hundred years later, Satan (Carradine) brings four maladjusted women for Perez to seduce and they all reject him. Several other unconventional characters enter the hectic picture: a mad inventor (Mitchell), a robot woman, a bank robber, a secret agent, and a crooked lawyer.

The robot falls in love with Perez and agrees to die for him. She short-circuits, causing an atomic bomb in a Latin American country to explode by mistake. The confusion ends with the major world powers utilizing their atomic weapons against each other.

Cameron Mitchell remembers Rathbone's enthusiasm for this project: "He thought it was a brilliant script and was excited at the fact that the part gave him the opportunity to recite passages from Cervantes. Basil's role was not unlike Don Quixote. Based on his performance, I think he would have made a superb *Man of La Mancha* . . . possibly better than anyone that has done the part thus far.

"He was in his seventies when he did this picture, but Basil was still very young at heart. I was shocked when he died a few months later. He seemed so immortal."

Rodriguez's finished picture was a muddled affair, which failed to attract much of an audience.

HILLBILLYS IN A HAUNTED HOUSE

(1967)

A Woolner Brothers Production. Color. Directed by Jean Yarbrough. Producer: Bernard Woolner. Screenplay: Duke Yelton. Released: 1967. 88 minutes.

CAST: *Woody Weatherby*: Ferlin Husky; *Boots Malone*: Joi Lansing; *Jeepers*: Don Bowman; *Dr. Himmil*: John Carradine; *Maximillian*: Lon Chaney; *Madame Wong*: Linda Ho; *Gregor*: Basil Rathbone; *Jim Meadows*: Richard Webb. *Also*: Molly Bee, Merle Haggard, Jim Kent, Sonny James, and Marcella Wright.

THE FILM: Rathbone's final film appearance was in a mediocre exploitation picture for the country/western market. Woolner Brothers had planned the project as a follow-up to their *Hillbillys in Las Vegas*, which had been a financial success. Although the cast of *Hillbillys in a Haunted House* featured some leading country singers (Ferlin Husky, Molly Bee, Merle Haggard, Sonny James, etc.), as well as horror stars John Carradine and Lon Chaney, the final result was both an artistic and commercial "bomb."

Hillbillys in a Haunted House: **With John Carradine.**

Hillbillys in a Haunted House: **With John Carradine.**

Briefly, the story deals with singer Woody Weatherby (Husky), his girl, Boots Malone (Joi Lansing), and their business manager, Jeepers (Don Bowman), who take refuge in a dark, forbidding old house, in order to escape a storm. The trio had been on their way to perform in the Nashville Country Music Jamboree.

A group of foreign agents, led by Gregor (Rathbone) and Dr. Himmil (Carradine), are headquartered at the house. The spies plan to steal the formula for a new rocket propellant from a nearby missile base and, to cover their activities, have set up elaborate equipment, so the house will appear haunted.

During their stay in the mansion, the three entertainers are terrorized by such things as dancing skeletons, sliding panels, and a gigantic gorilla. However, in the end, they are able to unmask the dastardly plot and aid the authorities in capturing the villains.

Producer Bernard Woolner recalls that Rathbone worked on the project for two weeks at a salary of five thousand per week. "He was a real gentleman," states Woolner, "and we all enjoyed working with him.

"There was one minor problem. The premium for the cast insurance on that picture really skyrocketed. When I inquired as to the reason, my agent told me it was because of Rathbone being in his seventies. Well, his age certainly didn't stop him from giving a good performance . . . and that was the important thing."

The production, budgeted at two hundred forty thousand dollars, had only limited bookings in the major cities, but did well in smaller towns.

Perhaps it's just as well that Rathbone's fans didn't get much of an opportunity to see the picture, since *Hillbillys in a Haunted House* was an unfortunate finish to a memorable career.

BASIL RATHBONE
June 13, 1892 – July 21, 1967

"He was a good actor and a nice guy"
— *Fredric March*